From Devotion to Total Surrender
Śaraṇāgati Yoga
In the Light of Indian Philosophy

From Devotion to Total Surrender

Śaraṇāgati Yoga

In the Light of Indian Philosophy

by

T.K. Sribhashyam

Alamelu Sheshadri

DK PRINTWORLD

Publishers of Indian Traditions

Cataloging in Publication Data — DK

[Courtesy: D.K. Agencies (P) Ltd. <docinfo@dkagencies.com>]

Sribhashyam, T. K.

From devotion to total surrender, śaraṇāgati yoga : in the light of Indian philosophy / by T.K. Sribhashyam, Alamelu Sheshadri.

p. cm.

Includes bibliographical references (p.) and index.

ISBN 13: 9788124606360 (Hb)

1. Śaraṇāgati. 2. Bhakti. 3. Hindu philosophy. I. Sheshadri, Alamelu, joint author. II. Title.

DDC 294.5512 23

First published in India in 2012

ISBN 13: 978-81-246-0636-0 (Hb) ISBN 10: 81-246-0636-6

ISBN 13: 978-81-246-0637-7 (Pb) ISBN 10: 81-246-0637-4

Published and printed by:

D.K. Printworld (P) Ltd.

Regd. Office: 'Vedaśrī', F-395, Sudarshan Park

(Metro Station: Ramesh Nagar)

New Delhi 110 015

Phones: (011) 2545 3975; 2546 6019; *Fax*: (011) 2546 5926

E-mail: indology@dkprintworld.com

Website: www.dkprintworld.com

To the revered memory of our Parents

Mucchukunte Sri T. Krishnamacharya

and

Srimati Namagiriammal,

with profound respects and gratitude

Life Sketch of Sri T. Krishnamacharya

Sri T. Krishnamacharya, also called Mucchukunte Krishnamacharya, was born in south India in 1888. Sri T. Krishnamacharya belonged to a family of philosophers and spiritual masters. He was the eldest of five children.

The majority of his studies were done at Varanasi (Benares) and Kolkatta, the two strongholds of traditional Hindu philosophy, where he quickly obtained the highest distinction in all the branches of Hindu philosophy. He mastered Hindu Yoga in the Himalayas and Buddhist Yoga in Burma, then part of India. Later, he went to Kashmir to study Sufism. He taught Hindu philosophy at the Banaras Hindu University and Calcutta University before accepting the King of Mysore's invitation to teach Hindu philosophy at Mysore Sanskrit College. Like his forefathers, he taught the king and was appointed a philosopher of the Royal Court.

As a Master of Philosophy, Sri T. Krishnamacharya was invited by many Indian royal courts and monasteries to participate in the philosophical debates, characteristic of Indian culture since time immemorial. He emerged victorious, not only in his arguments, but also in his ability to explain the application of Hindu philosophy, to the general public in a simple and convincing way. In addition to all this he had mastered 15 Indian languages, was an astrologer, musician, sportsman and a refined cook.

In the 1920s, Sri T. Krishnamacharya began teaching Yoga to the royal family and the residents of Mysore. With the passage of time, he gave increasing importance to the teaching of Yoga.

He always integrated the philosophical aspects of Yoga when practising or teaching. Around 1935, Sri T. Krishnamacharya taught his first batch of non-Indian students. These were Europeans, and as their numbers increased, he taught himself English in order to teach them in English. He lived in Mysore till 1954 when he moved to Chennai, where he lived until his death in 1989.

Sri T. Krishnamacharya had six children, three sons and three daughters. His wife, Srimati Namagiriammal as well as his children were taught by him. Sri T. Krishnamacharya continued to teach his family members until his death.

Sri T. Krishnamacharya never abused his position. He refused the rewards offered by the king and the royal courts and lived on the modest income he earned as an inspector of a coffee plantation, carrying sand and stones for construction projects and practising Indian Medicine (Āyurveda). He even conceded his rich inheritance to his brother and sisters in order to remain true to his philosophical principles.

Sri T. Krishnamacharya taught Yoga to his wife's brother, Sri B.K.S. Iyengar. Following the ancient tradition, Sri B.K.S. Iyengar, born in 1918, lived in his Master's house and began teaching Yoga at the age of 15. Apart from both the authors, Sri T. Krishnamacharya taught his eldest son, Sri T.K. Srinivasan, who was born in 1936, Indian philosophy and Yoga right from his childhood. The insights thus gained made Sri T.K. Srinivasan, also called Mucchukunte Anna, become an outstanding scholar in Mimāṁsā and Tarka philosophies. He lectures in Sanskrit in the traditional Vedānta monasteries, Sanskrit institutions as well as to PhD students of some universities in India. Furthermore, Sri T.K. Srinivasan holds a Degree in Law. Sri T.K.V. Desikachar, born in 1938, the second son of Sri T. Krishnamacharya, first completed his university degree before studying under his father in the 1960s.

Sri Krishnamacharya refused distinguished positions offered by the royal courts and monasteries in order to maintain his liberty and freedom in teaching. His wife, Srimati Namagiriammal followed his example and shared his simple life. For Sri T. Krishnamacharya and his children, she represented a living philosophy.

While Sri T. Krishnamacharya himself was an orthodox Hindu, he had great respect for all other religious, traditional or contemporary thoughts.

His open-mindedness brought him into contact with many spiritual heads of other faiths. Many religious chiefs, heads of states, yoga masters and philosophers came to learn under him. He honoured their need for confidentiality and never used these relations for his own personal benefit or advantage.

Genealogy

Ever since the ninth century the philosophy of Viśiṣṭādvaita Vedānta has been transmitted from generation to generation by the authors' ancestors. This traditional teaching has been bestowed upon both the authors of this book.

Srimathi Alamelu Sheshadri and Sri T.K. Sribhashyam are two of the six children of Srimathi Namagiriammal and Sri T. Krishnamacharya.

Paternal Genealogy:

Īśvaramuni also called Īśvara Bhaṭṭa (ninth century)

Nātha Muni (son of Īśvaramuni) (ninth century)

Īśvaramuni (son of Nātha Muni) (tenth century)

Āḷavaṇḍār also called Yāmunācārya (son of Īśvaramuni) (917-1042)

Devarāja (son of Āḷavaṇḍār) (949-)

Mahāpūrṇa Perianambi (son of Devarāja) (973-)

Śrī Kurukeśa (son of Mahāpūrṇa Perianambi) (1062)

Thirumalai Śrīnivāsācārya (fifteenth century)

Śrīnivāsā Tātācāriyar (sixteenth century)

Śrī Śrīnivāsā Brahma Tantra Parakāla Swamy (Spiritual Head of Śrī Parakala Maṭha, Mysore (1790-1860?)

Appaiah Dīkṣitar (son of Śrī Śrīnivāsā Brahma Tantra Parakāla Swamy (1800-69)

Śeṣa Dīkṣitar (son of Appaiah Dīkṣitar 1820-70?)

Śrīnivāsā Tātācāriyar (son of Śeṣa Dīkṣitar).

Śrī T. Krishnamacharya also called Sri Muchukunte Krishnamacharya (son of Śrīnivāsā Tātācāriyar) (1888-1989).

Maternal Genealogy (by courtesy of Sri B.K.S. Iyengar, the authors' maternal uncle).

Śrī Mudambi Varadācārya (brother of Śrī Rāmānuja, founder of Viśiṣṭādvaita Vedānta) — fourteenth century.

Śrī Mudambi Antācārya

Śrī Hastagiri Annan, disciple of Śrī Vedānta Deśika (a disciple of Śrī Rāmānuja). He conquered Śrī Narasiṁha Mishra, a great master of Advaita Vedānta, in a philosophical debate.

Śrī Antācārya — honoured by the king of Bangalore for his knowledge of Viśiṣṭādvaita and received the land of Vellur (at present Bellur, 50 km to the east of Bangalore) as a gift.

Śrī Vallur Alagiya Manavaḷa Perumāḷ

Śrī Vallur Govindācār

Śrī Vallur Anantācār

Śrī Vallur Aṣṭa Putra Śrīnivāsācār

Śrī Vallur Govindācār

Śrī Vallur Śrīnivasācār

Śrī Bellur (ex-Vallur) Rāmānujācār

Śrī Bellur Govindācār

Śrī Bellur Śrīnivasācār who propagated Viśiṣṭādvaita in Gujarat and Rajasthan

Śrī Bellur Kr̥ṣṇamācār

Śrīmati Bellur Namagiriammal (daughter of Bellur Kr̥ṣṇamācār) (1912-86)

Benediction by Sri B.K.S. Iyengar

I AM delighted to learn that my nephew, Sri T.K. Sribhashyam, and my niece, Alamelu Sheshadri, have undertaken to kindle the spirit of *bhakti* in order to experience the pure, unalloyed and untainted blissful state, which springs out from the path of love without the tinge of lust.

Patañjali deals with *bhakti-mārga* at the very beginning of the text with *Īśvara Praṇidhāna* (*Yogasūtra*, I.23). This is sufficient proof to trace that *aṣṭāṅga yoga* begins with *bhakti-mārga* as its practice takes the practitioner towards the realisation of God.

Actually, it is Patañjali who defines God as a Supreme Being, totally free from conflicts, unaffected by actions, untouched by cause and effect. *Kleśa karma vipāka aśayaiḥ aparāmṛṣṭaḥ puruṣaviśeṣaḥ īśvaraḥ* (*Yogasūtra*, I.24).

While concluding the text Patañjali explains that when one is freed from the fourfold aims of life (*puruṣārtha*), he transcends the qualities of nature (*guṇa*) and establishes himself in its purity of the self — the *puruṣa*.

With this foundation of pristine purity in the consciousness he automatically gets transformed to become a true *bhakta* (devotee) of God.

It means that one reaches God only after self-realisation. Or it also means that self-realisation is the springboard to leap towards experiencing God. In order to achieve this quality of pure consciousness, one has to make an one's arduous effort to sublimate one's *prakṛti śakti* (power of body), earn *yukti* (skilful intelligence or ripe intelligence) which definitely leads the *bhakta* towards *bhakti* and qualifies him or her to the noblest part of total surrender towards God — *śaraṇāgati yoga*.

When *jñāna* reaches that ripe state, the quality of surrender develops in *bhakti* and gets established in him. The *bhakti sādhaka* surrenders all his thoughts, works and actions to the Lord.

For an average individual, this approach to devotion consistently depends upon the way of developing *śārīrika śakti* and earning *jñāna* in order to attain the skilfulness or *yukti* for *bhakti* to grow.

The way to liberation (*mokṣa*) needs perfect knowledge, perfect action and perfect surrender to the Lord. The *bhakta* becomes a *bhāgavata* in every aspect; he not only knows and sees but also lives as a true servant of God, and thus, uses his words (*yukti*), work (*śakti*) and wisdom (*bhakti*) as if it all is for the grace of God, and leads a spiritually happy life with the utmost contentment (*anuttama sukha*) as if it is the words of God.

I pray to the Lord to bless the authors for their endless efforts in treading the pious path of *bhakti*. May all their works of action and words of wisdom touch the hearts of all readers so that they too move forward and reach this destination of total surrender, called *Śaraṇāgati Yoga*.

Pune, India
8 September 2006

Preface

> We meditate on that Supreme One, who has the neck and face of a horse, who has a radiant, blemish-free crystal body, who is the embodiment of Divine Knowledge and Bliss, and who is the support of all branches of learning.
>
> — An invocation to Lord Hayagrīva, the God of knowledge and wisdom

WORLDLY comforts and pleasures are not the means of happiness. Today we have in plenty all the needs of comfort and happiness, far more than our ancestors had. Yet, we are not better off than generations before. Even though the means of happiness have increased manifold over the century, our happiness has not increased. Our ancestors were happy, not because they had more objects of pleasure or fewer causes of trouble, but because they could preserve the steadiness of their mind, which gave them peace, contentment and happiness.

Devotion is not developed in one day. It takes several years to cultivate it, which would make God dwell in our heart. Even if it appears difficult to kindle and nurture, it is the one quality any human being can acquire. Sex, creed, language, nationality, profession, poverty, wealth, nothing will stand in the way of human being developing this emotion by which he can make his heart the abode of God.

There are different categories of devotees who gained liberation. Some gained it through worshipping their spiritual master, others through worship and service to devotees, yet others through pilgrimage, some others through the worship of divine representation, and still others through reading sacred texts. But they all had one device in common: the path of love. God does not look into the act, but into the love behind it. He does not go by the acts but looks into the hearts of the devotees and finds out that the love throbbing in them was the same, no more, no less.

Man's highest duty in life is to practise devotion to the Supreme, by whatever name one may call. All are eligible to practise devotion; the only qualification is an unfailing faith in Him. God is same to all, and he who takes refuge in Him, gets Him, while he who keeps aloof, excludes himself from God.

One who knows the itinerary can guide us in the right direction to reach the destination. Our father, Sri T. Krishnamacharya, infused Bhakti in his children and in his disciples from the beginning of their studies under him. His grace and God's blessings have helped us to undertake this work. It is our sincere hope and the earnest prayer that it will lead the readers on their path of *bhakti* to know the Supreme.

In the name of God, we dedicate this work to all travellers on the path of *bhakti* to know the Supreme Being.

In a work on Hinduism, it is unavoidable to use Sanskrit terms. The use of such terms has been minimized and the nearest English equivalent is given. An exhaustive glossary is appended. This work does fall short of the degree of excellence that it might have attained for which we request a comprehensive indulgence from the readers.

We offer our sincere gratitude to Cornelia Heyde from Germany for the sincere interest she has taken in our writings, going through the entire work, offering useful and valuable comments and thus helping in completing the work.

We owe our recognition to Shri Susheel K. Mittal of D.K. Printworld, who took a personal interest in publishing this book.

Without his encouraging support, perhaps, this edition would not have appeared.

We also owe our sincere thanks to all our well-wishers who helped us, in one way or the other, in making this book come to the light.

Let Peace and Harmony belong to the readers.

Oh! Almighty, from the death lead me to immortality.

— *Bṛhadāraṇyka Upaniṣad*, I.3.28

Presentation

We offer our humble salutations to the ancient sages, who fostered devotion (*bhakti*) with immense love and intense care.

The concept of devotion to the Supreme Being is as old as the Vedas themselves. The *Ṛgveda* refers often to this sentiment. Later, the Upaniṣads hailed the presence of such a sentiment.

The word *bhakti* has several meanings. Some of them are: "to serve", "to honour", "to love", "to adore" bringing to "devotion to God". Nārada says that devotion is the whole-hearted and supreme love of God. Such devotion makes man feel that he has gained the highest aim in life, he rises above fear of death; and he finds himself in unalloyed bliss.

There are many types of *bhakti*: Devotion is through peace (*śānta bhakti*) based on the feeling that the devotee is His. This devotion is predominated by knowledge and awareness of divine riches and culminating in absorption in God. Devotion through love is another type of *bhakti*. Here, the devotee feels that God is his, manifesting itself through the channels of personal affection. This is a widespread devotion wherein God can be considered as wife, husband, child, friend, or lover. Here attraction and attachment for God take personal forms.

Another type of devotion is through knowledge (*jñāna bhakti*). Curiosity, the origin of the search for knowledge, is as much an urge of the soul as any other passion. The *Bhagavad-Gītā* recognizes one who is an intellectual curious as a devotee. His curiosity takes an outward form and culminates in accepting and recognizing the Supreme Being. Ultimately, he merges in God and not in his ego. Moreover, this type of devotion produces the sense of adoration, which leads to complete self-surrender and unity with Him and acceptance of God as both Impersonal and Personal. It is like eating a morsel of food will simultaneously produce taste, satisfy the hunger and increase strength, so too, devotion through knowledge gives at once love and knowledge of God together with the spirit of renunciation.

Devotion through enmity (*videśa bhakti*) is one that might surprise many. This type of *bhakti* is more suitable to one who, for one reason or the other, is an enemy of the God. Indian epics and mythologies give ample evidence to such devotion. In all the incarnations of Viṣṇu or Śiva, the enemies of God were confronted in a manner appropriate to their attitude. God *blessed* these devotees by responding to their attacks but before killing them, liberated their soul of all their sins. Hatred and antagonism can produce as much absorption of the mind in an object or in a person as love and attachment can. If the object is God, concentration on Him, even though it is motivated by antagonism, would purify the soul, just as a potent medicine consumed, must necessarily effect a cure, whatever be the attitude of the patient towards it.

Man, caught up in bondage from a beginningless time due to *avidyā* (ignorance) assumes that the self belongs to him and that he enjoys full freedom, thereby developing a sense of egoism. After gaining philosophical knowledge regarding the true nature of the self and its relation to God, he realises that the self is absolutely dependent on God. Regretting over the wrong notion he had nourished so far and with all sincerity, he pleads before God that the self does not belong to him but to God and offers it to Him. This method is self-surrender (*śaraṇāgati*). This process implies renouncement of three types of egoism: (1) one is the agent of action, (2) it belongs to him and (3) the fruit of the act is for him.

Whatever be the type of devotion, it has to be deep-rooted so that the mind flows naturally and irresistibly towards God, as the Ganges flows to the ocean. This is the final fruit of devotion.

Just as vessels of different sizes, the rivers and the ocean are all full of water according to their respective sizes, even so, in respect of the souls, their fullness of bliss attained through devotion varies according to their intrinsic capacities. Those with limited capacities are satisfied with limited bliss and those with comparatively greater capacities reach fulfilment with still more. But each one's satisfaction would be full and complete in itself, according to one's saturation point.

The happiness and contentment that a seek erradiates, attract all those who meet him, inducing them to follow one of the paths.

All the presentations in the write-ups are taken from the great teachers of the past, who served the individuals as torch-bearers to achieve the goal of spiritual realization. We owe all our knowledge to these souls of the past, who invested much effort in making man reach his higher planes of consciousness, thereby helping him to develop his soul together with physical developments in the process of evolution of his life.

> I may be a man of little intelligence, alone, without any following, and unknown in distant places. Yet, this work of mine will not have to face disdain among men who are in quest of devotion. For look at the bees! What learning, what splendour of lineage, what power of personality, what noble virtues do they possess! Yet do not even refined connoisseurs welcome and taste with relish the sweet honey the bees collect!
>
> — The concluding verse of *Bhakti Ratnāvalī* by Vishnu Puri

Love is Divine, Divine is Love.

Contents

List of Tables and Figures

1

Dawn of Bhakti

When the powers of the organs of knowledge, as also of those of action, manifest as a unified mental mode directed towards the Supreme Being, spontaneous like an instinct and devoid of any extraneous incentive — that (state of mind) is called devotion (*bhakti*) to the Lord. — *Śrīmad Bhāgavata*, III.25.33

Those who are indisposed to contemplate on Thy deeds and glories are bound to go round and round the cycle of births and deaths, even if they are learned in philosophies and other branches of knowledge. For, toiling, all through day, they tire themselves out, at night the agitation of mind caused by the various desires within, disturbs their sleep; and the failure of their worldly plans and ambitions due to the stroke of destiny, engulfs them in disappointment. — *Śrīmad Bhāgavata*, III.9.10

DEVOTION (*bhakti*) is a peaceful emotion impregnated with divine knowledge. It is an emotion springing from the heart which is the centre of man's feelings.[1] It sprouts from God as pure essence of knowledge, resides in the souls, but in course of time gets polluted by its association with *prakṛti*.[2] The emotion of *bhakti* is not of an ordinary nature, it is the essence of the Divine. *Bhakti* is the essence of man's spiritual consciousness. It is a means to communicate directly with God. *Bhakti* has appealed to the masses in the right earnest from the Vedic period itself. *Bhakti* is

1. *Jīvātmā* is constituted of a set of concentric vehicles composed of matter of different degrees of subtlety. The common centre of all these vehicles is named as heart.

2. World of matter.

a deep affection for the Divine — the ancient and the only cause of the universe. To be one with God, one should put in all the sincere effort. Of course, no one is free from worldly temptations unless he or she has reached such an intense devotion, where only God and the service unto Him alone matters. A devotee understands that God is the creator of everything, and so everything is a part of God.

The steadfast devotion to God wipes out all the mundane disorders of the mind and links the mind with the Creator. Disorders of the mind are the result of a deep sense of ego. — "I-am-ness" that exists in man, and without which, man finds it difficult to survive. This ego is mainly responsible for all frictions and tensions in life. He, who contemplates on God, will be rid of this burden of ego. Once this ego sense is overcome, man finds solace and smoothness in his life's journey, with the grace of God.

The emotion of love towards God replaces all other mundane and materialistic emotions that otherwise agitate a man's mind. The emotion of love frees the mind of all other desires. Love is strength. A heart fully surrendered, is surcharged with a continuous flow of Divine Love as its own reward. The root of *bhakti* is in God and *bhakti* itself sprouts from God. Hence, offering prayers for the Divine is the right approach to reach Him. Man approaches God through what is divine in himself. The way of approach to the Divine is the joy of the soul. This joy is the outcome of a peaceful mind. It translates itself into *bhakti,* in its pure essence.

This process of establishing the connecting bond is *bhakti*. Through intense love, sages could succeed in their goal: finding the Ultimate Truth in what looked like nothing. God, who is referred to as the Ultimate Truth, is so subtle that one has to go beyond the spiritual consciousness to understand Him. He seemingly is formless, just nothing; but He reveals Himself to a dedicated discoverer within his Self. Vedic philosophers regard the whole creation on physical and metaphysical planes as a unified action of different forces, all being various forms of one and the same universal cosmic energy, which comes into manifestation from the all-pervading and all-powerful *Brahman*. *Brahman* is also named as *Ātman*.

In India, all religious practices are basically aimed at searching or discovering the creator, *Brahman* — the Supreme Being. Religious practices depend upon observance and the fulfilling of certain principles such as:

- That the worshipper must have a pure and strong mind,
- That whatever deity he entertains should be conceived in terms of truth, goodness and beauty,
- That the metaphysical basis of unity in diversity should be well established,
- That the ritual should be in keeping with the idea of unity, and
- That the unity should not remain a mere abstraction but must find a concrete form in social life, both internal and external.

Devotion is the constant worship of God. Vedic devotees considered the contemplation on the Divine not only in terms of one's own god, but also everybody else's god. The aim of *bhakti* proceeds with the idea of ultimate unity. "Even those devotees who worship other gods with faith really worship me, though in an irregular way."[3] It was the force of nature and her manifestations here on earth, the atmosphere around here and above in the heaven, that inspired the devotion, admiration and imagination of the Vedic poets. The plurality of Vedic gods is due to the strong belief in God. The hymns of *Ṛgveda* were all composed in praise of the gods — including terrestrial, atmospheric and celestial gods. They gave vent to their feelings of devotion presenting hymns, which in turn are known as Vedas. Veda means "to know, to understand".

3. *Bhagavad-Gītā*, IX.23.

Origin of Bhakti in Vedas

Bhakti is holding its supremacy as a delightful way of right from the Vedic period. The attitude of *bhakti* in which divine grace is the only source of spiritual progress is well expressed in the Vedas as no one by work attains Him (work is *karma-yoga*); Who works and strengthens ever more; Praised of all, resettles, valiant, bold in might.[4] God was praised and named as Indra during the Vedic period.

Yajurveda says,

> A devotee tries to unite his *bhakti* with the Divine, from whom it sprang through spiritual evolution.[5]

R̥gveda declares,

> You praise that ancient cause, the origin of R̥ta (Divine law) according to your knowledge. You will be freed of birth. If you cannot praise Him, recite His name. However, O Lord Viṣṇu! We devote ourselves to your light, attributes and form.[6]

Attributeless form also means having so many attributes that are too innumerable for a normal man, so he finds it better to praise as devoid of qualities.

Veda quotes,

> He who offers his all to Viṣṇu, the husband of Śrī (Lakṣmī), the primal cause, the creator, the ever new, he who recites the glorious birth and works of this glorious Being, that giver, that reciter, obtaining fame, reaches the Highest Abode.[7]

This unwavering devotion expressed in the Vedas has saved the Vedic religion through thousands of years.

Jīva, who has realised his own Self as self-luminous, universal,

---

4. *R̥gveda*, LXX.3.
5. *Yajurveda*, LXII.8.
6. *R̥gveda*, I.156.
7. Ibid.

inner principle is called Idam+dra, that is, "this seeing" on the strength of Upaniṣadic maxim: a knower of the Divine is the Divine himself. Such a *jīva* that has realised its ultimate nature of Brahmā is equally called Idamdra. By syncopating the syllable "dam", the same word Indamdra becomes Indra, the well-known designation of the Absolute Divinity. Just as *Bhagavad-Gītā* calls *Paramātman* as *upadraṣṭā*, Śaṅkara[8] points out that God's love should be referred to indirectly, that is to say, to be behind the veil, because they are worthy of great adoration.

Vedic prayers often become songs with the spirit of love. Love and devotion are the simplest form of worship of God in *bhakti*. Vedic devotees contemplated on Divinity as the Lord and in the most affectionate terms as father, mother, brother, friend, guest and so on. The worshippers seek divine help, protection, succour, mercy, benevolence, love and so forth. God is the saviour and the merciful one, protector and so on. He is worshipped as the most beloved one. To Vedic devotees, Divinity is common and universal. God is the Creator and Ultimate Being. He is the Lord of all existence — the supporter of the universe. He is the source of all strength, spiritual as well as physical. In Him, man has his ultimate refuge.

Vedic worship is both communal and universal. All are invited to worship without exception and without distinction. The power of the soul called *ojas*, the spiritual power, was cultivated by Vedic religion and is still upholding this cultivation. Vedic worshippers expressed their idealism in words like: To Him all pathways turn; He is the supreme goal of all; the best and easy path is *bhakti* and sung:

> *Come together ye all, with power of spirit,*
> *To the Lord of Heaven.*[9]
> *Who is only one, the guest of the people,*

---

8. The exponent of Advaita philosophy, philosophy of non-dualism.
9. Heaven here means the highest layer of spiritual consciousness.

To him, all pathways turn,
Verily He is one.[10]
God Indra! Thou art common to all.[11]
We invoke Indra who is common to all.[12]

Devotees expressed their love for God through songs of love. These songs echoed in the Indian sky down through the ages. This was their typical mode of worship; prayers in *bhakti* are the musical outbursts from the love-filled heart of man. The simple and direct prayer comes from the child as well as from the adult. A song in praise of God from the love-filled heart of man runs thus:

Sing, sing, ye forth your songs!
O! Priyamedhas, Sing!
Let children also sing!
Sing of Him, who is a refuge like the castle,
Now loudly let the Gargara (violin) sound,
Let the Godha (lute) send its resounding voice,
Let the string send its tunes around,
To God is our hymn upraised.[13]

God is one. Eventhough devotees named the varied ideas of the One Being differently. Their fondness for God is brought out in the lines:

He is our friend and father, our Creator,
Who knows all positions, existing things.[14]

Man should be pure in body and mind, in offering his prayers to God. Purity is godliness. A devotee is most God-like and his benevolence is like that of God, when he takes care of the naked, the sick, the blind and the crippled:

---

10. *Sāmaveda*, I.4.3.3 (372).
11. *R̥gveda*, VIII.65.7.
12. *R̥gveda*, VIII.99.8.
13. *R̥gveda*, VIII.69.8.9.
14. *Yajurveda* (*Vājasenayī Saṁhitā*, XXXII.10).

He clothes all that is naked
He doctors all that is sick
Through him, the blind man sees,
The crippled goes about.[15]

According to Veda, man sets up his relation with God in the mother's womb itself. This sense of the essential divinity of man is a special feature of the Vedic religion and spiritual idealism. The Vedas recognise the spiritual value born of love, besides recognising the values of truth, goodness, and beauty. Describing the presence of God in the body of man, the Veda says,

When they had fused the mortal man complete,
The Gods entered into Him.[16]

It is from this belief that religion is described as the manifestation of Divinity that is already in man. Man approaches God through what is Divine in him, the constant flow of love. The attitude of love as devotion was typical of the Vedic period. The word *bhakti* was introduced later to this attitude of Love. Through *bhakti*, man seeks God's help and grace to help him out of his sorrows and defects. According to the conception of the *bhakti* ideal, the sincere devotion of one's heart is sufficient for worship. These feelings of man are found in the lines:

God the Rescuer, God the Saviour, Mighty God,
Happily invoked at each invocation,
God powerful, invoked by many, I invoke,
May God, the bounteous, confer on us blessings.[17]

The spirit of *bhakti* hidden in the attitude of worship is found in the lines:

To thee I will bring oblation,
To thee I will send my prayer,
To thee who hast been adorable in our invocations

---

15. *Ṛgveda*, VIII.79.2.
16. *Atharvaveda*, XI.8.13.
17. *Ṛgveda*, LXVII.11 also in other 3 Vedas.

A fountain in the desert art thou, O, Deity
To the worshipful man, O Ancient King![18]

In a desert, a thirsty man is saved by a fountain of water found in an oasis. In the world, man is saved by the Divine grace. Divine grace and Divine protection find a mention in the Vedas frequently. A line in *Sāmaveda* reads: "Divine grace is the coat of mail within me".[19]

A warrior is clad in the coat of mail that as a shield, protects the vital parts of his body; but the grace of God is the coat of mail within him. Divine mercy is typical of the attitude of *bhakti* and is a feature of mass religion. The chief element in religion is the Divine grace, which is the most needed attribute by the humble and the distressed. The devotee constantly remembers and realises that all he has and all that he enjoys is from God, who in His infinite kindness has granted him with all this.

The Divinity as the refuge of man in the Vedas is addressed in the feminine gender as Mother. "As birds seek the shelter of the tree so we men seek the shelter of the Divine Mother, Sarasvatī."[20] The special feature of the religion of love is the worship of the Divinity as Mother. The word "most beloved"[21] also carries much sweetness in Vedic poetry. Conception of the joy of a stainless soul seeking the pure joy of the Divine is typical of Vedic culture. Man's worship is the opening of the floodgates of a joyous soul in front of the radiant glory of the source of all joy. Vedic hymns are compared to the streams gushing out of

---

18. *R̥gveda*, X.4.1.
19. *Sāmaveda*, 1872.
20. *R̥gveda*, VII.95.5. During the Vedic period, God's power was named as Sarasvatī. She is considered as the Deity of speech. The worship of Sarasvatī bestows man with the power of speech, which flows like a river, hidden in the ocean of spiritual consciousness.
21. "Most beloved" refers to divinity as mother in general. However, in this context, it refers to Sarasvatī, as Goddess. The idea of God being the most beloved is expressed in various ways.

mountains. "Like joyous streams bursting from the mountain."[22]

The ideas of worship through tender love, similar to the tender caressing of a child, are also found in, the Vedic songs. This conception of Divinity as a child appears in the *bhakti* cult as *vātsalya rasa*.[23] In the *Śrīmad Bhāgavata Purāṇa* the child Kṛṣṇa is made to symbolise the idea of the Divinity loved as the child. Singing was the means of expression of intense feelings of a devotee. Love of God expressed itself in songs. The eagerness and yearning of love are expressed as:

In my heart thoughts and feelings agitate,
Love yearnings proceed; thy fly to all the regions,
No comforter exists other than these;
In the Gods are my highest longings fixed[24]

This is the loving one, driving the issues of the many coloured;
The spring of light, in the chariot of splendour;
Him at the meeting of the waters and the sun.
The sages with their hymns caress as a child[25]

The one beautiful-winged (i.e the Divine)
He has entered the Sea (vastness of space)
He looks around this universe;
Him with a simple heart I have seen from near;
His mother kisses him and he kisses his mother.[26]

The spiritual and poetic significance is that the vision of Divinity corresponds to the vision of the exchange between child and mother.

The one who realises the Divine as the loving will find the whole world united in Him.

22. *Ṛgveda*, X.68.1.
23. Sentiment of affection and tenderness.
24. *Ṛgveda*, X.64.2.
25. *Ṛgveda*, X.123.1.
26. *Ṛgveda*, X.114.4.

A vision of a devotee is:

The loving sage beholds that mysterious existence wherein the universe comes to have one home
Therein unites and therefrom issues the whole;
The Lord is warp and woof in created beings[27]

Here the Divinity is expressed first as a personal experience; secondly as a mystery; thirdly the abstract conception of Divine is described as an essence, an existence and fourthly, in the Divine the whole universe is united in love, as birds in a nest. The idea of Divine presence as the underlying power of unity is in the metaphor of "warp and woof."

The attraction for love between the worshipper and the Deity has found wide space in Vedic devotion. The devotees were dependent on God. They prayed for His grace earnestly:

Truly God! We are thine, we are worshippers depend on Thee,
Except Thee, O much invoked, there is none
Mighty one to show us grace[28]

Supported by Thee O God! May we answer all who defy us.
Thou art ours and we are thine[29]

The Vedas sing beautifully from the depth of heart, such as:

O God! I would not sell thee for the highest price;
Not for a thousand, nor fifteen thousand;
O, Mighty one, nor for an infinite amount;
Lord of countless wealth.[30]

To Vedic devotees, love for God is not a mercantile transaction. Their spirit of pure love for God is selfless and is totally for God alone. The peculiarity in the Vedas is, though it contemplates many gods in different names and forms, it asserts each one as

27. *Yajurveda*, XXXII.8.

28. *Ṛgveda*, LXVI.13.

29. *Ṛgveda*, VIII 92.32.

30. *Ṛgveda*, VIII.1.5.

the Supreme Being. The devotional attitude towards the Divine remains unchanged even if the deities' names and forms are changed. All the deities are identified with just one Divine entity. Vedic worship is of the One Divinity though in many names and forms. The unity of God does not mean there is only one individual in the species called God but that the Divinity is supreme and all-pervading and all reality becomes unified in Him. He is the One, the One alone. All deities become One in Him.

Bhakti in the Brāhmaṇas

The idea of Vedic sages was to keep in constant touch with God, who is the origin of the world. They constantly reflected on this thought. The following hymn of *Ṛgveda* brings out clearly the philosophy of the wonderful mystery of the origin of the world:

Then there was neither being nor not-being.
The atmosphere was not, nor the sky above it,
What covered all? And where? By what protected?
Were there the fathomless bays_of waters?
Then neither death nor deathless existed
Of day and night there was yet no distinction,
Alone that one breathed calmly, self-supported
Other than it was none, nor ought above It.
Darkness there was at first in darkness hidden;
The Universe was undistinguished water.
That in which void and emptiness lay hidden;
Alone by the power of fervour was developed.
Then for the first time there arose desire,
Which was the primal germ of mind within it?
And sages searching their hearts discovered
In nothing the connecting bond of Being[31]

31. *The History of Hindu Philosophy* by Surendra Nath Gupta, vol. I, chap. II.

Vedas, Brāhmaṇas and their Philosophy

Ṛgveda, Yajurveda, Sāmaveda and *Atharvaveda* are the four collections of Vedas called Saṁhitā.[32] Brāhmaṇas are theological treatises. The word Brāhmaṇa signifies, that which relates to the prayer of *Brahman*.

The four goals in man's life called *puruṣārtha* are:

- *Dharma* (eternal laws),
- *Artha* (wealth as one of the objects of human pursuit),
- *Kāma* (desire), and
- *Mokṣa* (the final liberation of soul).

The Brāhmaṇas explain the sacred significance of different rituals to achieve these goals (*puruṣārtha*) in life. *Mokṣa* is the ultimate goal in man's life and the other three goals help and support this final goal. The hymns in Brāhmaṇas are composed for the sake of sacrificial ceremonies to invoke the particular God according to one's object of worship. They consist of sacrificial injunctions. It is a Vedic ritual to pour libations of clarified butter in the sacrificial fire. The injunctions introduced in Brāhmaṇas influence and ignite man's mind to approach God. A feeling of devotion arises, as a result of offering libations to the fire in *yajña*.

Vedic scriptures divided man's life into four stages, *āśrama*:

1. *Brahmacarya* (student life, where one is initiated into higher life),
2. *Gṛhastha* (stage of householders),
3. *Vānaprastha* (to lead the life in forest resuming *brahmacarya* again), and
4. *Saṁnyāsa* (following the ideal of complete renunciation).

Bhakti is cultivated gradually during these four stages. The word Brāhmaṇa also means "one, who is engaged in the search

---

32. All the Vedas "put together" are known as *Saṁhitā, saṁ* = together, *hitā* = pleasing.

of *Brahman*". The spiritual injunctions prescribed for sacrifices are intended for *gṛhastha*. *Yajña* is the Vedic ritual of offering libations into the sacrificial fire, lighted on an altar. Whatever may be the names of deities worshipped, the ritual is the same. The Vedic ritual is picturesque, accompanied by chanting, singing (*Sāmaveda*), etc. There is the simple domestic ritual called *Agnihotra*, in which the family offers its daily prayers by assembling around the sacrificial fire, in which libations of clarified butter are poured into this fire. There are also sacrifices held in open spaces during different seasons and attended by masses. All the sacrifices, though conducted in the material sense, induce *bhakti* in the heart of the performer as well as in the masses. Love pours where the mind contemplates. The Brāhmaṇas explain the procedure for all these sacrifices. The performance of sacrifice is the foundation for *jñāna*, which is essential for man's spiritual evolution. When one reaches perfection in *jñāna*, then one performs *jñāna yajña* — offers his *jñāna* in the fire of spiritual sacrifice, that is the sacrifice in the form of wisdom or worshipping God through knowledge. This is *bhakti* in the real sense! God resides in the hearts of all, which is the place of the highest learning. God's glow is like that of a pure crystal. He (God) must be visualised mentally before offering knowledge. This is a spiritual sacrifice. This type of sacrifice is recognised as far superior to other sacrifices conducted with the help of material substances. The fire of spiritual sacrifice is the fire of knowledge.

In a *yajña*, the materials used, the colour, the sound, the fragrance, etc. are at their full play. The glorious lustre of the blazing fire, the sweet perfume of the burnt *ghee*, the blades of glass, the cooked offering, the crushed *soma* (creeper called *guḍūcī*)[33] and the other materials of *yajña* have their direct and purifying effect on the mind of the worshipper: igniting *bhakti* in man as well as the masses. The five systems of *yajña*, namely

33. *Guḍūcī* (*Tinospora cordifolia*) means one that protects the body.

agnihotra (domestic sacrifice), *brahma yajña* (study and teaching of Vedas), *nara yajña* (service of the guest), *bhūta yajña* (giving food to the animals and birds) *pitṛ yajña* (offering of oblations to ancestors) are recognised as *mahāyajña*s (great sacrifices). Though these are the material aspects of *yajña* related to fire, fuel and oblations, they are highly symbolic — a strong base for *bhakti* is found in these *yajña*s. They also form the spiritual discipline (*yajña* of *tapas*) in which the fire of restraint is lighted and the senses are the offerings. In the *brahma yajña*, sacred studies, the knowledge is offered to the fire of Self. For a man of spiritual discipline and self-dedication, the most important ideal for *bhakti* is the *yajña* of *jñāna* in which *Brahman* is fire, fuel and oblation. *Brahman* here stands for the Supreme Being or Supreme Reality. The Self has *Brahman* as its self. To realise its own nature, the aspirant offers wisdom as the oblation in the fire of *Brahman*. This means the Self meditates on Him in all his works.

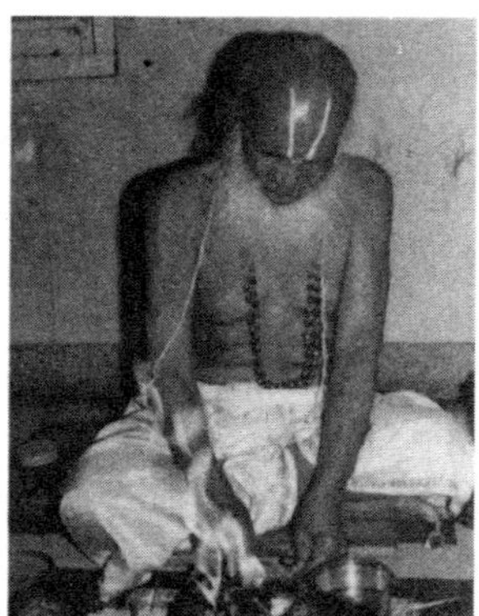

fig. 1: Author's father, Sri T. Krishnamacharya invoking Agni (Photography: T.K.Sribhashyam, France)

Brāhmaṇas prescribe the material part of *yajña* to ignite devotion in a systematic process like *karma*, *jñāna* and *bhakti*. *Bhakti* is the combined effect of *karma* and *jñāna*. The act of offering *jñāna* to God, and only for God, is devotion. The Vedas accepted action as an essential part of life. *Bhakti* requires the sharpening of the mind, which is the main connecting thread between man and God. Man should approach God by developing divine qualities in him. "God desires the man, who presses the juice" (that is, who performs a spiritual sacrifice).[34] A devotee while performing *yajña* offers oblations to *agni* (fire god) not for his own welfare, but for the good of mankind as a whole. He sees the spiritual vision of God as residing in all. The nobility of the moral ideal deserves special attention. While performing a sacrifice, the devotee prays for the removal of sins of all:

> *Agni! Lead us by right path, to well-being*
> *Thou, God! Who knowest all duties,*
> *Remove from us the sin that makes us go astray*
> *We will offer Thee our fullest adoration.*[35]

Goodness is divine. The foundation of a good life is goodwill in the mind. The spring of action proceeds from the mind of man. If the will that comes from the depths of a man is good, then his whole conduct would be good. This inherent goodness in man helps develop devotion.

The significance in the Brāhmaṇas is that by earnest determination, one dedicates oneself to the higher ideals and through this self-dedication, one enters spiritual life. Achievement of spiritual refinement brings God's grace.

Bhakti in the Āraṇyakas

Āraṇyaka means forest treatise. As seen earlier, there are four well-known divisions of the Vedas: *Ṛgveda, Yajurveda, Sāmaveda* and *Atharvaveda*. The Brāhmaṇas were annexed to these Vedas and the Āraṇyakas were supplementary to them. The Upaniṣads were also included by the names of the respective Vedas, to which they belonged. The Āraṇyakas occupy an intermediate position between the Brāhmaṇas and the Upaniṣads, both in

34. *Ṛgveda*, VIII.2.8.
35. *Ṛgveda*, I.189.1.

form and spirit. The Āraṇyakas consist of the principles of meditation with devotion on certain vital points in the body or symbols that are supposed to be of great merit. They replace Vedic rituals.

The Vedic rites are of two kinds. One is entirely a mechanical procedure and the other is coupled with meditation. The results obtained through meditation are more symbolic, for they lead the one who practises meditation on the path of *bhakti,* enabling him to develop direct contact with God. The core of *Brahma-vidyā*[36] through meditation is taught in the Āraṇyakas by the sages. Āraṇyakas stood for the spiritual form of worship, which the householder has to perform. Devotion is uninterrupted meditative love for God who dwells within the man as his protector. Sages replaced the performance of elaborate, complicated ceremonial sacrifices with meditation because of the non-availability of such accessories and articles as were required for the sacrifices, in the forest. The main characteristic of Āraṇyakas is that it supplies the esoteric meaning of the great Vedic rituals.

An aspirant of spiritual studies retires to the forest, after having led the life of *brahmacarya*[37] and *gṛhastha*[38] for some time, to

36. *Taittirīya Upaniṣad,* III.1 describes, "that from which these beings are born, by which they live after birth and into which they enter at death . . . try to know that. That is *Brahman.*" *Brahman* is defined in *Vedānta Sūtra* as: "That omniscient, omnipotent, all-merciful being from whom proceed the origin, sustenance and dissolution of this varied and wonderfully fashioned world" (*Vedānta Sūtra* 1.1.2). According to Rāmānuja, one has to regard the Supreme *Brahman* as the Self of the soul even as the soul is the Self of the body, for all souls constitute the body of *Brahman,* the Lord. *Brahma vidyā* means "knowledge of *Brahman*". It consists of answers to the question like: "What is the final cause of this universe? Is it *Brahman*? Where is *Brahman*? Is he related to things in universe? If not, how can Absolute *Brahman,* unrelated to anything, be the course of any thing? What is his nature? When are we born? Why do we live?" and so on.

37. Period of study.

38. Period of householder.

continue his studies. The influence of holy men, who live in the forest, also supports them to devote their remaining life to the contemplation of God. Birth as a human being is the most precious gift of God. Man is privileged to shape the course of his life in a planned manner to a great extent by using his intellectual faculties. For this, he has to follow certain principles that suit the conditions of his life in various stages. The third stage of *vānaprastha* is a life of hardship. However a devotee is unmoved by the sufferings in his life. His goal of keeping in constant touch with God gives him enough strength to bear the hardships that come along.

Āraṇyakas prescribe *mantras* along with meditation which relates man to God. For example, in *Aitareya Āraṇyaka*, Gāyatrī and Mahāvrata[39] are identified with *Brahman*. *Puruṣa*, the Cosmic Intelligence, is designated as Prajāpati.[40] Meditation on these is equal to the meditation on *Hiraṇya Puruṣa* — the innermost essence of the visible universe. The power of speech, *vāc*, is extolled as conscious and unconscious energy animating the body and is equated with *ātman* or *prāṇa*. *Prāṇa* (the life energy) is stated to be at the root of the speech. *Prāṇa* is the spirit immanent in the universe. The knowledge of the whole universe rests on the root of speech — *prāṇa*. *Aitareya Āraṇyaka* suggests meditation on *prāṇa* by identifying it with *Brahman* (*Brahman* is equated with *ātman* too): "Thou art *Ukta*,[41] thine art all this, we are thine and thou art ours".[42]

Man's desire to keep constant contact with God is upheld here. Meditation on speech is equal to the meditation on *prāṇa*, which is again equal to meditation on *ātman* or *Brahman*. *Prāṇa* is

39. *Gāyatrī* = *Gāyati iti gāyatrī* = That which sings. *Gāyatrī* is a metre of 8 letters. *Gāyatrī mantra* is 8 × 3 = 24. *Mahāvrata* is the name of a great sacrifice.

40. Another name for creator.

41. Eulogy, praise. Name of a Vedic sacrifice.

42. *R̥gveda*, VIII.92.32.

upgraded as Absolute Being in this Āraṇyaka. Again, it is said that from the five aspects of *prāṇa*[43] the whole universe sprang up and subsists in the relation of matter and spirit. Man recognises the manifestation of *ātman* more clearly in herbs, trees and animals by meditating on these. Human personality is the sphere in which *ātman* dwells as witness. Being endowed with intelligence, man recognises the manifestation of *ātman* in a greater degree.

Prāṇa, the life principle, entered man from the forepart of his feet. It proceeded higher up to the thigh, stomach, heart and the head and finally ramified into sight, hearing, mind, speech and vital breaths. Sages proclaim meditation on *Brahman* in the stomach or in the heart, the former as the seat of *Brahman* named *Vaiśvānara.*[44] Meditation on the cosmic forces is taught in many ways by different sages in Āraṇyakas. All the sages found out a gradual union of speech, *prāṇa,* wind, all gods, the heavenly world and *Brahman* through meditation.

The Cosmic Being, Prajāpati, is not only considered as "Time" but is also an object of meditation. The feminine symbol of time is the Deity Kālī, the dynamic aspect of Reality. Time is the undivided and united principle. It is identical with the Cosmic Being and the principle in the Sun. Sun is the essence of the year, because it is the measure and condition of appraising time. Meditation on the Sun in the sky is glorified, identifying it with the Cosmic Being. The Sun in the sky also corresponds to the manifestation of *ātman* in the right eye, because *ātman* is most manifested in the right eye. While entering the human body, *ātman* is differentiated as *jīva* and *prāṇa.* While the former enters through the fontanelle, the latter enters through the forepart of the feet. Like a charioteer, it controls the body. Meditation on the crown of the head corresponds to the meditation on *ātman* directly.

---

43. The five aspects are: *prāṇa, apāna, vyāna, udāna* and *samāna.*

44. *Vaiśvānara* is the name of the digestive fire.

Meditation on the full moon in the sky corresponds to the meditation on the heart. Moon is equated with mind.

Agni is considered to be the intermediary principle between God and man. This is why man offers all oblations to God through *agni*. Meditation between the eyebrows (*bhrūmadhya*) corresponds to meditation on *agni*.

The psychological conception of the Self as consisting of sight, hearing, mind, speech is of theological speculations identified with *Brahman* and meditated upon.

In *Īśavāsya Upaniṣad*, Fire and Sun are worshipped and meditated by the devotee, considering them as personal Gods.

Brahman is spoken of by the sound *OṀ*, *OṀ* being the designation of God. Meditation and reflection on the sound *OṀ* is the best means of realising *Brahman*. Meditation on *OṀ* elevates the spiritual consciousness. The *Bṛhadāraṇyaka Upaniṣad* describes the body of the sacrificial horse as the cosmic form of Prajāpati, the presiding deity of the horse-sacrifice (*aśvamedha yajña*). It is stated that the horse, which is the most important object in this sacrifice, is to be meditated upon as Prajāpati, the Cosmic Being. This meditation is like the superimposition of an idol as deity. It purifies the horse and defines it as Prajāpati. In the absence of the horse, the performer of the sacrifice imagines himself as the sacrificial horse and meditates upon the parts of his own body as different parts of the Cosmic Being. This moving universe is the horse. Thought activity as meditation is an external worship in the form of sacrifices. This meditation will take man's spiritual consciousness to the highest level, the *Brahman* consciousness.[45]

Again, in a sacrifice called *jyotiṣṭoma*, the vital force is invoked as Prajāpati. Meditation on the vital force (even without following any principles) is said to subdue subconscious forces, thereby assisting the devotee with the realisation of *Brahman* consciousness. The vital force *prāṇa* is the cosmic life, and *puruṣa*

45. *Bṛhadāraṇyaka Upaniṣad*, I.1 calls it *Aśva Brahman*.

is the cosmic personality. Both are the same Divine principle, embodied in the universe. *Prāṇa* is considered as the spirit immanent in the universe. *Prāṇa* is meditated upon because it is in all beings, in all places, it has entered all creatures. Before manifestation, the whole universe was present as an idea in *Brahman*, and *prāṇa* is the spirit immanent in that universe. *Prāṇa* is thus meditated upon.

The third section of *Bṛhadāraṇyaka Upaniṣad* describes the two forms of *Brahman* as gross and subtle and suggests the meditation on these forms. The gross form is made of earth, water and fire, and the subtle is formed of air and ether. The superimposition of *Brahman* on these forms — collectively or individually — leads to the realisation of the Self. The result of Self-realisation is that the *jīva* understands, within his own consciousness, the immanent principle of all existing objects as the very Being of the universe. This (*jīva*) appears as his mind through the intellect principle which constitutes his very soul. Thus, he realises *ātman* (also called *Brahman* by many sages) as the most pervasive principle.

Man is capable of dissolving his lower principle in the next higher principle through meditation. For example,

> Hearing from Arjuna the news of Lord Kṛṣṇa's departure to heavens, Yudhiṣṭhira, traversing the whole course of Yoga step by step, dissolved the lower principle into the next higher and finally effected the merger of his personal consciousness into the universal.[46]

The meaning is: Disregarding all his ornaments and garments, cutting himself off from all his personal consciousness, he offered his speech as oblation into the fire of his mind, he offered his mind into *prāṇa*, his *prāṇa* into *apāna*, thereupon *apāna* into death and death into the five principles of earth, water, fire, air and ether. Having thus offered, Yudhiṣṭhira offered everything to the fire of the Self, which effected a complete merger of his

46. *Śrīmad Bhāgavata Purāṇa* (I.15.40.42).

Self into the eternal *Brahman*.

Explaining the above process the *Bṛhadāraṇyaka Upaniṣad* says,

> The universe is nothing but *Brahman* at the time of origin and during its continuance and also at the time of dissolution.[47]

So, in the absence of all objects and organs, only the Self, the "one" without a second remains. The world is wholly dependent upon the relative consciousness of the individual soul (*jīva*). When the soul begins to examine the nature of the object of worship through meditation and understands the true meaning of the plurality of its visions, it feels *Brahman* as the only first principle. This transcendence of individual consciousness into *Brahman* is called Realisation of *Brahman*.

The Āraṇyakas adopt the process of meditation and contemplation, which is *bhakti* itself. Through intense love to God alone, the goal in meditation can be achieved.

Bhakti in the Upaniṣads

Brāhmaṇas, Āraṇyakas and the Upaniṣads do not reveal *bhakti* directly. They provide the methods essential for reaching the spiritual goal in life. This goal is the perception of the Highest Truth. *Bhakti* is hidden in all the methods directed in these scriptures.

Directing the mind towards this goal, while performing the prescribed sacrifices is a meditation, which is *bhakti* itself. The four Vedas are divided into three sections: *Mantra*, Brāhmaṇa and Upaniṣads. The *mantra* section contains the praises of Gods with names: Indra, Agni, etc. The sages were attracted by the beauty of the nature and its power. Sun, moon, stars, wind, water, rain, lightning, etc. gave experiences to the sages to extend their search of the Real Cause behind these. The praises were prolonged by their experiences. The part of the *mantra*, which was recited during sacrificial ceremonies, was named Brāhmaṇa.

47. *Bṛhadāraṇyaka Upaniṣad*, II.4.11.

The Brāhmaṇa also gives the detailed procedures of performing every single sacrifice and their expected results.

The important part of Upaniṣad is known as Vedānta,[48] because it is a secret doctrine.[49] The essence of the Vedas lies hidden in the Upaniṣads. There are many Upaniṣads, but not all are of much importance. Some of the important Upaniṣads are *Aitareya* and *Kauṣītaki* from *R̥gveda*, *Chāndogya* and *Kena* from *Sāmaveda*, *Taittirīya*, *Mahā Nārāyaṇa*, *Kaṭha*, *Śvetāśvatara*, *Maitrāyanīya Upaniṣad* are from *Kr̥ṣṇa Yajurveda*, *Īśa* and *Br̥hadāraṇyaka* from *Śukla Yajurveda*. The aim of the Upaniṣads is the search for God (*paramātmā*) in the soul of man (*ātmā*). Upaniṣads direct the paths to grasp this highest truth in the form of direct perception. The seers of the Upaniṣads gave preference to the realisation of *ātmā*, which in turn leads to the realisation of *paramātmā*.

It is to be noted that the Upaniṣads use the terms *paramātmā*, *Brahman*, *ātmā* and many other names like *Īśvara*, God, Divine, etc. for the One Supreme Being, the Highest Divinity, who is the Creator of the universe. The extreme love and intimacy towards this Supreme Being made the seers praise Him with different names. They sometimes explained His secrets in various ways, depending upon the state of consciousness they reached spiritually. Their effort of contemplation in reaching their goal is *bhakti* itself, though the word *bhakti* is not often used.

The word Upaniṣad is derived from the root *ṣad* with the prefix *ni*. *Upa* means "near", *ni* denotes "to sit" and *ṣad* indicates "removal of ignorance". Upaniṣad also means that *Brahman* is close by in Upaniṣad, and is to be learnt by sitting down near the spiritual master. The hidden knowledge of spirituality in the Upaniṣad is to be experienced with the guiding of a spiritual master only. The real names of the authors of the Upaniṣads are not to be found anywhere, though there is a mention of names

---

48. *Veda* = Knowledge, to know; *anta* = end.

49. *Śvetāśvatara Upaniṣad* (V.6).

indirectly. The practices prescribed in the Upaniṣads are mostly suited to man at the stage of *saṁnyāsa* (complete renunciation).

In the Upaniṣads, God is pictured as existing inside the living beings as well as outside, and He transcends these two. Devotional attitude does not spring up suddenly and flow down fast in the Upaniṣad. Devotion therein is portrayed as a slow moving, hidden river covered with sand. If a little sand is removed, the clear water can be found. This is the picture of *bhakti* in the Upaniṣads. They reveal knowledge in abundance with *bhakti* hidden but always flowing. This *bhakti* in the knowledge provided meaningful material for the scriptures on devotion.

All types of emotions and sentiments (*nava rasas*[50]) are expressed in their climax and culmination in the Upaniṣads. The sages of the Upaniṣads were highly sentimental and they were also good poets. When their hearts were inspired by God, the Upaniṣads came forth. *Taittirīya Upaniṣad* says,

> That (the experience of knowledge gained) is joy of love. Having obtained this taste (filled with *nava rasas*) man becomes blessed; for who can breathe out or breathe in, if this joy of bliss essence were not there in the cavity of the heart and this *Brahman* Himself brings us joy."[51]

It indicates that the Self, which is a spark of *Brahman*, is full of *rasa*[52] (bliss essence). The Upaniṣads explain that the experience of the Self (as *Brahman*) in the self (as *jīva*) is a positive joy, so perfect in itself that all the sensuous objects put together can never give even a trace of its eternal perfection. Having experienced this spiritual centre (*Brahman*) with supreme love to Him, the individual becomes blessed. *Bhakti* is the only path to enjoy this experience.

---

50. The nine primary emotions (*nava rasas*) are love or passion, humour, patheticness, anger, heroism, fear, disgust, marvel and peace (*śṛṅgāra, hāsya, kāruṇya, raudra, vīra, bhayānaka, bībhatsa, adbhuta* and *śānta*).

51. *Taittirīya Upaniṣad*, Brahmānanda Vallī, Sec. 7.

52. *Ānanda rasa*.

God not only resides in the heaven (*Brahman* consciousness) but He also exists in every vibration of man's thought. He can be addressed by any name and can be given any form. He can even be called "This" and "That". Everything in this ever-changing universe is drawn by Him. The Upaniṣads do not forbid the pleasures of material life. But they lay stress on the idea of understanding the secret of joy and experience in the world.

If observed closely, it will be found that the attitude of *bhakti* does need the presence of ego sense, but more so a peaceful state of mind. There should be a God to rule the people and there should be a world, where all live. Without the ego, the world and the God, the feeling of *bhakti* would not develop in man's heart. No doubt, the Advaita[53] view, expressed in the Upaniṣads, gives predominance to the formless, attributeless Supreme *Brahman* (*Nirguṇa Brahman*). It also speaks of *jīva* merging in *Brahman* by becoming one with Him. But the Upaniṣads also accept the view that there should be a *Brahman* with attributes (*Saguṇa Brahman)* before reaching the state of attributeless *Brahman* (*Nirguṇa Brahman*). The Upaniṣads also accept the presence of a ruler (God), who controls all beings, before each *jīva* merges in Him. He is the creator, the protector of His creations and He is the cause of dissolution. He fashions the *jīva* to experience the results of his own actions, keeping the whole world under His check. A devotee, by his meritorious actions, obtains supreme joy to enjoy this divine experience.

Kaṭha Upaniṣad says,

> As the moving (Sun), He dwells in the heaven (as air). He pervades all and dwells in inter-space (as fire), He resides on the earth (as *sama*), He stays in a jar, He lives among the men, He lives among the Gods, He dwells in space, He is born in sacrifice, He emerges from mountains, He is unchanging. He is great.[54]

---

53. One of the branches of Vedānta.

54. *Kaṭha Upaniṣad*, II.2.

The Upaniṣad continues:

> It is out of fear for their master (God is referred to as master) that all regulated activity is going on in this world. From fear of Him, the fire burns, from fear shines the Sun, from fear run Indra, air, and death the fifth.[55]

We find similar ideas in *Taittirīya Upaniṣad*:

> Through fear of Him blows the wind, through fear of Him rises the sun, through fear of Him again fire and moon and lastly the fifth, death proceed to their respective duties.[56]

To induce *bhakti* in the aspirant the *Muṇḍaka Upaniṣad* says,

> From Him who is all-wise and omniscient and all-knowing in detail (to minuteness) and whose austerity is constituted by knowledge, evolve this derivative *Brahman*, name, colour and food.[57]
>
> From Him emerge *sāma* and *yajur mantra*s, initiation, all sacrifices — whether with or without the sacrificial stake, offering of brāhmaṇas, the year, the sacrifices, and the worlds where the moon sacrifices all and where the sun shines.[58]

Addressing the aspirant with friendly terms to ignite love in the Creator, the spiritual teacher of *Muṇḍaka Upaniṣad* says,

> Luminous, subtler than even atoms, that imperishable *Brahman* in the abode of the world and all its inhabitants. It is life, speech, mind, reality, and immortality. That is the mark, which should be penetrated by the mind. Penetrate It, O my friend.[59]

It is the perfect concentration and contemplation alone through which this mark can be attained. Unless there is uninterrupted contemplation, the mark of *Brahman* cannot be reached. This is

55. *Kaṭha Upaniṣad*, II.3.3.
56. *Taittirīya Upaniṣad*, Brahmānanda Vallī, 8.
57. *Muṇḍaka Upaniṣad*, I.1.9.
58. *Muṇḍaka Upaniṣad*, II.1.6.
59. *Muṇḍaka Upaniṣad*, II.2.2.

an indirect way of bringing the attitude of devotion into the aspirant's mind. Even if man accepts the formless, attributeless *Brahman* (God is referred as *Brahman* here) he will have to accept a God who rules the world and the individual souls, so long as he sees them exist. Here, the Supreme God and the God who rules the world are not different. Seeing from the aspect of space, time and cause, the Supreme God (*Brahman* of the Upaniṣads) Himself transforms into God of love and religion. It is the personal God alone, who makes man understand the hidden truth behind the world, if he goes a little further away than the existing world. This is to be reached through the mind. The God of love is the only one, the most loveable one, who is very near to all. None other than Him can be loved so much. The culmination of knowledge, power, and divinity are in Him only. If one understands the God of his religion, then he understands the Supreme God. "God without attributes" and "God with attributes" are like the two sides of a coin. It is the power of the Supreme God that stands over a man to direct him to reach his goal of perceiving Him and then merging in Him.

Kena Upaniṣad uses a story to bring to light the power of *Brahman*: Once there was a war between gods and demons. The gods won due to the power of *Brahman*; but due to ignorance, they thought it was due to their strength. *Brahman* thought of eliminating their pride. As they were congratulating each other on their victory, a strange figure appeared before them, whose identity they could not make out. They sent Agni, Vāyu, etc. to find out who he was. But they failed in their efforts. When Indra went near that strange figure, it became invisible. Instead, the lustrous, beautiful Umā (considered as the wife of Lord Śiva, also the brilliance of white) stood in that place. She revealed the truth to Indra.[60] Umā here represents *Brahman* with attributes. Through her, the gods understood the real nature of *Brahman*.

60. *Kena Upaniṣad*, III.

The above story demonstrates how *Brahman* without attributes (*Nirguṇa Brahman*) can be known through *Brahman* with attributes (*Saguṇa Brahman*). The same *Upaniṣad* says through an instruction on *Brahman*,

> It is the mind that reaches as it were that (*Brahman*) and by which the aspirant constantly reflects upon that *Brahman*. This is the way he should direct his mind.[61]

Unless there is the attitude of devotion in the aspirant's mind, it is not possible to reflect constantly on *Brahman*. When the mind is filled with devotion, it becomes free from ego[62] and becomes powerful enough to be near to *Brahman*. Yama (the God of Death) tells Naciketā (son of the sage Vājaśravasa):

> This Supreme Self cannot be known through much study, nor through intellect, nor through much hearing. It can be known through Self alone that the aspirant prays to. This Supreme Self of that seeker reveals its true Supreme nature.[63]

Only to a man without desire, who seeks for the Self alone with devotion, the Supreme Self becomes known. *Kaṭha Upaniṣad* (1.3.9) describes the highest state of man's spiritual consciousness as "The man however, who has, as his character, a discriminating intellect and who has under control the reins of the mind attains the end of the road." This end of the road is the state of highest spiritual consciousness that unites man with God. The same Upaniṣad describes the end of the road as: "By the seer of subtle things, He is seen through a pointed and fine intellect."[64] When the mind gains perfection through concentration, the intellect

---

61. *Kena Upaniṣad*, IV.5.
62. Ego of lower attitudes does not induce *bhakti* in the mind. Free from ego means that the mind forgets even the mere "I" sense and thinks he is God's and belongs to God.
63. *Kaṭha Upaniṣad*, I.2.23; *Muṇḍaka Upaniṣad*, II.2.3.
64. *Kaṭha Upaniṣad*, I.3.12.

becomes extremely subtle. Then immediate perception of *Brahman* comes to man. One can read, hear, discuss on the Self. But it cannot be attained through these alone. One has to pray to Him constantly to reveal His grace, then only it is possible to understand Him.

Śvetāśvatara Upaniṣad stresses the importance of God's grace:

> In this infinite wheel (changing universe) of *Brahman*, in which everything lives and rests, the pilgrim-soul is whirled about. Knowing the individual soul (*jīva*), hitherto regarded as separate, to be itself the Moving Force, and blessed by Him, it attains immortality.[65]

The spiritual progression is compared to a pilgrimage. Again, *Śvetāśvatara Upaniṣad* praises supreme devotion as:

> These truths, when taught, shine forth only in that high souled one, who has supreme devotion to God and an equal degree of devotion to the spiritual teacher. They shine forth in that high-souled one.[66]

Devotion should be for devotion's sake. Only then, devotion transforms into supreme devotion. There should be no transaction of giving and taking involved. The only gain is the gain of bliss through the love for God. God alone is worthy of love. He is the *Brahman* and *Īśvara*, the Supreme Self. Just as the rivers join and merge into the sea, the devotees' spiritual consciousness flows towards God and mingles with Him.

The Upaniṣads lay stress on the importance of a spiritual *guru* to kindle *bhakti* towards God in an aspirant. The *guru* acts as a guide. Hindu scriptures uphold the *guru*'s status equal to that of Brahmā, Viṣṇu and Maheśvara, the three aspects of the Supreme Self. However, self-effort, exceptional renunciation and God's grace are also essential for the realisation of the Highest

---

65. *Śvetāśvatara Upaniṣad*, XI.6.

66. *Śvetāśvatara Upaniṣad*, VI.23.

Truth. One cannot have self-realisation as a gift from a *guru*. While introducing the concept of devotion, *Īśāvāsya Upaniṣad* says, "All this (what ever moves on this world) should be enveloped by God."[67]

Whatever one sees, hears and experiences should have the idea of God in it. If whatever one sees is as if soaked in God, and makes Him drip in that, one will not be bound by any bondage. When one forgets God, one falls into the sea of ignorance. There is only one way to come out of ignorance, namely contemplating on God uninterruptedly. All, the entire world, should be covered by Him.

An aspirant in *Īśāvāsya Upaniṣad* prays to his personal God, the Sun, for His grace

> O Sun! Thou controller and supporter of all, contract Thy rays, Gather Thy light. Through Thy grace, I behold the most blessed form of Thine.[68]

One is certain to obtain God's grace through constant prayers. *Taittirīya Upaniṣad* portrays devotion by praying Indra[69] for the knowledge of *Brahman*. Indra here is not merely the god of other gods (minor gods) but is the Supreme *Brahman*, who is omnipresent, omniscient, whose form is manifold.[70]

Only if Indra bestows his grace, is the knowledge of *Brahman* bestowed upon the devotees. Attaining this very knowledge makes man see *Brahman* in all. However, before that, there is the need of a *guru* (spiritual master, who has practically gained the knowledge of *Brahman*), who acts as a guide to make one acquire the knowledge of *Brahman*. An individual can attain the knowledge of *Brahman* under a *guru* only if he is keen in his

---

67. *Īśāvāsya Upaniṣad*, 1.
68. *Īśāvāsya Upaniṣad*, 16.
69. One of the primal Vedic divinities.
70. *Taittirīya Upaniṣad*, Brahmānanda Vallī, 4.

personal efforts of making *Brahman* reside in each and everywhere in him.

In the *Taittirīya Upaniṣad*, the Supreme Self is described as truth (*satyam*), knowledge (*jñānam*) and infinite (*anantam*). In Vedānta philosophy, *satyam* indicates the Real — the changeless substratum for all change and modification. It is the intelligence itself. *Jñānam* indicates the consciousness or conscious principle, beaming around in its awareness, illuminating all objects that it comes across. *Anantam* means infinite, unborn and eternal; that truth reveals itself as infinite and consciousness.

Desire is a mental disturbance. Only when there is an end to this disturbance, the peaceful mind allows the joy of the soul to beam out. The repository of all joy is the Self. The pure awareness or Reality is itself Absolute Bliss. *Taittirīya Upaniṣad* declares that all joys come from the Self and they are seen through the intervals of peace in the mind's natural state of thoughts. Generally, man identifies himself with sensory perceptions and thereby suffers. But when he understands that he is not the body nor the senses, and that he is beyond everything, he does not come back to the lower level of consciousness. At this stage, the ego-consciousness dissolves and the mind becomes pure. The devotee keeps direct contact with God; he will be near to God.

The word Absolute Bliss is generally referred to as the place of Heaven (*svarga*). It means the state of unmixed joy and happiness, the state of unvarying bliss that stems from consciousness, while in constant contact with God. The goal of the devotee is attained in this state. He considers God in a higher status and above Him and worships Him with utmost respect. This respectful worship makes him know more and more about God. God is different from all objects — known or unknown. The knowledge of God flows from the flawless intellect. It is a revelation that comes instantaneously to a devotee. God is the essence of everything and the indwelling spirit of all existence is limitless. All the Upaniṣads teach unceasingly the methods of investigation. When one attains God at all levels of one's consciousness, one attains the true knowledge of Him.

Just as a thread runs through the jewels in a necklace, God — as awareness (*caitanya*) — is present through all mental experiences of a man. Just as a lighted lamp illumines all objects kept in a room, the mind in all of its functions is illumined by God. So, the mind should be constantly preserved in moral and spiritual refinement.

The Concept of Bhakti in the Purāṇas

The word *purāṇa*[71] means "belonging to the past". Purāṇa became the traditional mode of teaching in the past to make the ordinary mass understand the inner essence of the Vedas. Purāṇa adopted the path of devotion.

The world changes its attitudes in the minutest split of every second. Man is incapable of observing the changes that are taking place right in front of his eyes. These changes made it difficult for him to adopt the principles laid down in the Vedic traditions. This failure in adopting the principles brought about a total agitation in his mind. He needed some solace to bring his mind back to a balance. Devotion to God was born at that moment to bless man.

In the *Śrīmad Bhāgavata Purāṇa*,[72] the divine sage Nārada says that the easiest path to the Lord is the path of devotion. All other paths of Yoga are harder paths which lead to the feet of God. The praises of God (Nārāyaṇa), even if they are couched in wrong words, even if they are sung out of tune, will assure man of the grace of the Lord. Like a piece of *araṇi*[73] (a kind of tree) which, when churned, will give smoke first and fire later,

71. *Pura Bhavam* — of the Past.

72. One of the 18 Purāṇas.

73. *Araṇi* is a fire producing plant. Pieces of wood of *araṇi* are used for kindling the sacred fire by attrition.

which will consume the wood itself, even so, the mind of man, when churned by constant devotion to the Lord, will make all evil in him come out on the surface. The true *sāttvika* nature of man will then blaze forth and like fire, it will consume the bondage of *karma* and grant him liberation forever. Even if a man fails in the duties ascribed to him, even if he is a sinner, but if there is a spring of love, of devotion to God in his heart, that will wash away his sins, and he will be dear to Him. The highlights of Purāṇa thus began to illumine the mind of the masses.

There are many Purāṇas. According to all orthodox estimates, Purāṇas derive their validity from the Vedas. The philosophical elements of the Upaniṣads and the *Brahma-Sūtra* are also preserved in the Purāṇic tradition.

In the mythological compositions of the Purāṇas, gods are presented as the actual personalities and the characters in them have the element of joy and sorrow like mortals on earth. Through god-related tales, the great saints of the past enjoyed an immersion in the ocean of God's bliss within their hearts. Purāṇas advice the mind to find solace in God, by bringing it in direct contact with Him. A special section in all the Purāṇas is devoted to the treatment of creation and dissolution, bringing out philosophical speculations.

All Purāṇas speak — directly or indirectly — of *bhakti* with its different aspects; e.g. in *Padma Purāṇa,* there is a mention of *brahma bhakti,* which can be by word, deed or thought. It distinguishes between *sāṁkhya bhakti* and *yoga bhakti.* The knowledge of 24 principles and their distinction from the ultimate principle *puruṣa,* as also the knowledge of the relation among *puruṣa, prakṛti* and the individual soul is known as *sāṁkhya bhakti.* The practice of *prāṇāyāma*[74] and meditation (*dhyāna*) upon the mind constitute *yoga bhakti.* The term *bhakti* is used in a special

74. The general technique of *prāṇāyāma* is: Facing east, sit cross-legged with an erect back. Fold the index and the middle finger of the right hand. Bend the right arm to bring the right hand in front of the nose. →

sense in *Padma Purāṇa*. They narrate the stories of the Lord and many of His incarnations (*avatāra*) to establish *dharma* or righteousness on earth.

Avatāra means "descent" or "the one, who has descended". The Divine, from time to time, comes down to the earthly plane to raise its creation to a higher status. The goal of the *avatāra* is to establish a new *dharma*. Whenever there is an excess of unrighteousness (*adharma*) in life and all sorts of materialism invade the heart of human beings, God descends to the earth to preserve the equilibrium — assuming a human form and nature. God is incomprehensible, not bound by anything, including the chain of cause and effect, which makes ordinary man live through the cycles of births and deaths. God is beyond all these shackles. But man is not great enough to realise Him. Man can only see through human eyes, perceive through the senses and he grasps things only through human intellect. God in His infinite kindness has assumed many forms of living beings so that people could see Him. These forms helped the people. He established *dharma*, whenever there was a threat of *dharma* being eclipsed by *adharma*. By His teachings and examples, He showed, how a human being could raise himself to a higher quality of life. Love and mercy are more powerful than hatred and cruelty. *Dharma* will eventually conquer *adharma*. The reality, which is Being, Intelligence and Bliss will overthrow sin.

Dharma literally means "mode of being". It is the essential nature of a being that determines its mode of behaviour, so long as our actions are in the right spirit. *Adharma* is a non-conformity

→ Then close the right nostril with the thumb and inhale through the left nostril. At the end of the inhalation, hold the breath for 5 or 10 seconds according to your capacity. Close the left nostril with the ring and the little finger. Open the right nostril and exhale through the right nostril. Keeping the left nostril closed inhale through the right nostril. Again, hold the breath for 5 or 10 seconds according to your capacity. Then close the right nostril, open the left nostril and exhale through the left nostril. This forms one cycle.

to our true nature. It is the privilege of God to keep the world going on the lines of righteousness. He assumes *avatāra* to re-establish the right when wrong prevails.

There are ten significant incarnations according to the Hindu concept. They are in the following order: Matsya (the fish), Kūrma (the tortoise), Varāha (the boar), Narasiṁha (the man-lion), Vāmana (the human dwarf), Paraśurāma,[75] Śrī Rāma, Śrī Kṛṣṇa and Buddha (all the four as human beings) and Kalki, which is yet to take place.

Contemplation on God becomes difficult for man due to the circumstances under which he is forced to live. By listening to stories of God in His many incarnations, even the worst sinner can be saved. Purāṇas speak of His *avatāra*, apart from many other stories, glorifying God. The path to the Lord is devotion — *bhakti mārga*. *Bhakti* is seen as the golden thread running through the stories in the Purāṇas. This helps man to contemplate on God, to realise Him and to reach Him. Listening to the stories of Gods' glories is also a spiritual exercise. Based on the concept of the 10 incarnations, it is found that the presence of God is in each creation. His stories are the driving force in inducing devotion among the masses.

Many divine experiences of devotees, who had the direct vision of God through their immense love for Him, are also found in the Purāṇas. All Purāṇas reveal one Single Truth: the existence of God. Truth is characterised by its universality, though devotees speak of their experiences according to the language specific to their tradition. A tradition is authentic, when it evokes a satisfactory response to the reality presented by it. It is valid, when the minds of the people thrill with it and vibrate with its content.

A devotee may refer to the Ultimate Reality as Nārāyaṇa, Viṣṇu, Rāma, Kṛṣṇa and so forth, or as Śiva, Śambhu, Śaṅkara,

75. A great and powerful sage defeated by Lord Rāma. He is a minor incarnation of Viṣṇu.

Parameśvara and so on. The former is called Vaiṣṇava[76] and the later Śaiva. But the value of their spiritual experiences does not vary.

The human eye can see only outward forms. The eye of the spirit perceives the inner soul. There is a type of knowledge that one can acquire by one's own efforts, the knowledge based on the activities of senses and intellect. Another kind of knowledge is possible, when one is under the influence of God's grace; this is a direct knowledge of spiritual realities. God's vision is a gift of God. This vision is not a mental construction, but a disclosure of a truth, which is beyond the finite mind. The directness of experiences and the spiritual visions of devotees are found in the Purāṇas.

Men, in different stages of their spiritual development, worship Gods, the ancestors and the spirit of the dead, but being limited in metaphysical forms, men routinely fail to acquire the peace, that is beyond all understanding. These worships in limited forms give only limited results. No devotion will fail in its highest reward. Any sincere devotion is a search for this highest God.

Purāṇas throw light on the subtle aspects of a spiritual life to the devotees. According to the Purāṇas, spiritual knowledge cannot be acquired directly from the scriptures without divine grace, which is canalised through a spiritual preceptor.

The relation between God and His devotee is unique. The Almighty, who is omnipotent and invincible, allows Himself to be charmed by His devotees. A true devotee is not swayed by the worldly attractions and remains devoted to God, even when beset with misfortunes. Purāṇas deal with the life of such devotees. All the Purāṇas significantly point out, how the unique relationship between God and His devotee is forged due to love and devotion respectively. Just as a father who is happy when

76. The follower of Viṣṇu is a Vaiṣṇava; the follower of Śiva is a Śaiva.

his child outshines him in life, God delights in the spiritual progress of His devotees.

Through stories, the Purāṇas give a description of the universe with God's outstanding glories that raise man to the highest level in his spiritual progress step by step.

Kaṭha Upaniṣad says, "Consciousness should be raised step by step. The higher the consciousness is raised, the more free men are."[77] Purāṇas support this statement, describing God's manifestations and their glories.

The universe consists of an infinite number of objects and an infinite number of creatures. For the proper regulation and control of these diverse orders of creation, they have been classified into various divisions under God's immutable laws and each division has been placed under the control of a supervisor or chief, so that the process of their creation, maintenance and destruction may be carried on, strictly according to the law. The Hindu Vedic chiefs are Rudra, Āditya, Sādhya, Viśvedeva, Marut, Pitṛdeva, Manu, Saptarṣi, etc. They are believed to have both, an embodied and unembodied form. All of them are nothing but the representations of some of God's glories.

Viṣṇu Purāṇa says,

> All the Gods, all Manus, the seven seers, as well as the sons of Manus, Indra — the chief of Gods — all these are special manifestations or glories of Lord Viṣṇu.[78]

These representatives are duly chosen from various orders of creations for the proper functioning of creation. In the selection, the choice particularly falls on those who manifest God's lustre, energy, strength, learning, knowledge and power. Purāṇas speak of the essentials of all these to enable man to understand the process of creation.

---

77. *Kaṭha Upaniṣad*, III.10.

78. *Viṣnua Purāṇa*, III.1.46.

Great Devotees of the Purāṇas

The concept of surrender emphasises the Almighty's Lordship of the entire creation and hence, when a devotee seeks refuge in Him, the responsibility of granting succour to him rests upon the Lord. The *Śrīmad Bhāgavata Purāṇa* speaks of many such instances: Prahlāda, the son of a demon-king; Gajendra, an elephant; and Draupadī, the wife of Pāṇḍavas.

PRAHLĀDA

The demon-child, Prahlāda, was a staunch devotee of Lord Nārāyaṇa. His demon-father, Hiraṇyakaśipu, did not like his son's love and respect for Nārāyaṇa. An argument ensued between them and the enraged father was about to cut-off Prahlāda's head with his drawn sword, when a terrible noise was heard and a pillar in the royal hall split into two. Out of it emerged Lord Nārāyaṇa with the face and the chest like that of a lion and waist-downwards of a man. This form is the Narasiṁha incarnation (man-lion form). Hiraṇyakaśipu had a boon from Brahmā: None of Brahmā's creations should be able to kill him, and he should not be killed with any weapon. So God assumed a unique form not created by Brahmā. With His nails and His teeth, He tore the entrails of Hiraṇyakaśipu out. The sight was dreadful, as Hiraṇyakaśipu's end had come. The child-devotee, Prahlāda, fell at the feet of Lord Narasiṁha, washing them with tears. The Lord placed His hand on the head of this child-devotee and raised him up. Overcome by emotion, Prahlāda prayed for the everlasting presence of God's form in his heart. As God does not expect anything from a devotee, except devotion, He saved Prahlāda, whose devotion was limitless.

Prahlāda says,

> He who has motiveless devotion to Śrī Hari (another name of Viṣṇu, the Supreme Being), in him all virtues and all divinities abide. If one has no such devotion, how can noble qualities (like renunciation, discrimination, universal love, etc.) arise in one, as a

mind without devotion to God always goes outward to petty objects and imaginary sense enjoyments? Just as water is to fish, so is Śrī Hari (another name of Viṣṇu, the Supreme Being) to the life of a devotee. People who ignore His majesty and get attached more to domestic felicities — how can they pretend to be, or be accepted as, great men? To do so is as ridiculous as the world's convention of recognising the superiority of married couples merely by considering their age.[79]

GAJENDRA

Gajendra was an elephant. Instigated by fate, a crocodile, which had been living in the lake for a long time, grasped the leg of the elephant Gajendra (who had gone to the lake to drink water), with its mighty jaws. The elephant winced in pain and tried to shake off the crocodile. But even after much effort, it was impossible for the elephant to free itself from the crocodile's clutches. The tussle went on for hours. The crocodile was gaining ascendancy and found himself stronger and more powerful. At that moment, the elephant realised that his life would soon leave his body. Now, seeing everything in the proper perspective, he surrendered to the Lord, who is the refuge of even Gods like Brahmā. Touched by the elephant's plight the Lord appeared before him, killed the crocodile and pulled the elephant out of the lake.

This is one of the instances when God rushed to save His devotee. This incident has a special significance, because it reveals God's assurance of His grace to a devotee, although the devotee is a sub-human. God protects all His creations in their different forms.

DHRUVA

Human birth is the long process of evolution wherein the *jīva* — by its own merit — is blessed by God. The life of Dhruva, the child-devotee illustrates this truth. Spurned by his father, Uttāna-pāda, at his stepmother's behest, who wanted her own child to be doted upon, Dhruva was stung by the treatment meted out to on

79. *Śrīmad Bhāgavata*, V.18.12-13.

him. He was hardly five-year-old then. His mother, Suniti, tried her best to console him saying that one must not entertain evil thoughts about others. She pointed out that a man reaps in this life every suffering he has inflicted on others in a previous existence. She instead diverted his mind, advising him to adore the Almighty, who was capable of blessing him with all he desired. Dhruva, intent on winning back his father's love, immediately left for the forest to perform intense penance. Sage Nārada, who learnt about it, tried to dissuade the child, saying that he was too young to undertake such austerities, but seeing his determination he blessed him and taught him the method of winning the Divine grace by initiating him into the *vāsudeva mantra*.[80] Dhruva was blessed with the vision of the Lord in a very short period, though very young, because of his one-pointed devotion. He got all he desired — Dhruva was speechless, when he beheld the Lord and his heart overflowed with devotion for Him. The Lord sensed that the child wanted to enrol him, but did not know how to do so. He touched the child's cheek with His conch, which is considered to be the concrete form of the Vedas. Dhruva was instantly blessed with spiritual knowledge and sung the glory of the Lord. God granted the child his heartfelt desire and a permanent place in the Divine abode.

In *Śrīmad Bhāgavata Purāṇa*, the Love for God is treated in two main forms. These are *jñāna bhakti* and *bhāva bhakti*. In *jñāna bhakti*, love is based on a vivid awareness of Divine majesties and makes one sink into Him in utter self-surrender and becomes one with His being, through His grace. *Bhāva bhakti* (sentimental devotion) is based on the sense of loving intimacy with Him. It does not seek dissolution in Him, but essential service to Him.

The profound teachings by Kapila[81] on *ātma vidyā* to his mother Devāhuti are also found in *Śrīmad Bhāgavata Purāṇa*. Kapila

---

80. Certain syllables, when arranged in a particular way, bestow certain powers hidden in them, when repeated for a prescribed number of times with faith. The *Vasudeva Mantra* is *oṁ namo bhagavate vāsudevāya*: Salutations to God Whom is the Divine Source, the indweller of all.

81. Considered as an incarnation of Mahā Viṣṇu.

(who propounded Sāṁkhya philosophy) kindles *bhakti* in his mother's mind through *ātma vidyā* (also known as *brahma vidyā*). *Ātman* is the *Puruṣa*,[82] who has no beginning and no end. He is self-ruminant, pervades everything and is eternal. *Prakṛti* is the cause of the conditioning of *Ātma*. *Puruṣa* pervades the world of plurality. Kapila suggests his mother Devāhuti to follow the path of devotion to be free from the two forces of *avidyā* and *māyā* that capture *jīva*.

Devotion to God gives rise to pure knowledge and non-attachment. Love for God makes one indifferent to other loves, and thereby non-attachment is achieved. When a devotee realises that the only aim in life is to reach God and strives for it, he has learnt the truth, and his ignorance (*avidyā*) vanishes. It is the *Brahman*, *Puruṣa*, *Īśvara*, or *Bhagavān* — according to different paths — which seek Him, who is revealed in all manifestations in the world of plurality. Realising *Brahman* is not a knowing but a becoming.

The life of man on earth can be compared to a boat on the sea, by the name *saṁsāra* (voyage of worldly life — mundane existence). So that the boat reaches across safely, it should be rowed properly, otherwise the boat will sink. This proper rowing is *bhakti*. When *bhakti* springs in man's heart, he will surely reach the coveted liberation from all bondage.

Whether it is a full-grown human, a child, a sub-human or any other species, created by God, he — and she — will surely be graced by God, who is the embodiment of compassion, if he is devoted to God.

HANUMĀN[83]

Devotee poets hail Hanumān as the one who protected the lives of those dear to Rāma. He was a great devotee of Rāma.

---

82. One, who resides in the city of the body.

83. He was the son of Añjanā by the God of wind. He is represented as a monkey of extraordinary strength and powers. He as a Minister of Sugrīva, played an important role in the Great War at Laṅkā.

Devotion is of three types — motivated, unmotivated and ultimate. In the third kind of devotion, the devotee sees the Lord as immanent. There have been innumerable devotees, who have done yeomen service not only to the Lord, but also to the Lord's messengers and His ardent devotees. But an exceptional example of the ultimate type, who dedicated everything — his body and soul — to Lord Rāma was Āñjaneya (Hanumān). He realised that Rāma was an incarnation of the Supreme Being and served Him with pure love and devotion, without expecting anything in return. He was humble, brave, wise and possessed all the virtues expected of a true devotee.

Hanumān's prayers were answered. He saved Sītā just in time. It was Hanumān in the epic *Rāmāyaṇa* who displayed courage, foresightedness and — above all — deep faith in the Divine wealth.

From the moment Hanumān considered Rāma to be an incarnation of the Supreme Being, he showed untainted devotion and lived for Him and Him alone. He had no other interest in the world except serving Rāma. He was the true possessor of the wealth of *Rāma Nāma*.[84]

While Rāma granted Liberation to all animate things, who lived in Ayodhyā, Hanumān was not willing to leave this world, where Rāma lived. He only wanted to continue living with Rāma in the world, where he could listen to the glory of Śrī Rāma. It is apparent from Hanumān's own words that he is present wherever the Lord's glory is recited, as said in the epic, "As long as your Divine tale will circulate on this earth, so long shall I stay on the earth. . . ."[85]

His devotion of God was not a means to the realisation of God, but an end in itself; such devotion does not seek anything in return and one's unbounded love of God expresses itself in the acts of service to Him and is very rare to attain.

84. All the powers are hidden in the word Rāma.

85. *Rāmāyaṇa*, Uttara Kāṇḍa, 108.36.

BHĪṢMA

Bhīṣma, the son of King Śāntanu of the lunar race, was the "elder" of both the Pāṇḍava and the Kaurava. When he renounced the kingdom and the worldly pleasures, for the sake of his father, he was given the name Bhīṣma, which means "terrible". Having lain on his bed of arrows for full 50 days and eight, Bhīṣma resolved to give up his physical body with embodied soul on the day the Sun turned towards north, and spoke to Lord Kṛṣṇa, as "O Lotus eyed one, O highest person, pray redeem this soul". "Kṛṣṇa, I Pray allow me to cast off my body. Leaving this body with your leave I shall attain the Supreme state."[86]

The Lord gave His assent. Thereupon Bhīṣma stopped his breath through Yoga and gradually began to push it upwards. As the outgoing breath left a particular part of the body in its upward journey, the shafts stuck into that part got detatched and the wounds got healed. In an instant all the arrows dropped out of Bhīṣma's body, not a single wound was left and his vital breath forced its way upwards — through what is known as *brahmarandhra* (an aperture in the crown of the head). People saw that a column of light issued from the *brahmarandhra*, which disappeared into the sky in the twinkling of an eye.

DRAUPADĪ

Being kept as wage by Dharmarāja, the eldest of the Pāṇḍavas, the wife of Pāṇḍava, Draupadī, had been won by Prince Duryodhana in the game of dice. As per the rules of wage, she should become the property of Duryodhana (the eldest of Kauravas). She was brought to the Royal Hall by Duḥśāsana, the second of the Kauravas, who started dragging at the upper cloth of the enraged queen Draupadī to publicly insult her. Overcome by agony, she folded her palms together and surrendered completely to Lord Kṛṣṇa. Then a miracle happened: Draupadī's clothes kept on getting longer and longer

86. *Mahābhārata*, Anuśāsana Parva, 167.45.

and clad her like the infinite kindness of God. Duḥśāsana tired, could no longer continue pulling her clothes. At last, exhausted, he gave up the attempt and sat down with chagrin written all over his face. Draupadī's modesty was thus saved by Lord Kṛṣṇa, whose great devotee she was.

Representation of God in the Created World

The Purāṇas speak in very high terms of the presence of God in every human being, sub-human being, trees, plants and so forth. Speaking of the fig tree (*aśvattha* tree), it is said: In the root of the holy fig tree resides Viṣṇu, in the trunk, Keśava, in the branches, Nārāyaṇa, in the leaves Lord Hari, and in the fruits abides Acyuta in conjunction with all Gods.[87] There is not the least doubt in this. This tree is Viṣṇu Himself appearing in a concrete form.[88] In addition, Śrī Kṛṣṇa says in the *Bhagavad-Gītā*:

> Of the trees, I am *aśvattha*. Exalted souls worship the sacred root of this tree. Dependence on this tree wipes out thousands of men's sins, grants their prayers and bestows merits.[89]

These types of stories and explanations instil a devotional attitude into peoples' minds. Of special attraction to devotion in the Purāṇa are the visions God blesses with to some of his devotees. *Śrīmad Bhāgavata Purāṇa* describes the vision of the universe, as seen by Yaśodā, the foster-mother of Lord Śrī Kṛṣṇa: As an infant, Śrī Kṛṣṇa had been giving incomparable joy to the hearts of His mother Yaśodā and men and women of Vraja (the city where Śrī Kṛṣṇa used to live) by his childish plays and pranks of marvellous nature. One day, he ate up a huge quantity of mud. Thereupon snubbing him, the mother said "O, wilful child! Why should you have stealthily eaten up mud?" To this, the Lord opened his mouth to show her that he had not eaten the mud. Looking into the mouth, Yaśodā was taken aback in absolute

87. Keśava, Nārāyaṇa, Acyuta are the other names of Viṣṇu.
88. *Skanda Purāṇa*, Nagara Kāṇḍa, 247.41, 42, 44.
89. *Bhagavad-Gītā*, X.26.

wonder. She saw, in the small mouth of the baby Kṛṣṇa, the entire creation, the cosmos including the animate and inanimate worlds: the sky, the 10 cardinal points, mountains, islands, oceans, the earth, air, fire, the moon, stars, the deities presiding over the senses, the senses and the mind, the sense objects like sound, etc. the *jīva*s and their various forms and the whole of Vraja. She wondered whether she was awake or dreaming. Finally, she was seized with fear and surprise and, bowing to Him, surrendered herself to Lord Śrī Kṛṣṇa.

Who will not be spellbound by listening to these intense stories of philosophical speculations? Another devotee, sage Mārkaṇḍeya, describes his vision of God as

> The entire universe was water-flooded. Nothing could be seen except water. At that moment Lord Nārāyaṇa appeared in the form of a child lying on an *aśvattha* leaf (fig leaf) with his lotus hands holding the great toe of his lotus foot to his lips, with a smile of contentment lighting his face.[90]

Śāṇḍilya's and Nārada's Aphorisms on Bhakti

Śāṇḍilya Bhakti Sūtra and *Nārada Bhakti Sūtra*[91] form the classical authority on the philosophy of devotion. The aspirants of the doctrine of devotion should study the views of Nārada and Śāṇḍilya on *bhakti* to understand the subject clearly. Both these sages adorned the spiritual horizons of India. They both dealt with the subject of devotion, but the modes of approach were different. While Śāṇḍilya's approach is more intellectual, Nārada deals the subject in a more emotional and realistic way. That is to say, Śāṇḍilya has evolved a philosophy of devotion whereas Nārada has made it a practical religion of devotion.

The exact date and life of Śāṇḍilya are difficult to ascertain, because in olden days Indian mind was indifferent to history.

90. *Śrīmad Bhāgavata Purāṇa*.

91. *Sūtra*s are aphorisms.

Indians bent only towards the knowledge a sage possessed. On the one hand, he seems to have lived between 500 BCE and CE 900 from the commentaries on *Śāṇḍilya Sūtra,* on the other hand, his date is restricted to the period between CE 200 and 900. Whatever may be his time, while going through his aphorisms on *bhakti;* the reader appreciates and enjoys his intellectual approach to the subject forgetting about the period he belonged to. Nothing much is known about his life too. That was the way, a true devotee used to live.

As far as Nārada is concerned, it may be gathered from certain passages in *Śrīmad Bhāgavata Purāṇa* that Nārada was the son of a maid servant; through the grace of some great souls he became a man of God. All the Purāṇas contain many references to him, because the heavenly melodies and the invention of the lute (*vīṇā*) are credited to him. "He (Nārada) rejoices himself by playing on his divine lute, and singing the glories of the Lord, he delights the afflicted world".[92] Nārada's divine love is equalled by his divine wisdom, acquired through austerities and the contact with sage Sanatkumāra.[93]

Once Nārada admitted to Sanatkumāra, the great sage, that he could not remove the burden of sorrow by the study of Vedas, its auxiliaries, the secular sciences like mathematics, physics, medicine, chronology, polity, archery, logic and the rest. Then Sanatkumāra enlightened him about the infinite Bliss *Bhuma.*[94] *Bhuma* is another name for *Brahman.*

The *Mahābhārata* (XII.194-95) describes how he contemplated for 100 years with great zeal under touch ascetic discipline, how he arrived at the infinite form of Śrī Kṛṣṇa sporting in Vraja (a village in north India) and how the Lord taught him the need of unswerving devotion. It is also said that he first got the vision

92. *Srīmad Bhāgavata Purāṇa,* I.7.38.39.

93. Sanat is one of four sons of *Brahman.* As he is blessed with a special power to remain young forever, he is called Sanatkumāra, Kumāra meaning young.

94. *Chāndogya Upaniṣad,* VII.1.2.

of *Sāvitri* and then of Lord Viṣṇu, while performing great austerities near a Himalayan lake.[95]

Nārada is the divine messenger in the Purāṇas, the friend, philosopher, guide and console of all minor gods, men and demons; the intermediary between God and His creation. The name Nārada means "the great person, who infuses the knowledge of God in the mind of human beings". This is the exalted role of the divine sage Nārada. He took the view that the first duty of a creature is to realise the Divine Truth, and then only should he enter upon the worldly life.

Commissioned with a divine mission, Nārada is one of those who represent a man of true knowledge, a *yogī* and a devotee. He, however, preferred to deal with *bhakti* as being the most efficient and easiest of all paths, which is available for all — irrespective of caste, creed and gender.

The three functions of the mind — intellect, emotion and will — have to be purified of the dirt of ego. *Jñāna yoga* purifies the intellect, *karma yoga* the will and *bhakti yoga* the emotions. The sole condition of knowing God is to aim at the purity of mind. Jesus Christ puts this great truth in his words as "Blessed are the pure in heart, for they shall see God".

The *Nārada Bhakti Sūtra* advocates a way of purifying the emotions, to provide a clear background and motive for the service of God and man.

ŚĀṆḌILYA'S VIEW ON BHAKTI

The 100 aphorisms on *bhakti* by the sage Śāṇḍilya are full of intellectual essence. He starts his *sūtra* on *bhakti* saying "the desire to know about *bhakti* (must be cultivated)".

The earliest commentator on the *Bhakti Sūtra* of Śāṇḍilya is the great philosopher Svapneśvara. Commenting on the first *sūtra* he says,

95. *Mahābhārata*, XII.190.

> The soul (*ātman*) is all-pervading in nature. So it is bound to pervade the mind (*antaḥkaraṇa*) which is by nature limited and finite, as the mind is made up of three *guṇa*s of *sattva, rajas* and *tamas*. These *guṇa*s of the mind cause the erroneous perception that *ātmā* is itself body and mind. To remove this wrong perception that creates the sense of bondage some method should be adopted. By the knowledge of *ātman,* it cannot be removed, though this knowledge purifies the mind. This knowledge is incapable of removing the superimposition of the characteristics of the mind on *ātman,* since it is directly connected with it. It cannot be possible to remove *ātman,* which is the very basis of existence and manifestation. Removal of the sense of bondage is possible only by the removal of the limiting adjunct, that is, working the *buddhi* back into its original cause. This can be done only through the devotion to God.

Citing the example of the *Bhagavad-Gītā,* he concludes that it can be done only through the devotion to God. "And he who serves Me with an unwavering devotion transcends the three *guṇa*s of *sattva, rajas* and *tamas* as is fit to become *Brahman*."[96] The knowledge of jaundice cannot prevent a jaundice patient from seeing a white object as yellow. Inquiry into devotion bears the fruit in the form of the highest good. It is the highest love for God.[97]

Devotion is defined as the highest love of attachment to God. It is the highest attachment to the object of worship. This attachment is associated with pleasure. Devotion is nothing but the love to be cultivated towards the being that is to be propitiated. This love to God should remain unshakeable, like in the prayer of Prahlāda:

> O Lord, even though I may have to pass through thousands of wombs, let there be in me for ever, O! Acyuta, unshakeable devotion to thee, in each of these births.[98]

---

96. *Bhagavad-Gītā,* XIV.26.
97. *Śāṇḍilya Bhakti Sūtra,* 2.
98. *Viṣṇua Purāṇa,* I.20.16.

Bhakti, according to Śāṇḍilya, is the sole means of Liberation. It is defined as the supreme attachment to God and love for God. All are entitled to tread the path of devotion and is considered excellent.

> The path of devotion is indeed excellent, because it contributes to well-being in every way and because it is free from fear of every kind.[99]

It is the highest love to God. Śāṇḍilya says, through devotion Liberation can be attained as in the case of the milkmaids of *Śrīmad Bhāgavata Purāṇa,* even though they are devoid of learning.

According to traditional scriptures, devotion can only come through three stages: hearing (*śravaṇa*), reflecting (*manana*) and meditation (*nidhidhyāsana*). By removing impurities in the mind, knowledge causes devotion, which in turn gives Liberation. But devotion cultivated directly will also burn these impurities and give the fruit of Liberation. As long as one is devoted to God, there is no need for knowledge. "Through devotion he (aspirant) recognises me."[100] Though devotion is of the nature of attachment it cannot be devalued — taking it as sensual pleasure — because the object of that attachment is God. Devotion cannot be identified with work (*kriyā*), will or wish (*icchā*) nor even with faith (*śraddhā*). Śāṇḍilya gives importance to the means given in the Yoga of Patañjali. He says Yoga is useful to both — knowledge and devotion — because concentration of mind is necessary in both. Concentration transforms into meditation, when it becomes steady and firm.

Śāṇḍilya classified devotion into two — supreme and secondary — devotion. However, supreme devotion is *bhakti.* The secondary is also essential, because it leads to the rise of supreme devotion — though in a secondary sense. Śāṇḍilya gives a long list of the signs by which the maturity of devotion can be

99. *Śrīmad Bhāgavata,* VI.1.17.

100. *Bhagavad-Gītā,* XVIII.53.

inferred. They are respect, high esteem, delight, doubting other objects, praising the greatness of God, holding the life for His sake, considering everything as His, regarding Him as existing in all beings, not resisting His will and so forth.[101] These are not only the signs by which supreme devotion expresses itself, but are also the means to attain supreme devotion when they are consciously practised. While practising, they become secondary devotion. The other types of secondary devotion, as mentioned in the *Bhagavad-Gītā*, are: praising Him, paying obeisance to Him, thinking of Him but none else, worshipping Him, offering anything with love, offering everything one does or enjoys, etc.[102]

All these actions purify the heart and facilitate the rise of supreme devotion. There is no rule laid, while practising them. Anyone who practises sincerely and intensely can please God and thus become a devotee of supreme devotion. The doctrine of *bhakti* assures that all these methods are capable of destroying even the great sins and can take the place of difficult expiations. However, sincere repentance is a pre-condition, and these practices must be continued until one's death.

Śāṇḍilya expresses that though all are entitled to the practice of devotion, not all can attain supreme devotion before they die. Such devotees are said to be reborn in the world of God, where they will continue with their devotional practices, and finally attain the supreme devotion and Liberation through it. Śāṇḍilya says that it is not knowledge of *ātmā* that destroys this bondage, but the supreme devotion. Liberation is of the nature of immortality and is to be obtained through devotion to God. The supreme devotion destroys the limiting adjuncts (*upādhi*) of the individual soul,[103] thereby liberating it. The liberated soul lives as *jīvan mukta*, as long as the body lasts owing to the

101. *Śāṇḍilya Bhakti Sūtra*, 44.

102. *Bhagavad-Gītā*, IX.

103. The intellect (*buddhi*) and the ego (*ahaṁkāra*) are usually considered as the limiting adjuncts.

momentum of his past *karma*, which has fructified giving him this body. At the time of death, he is merged in God.

According to Śāṇḍilya, though the individual soul is actually identical with God, it also appears as many because of the multiplicity of intellect (*buddhi*). It is like the one Sun appearing as many, being reflected in several mirrors. When they are removed, all reflections merge in the Sun.

Liberation can also take place progressively. Lower devotion gives gradual Liberation, whereas supreme devotion provides immediate Liberation. Even lower devotion is given importance because it matures into supreme devotion, either in this world or in the higher realm.

> Desire, deliberation, doubt, faith, lack of faith, steadiness, impatience, shame, intelligence and fear — all these are nothing but forms of mind.[104]

Like the sensations of pain, the sense of egoism is also directly perceived in the intellect, because all the intellects associated with the individual souls have arisen from the ego-principle of *Īśvara* (or *Brahman*). This means there is no need for any evolution of intellect itself.

Pleasure, pain, etc. are qualities which reside in the intellect. When reflected upon the soul, they are wrongly attributed to the latter.

Since the intellect of the individual soul springs from the Lord, it must be capable of grasping the external world made up of these elements, namely the gross elements, the subtle elements, the sense organs, etc.

NĀRADA'S VIEW ON BHAKTI

> O Nārada! I do not reside in heaven nor even in the heart of *yogīs*,

104. *Bṛhadāraṇyaka Upaniṣad*, I.5.3.

> but wherever My devotees are engaged in singing My praise, it is there that I am invariably present.[105]

The mention of the name Nārada infuses devotion (*bhakti*) into the Hindu minds, such is the intensity of his devotion (*bhakti*). His teachings on *bhakti* are non-sectarian. Throughout his work, Nārada avoids a definition of God, for he feels that to describe God is to bring Him down to the level of the finite objects of relative knowledge. To a right thinker, each view of God is only a partial view of the whole truth. Each aspirant may conceive God in his own way as the perfect ideal of his thinking and can worship his chosen ideal according to his own capacities and needs, giving the same freedom of thought to others. Each one must keep in mind that God is his own view of the Divine Truth from his own level of spiritual development. Another person may have a different outlook of the same truth. In an aspirant of *bhakti,* it is not the difference in view that is to be taken seriously, but how intensely he directs his thoughts on God. In all, *bhakti* is the firm love of God that can never be destroyed.

What is called *bhakti* is nothing but the enjoyment of the Lord, the master of the senses, with the senses purified by the simple nearness of Him, without laying any condition whatsoever. "That (*bhakti*), verily, is of the nature of supreme love of God."[106] In his third aphorism, Nārada describes, how divine love and Liberation go hand in hand. "And in its own intrinsic nature, Divine love is nothing less than the immortal bliss of freedom itself (*mukti,* Liberation), which comes unsolicited by the grace of God and self-sacrifice."[107] The essential characteristics of devotion are the consecration of all activities by complete self-surrender to Him and extreme anguish if He were to be forgotten.[108]

---

105. *Mahābhārata* (Anuśāsana Parva); *Padma Purāṇa.*

106. *Nārada Bhakti Sūtra,* I.2.

107. *Nārada Bhakti Sūtra,* I.3.

108. *Nārada Bhakti Sūtra,* II.1.19.

The word love in devotion (*bhakti*) is not used in the sense of lust, because it is a form of renunciation. It is the love of the human spirit for the cosmic spirit. Dedication of all activities of the mind and body is to be utilised for the sake of love (of the human soul) for the cosmic soul. In this way, renunciation is essential in devotion (*bhakti*). Through love, all the powers of the mind and the body are surrendered to God, to achieve the union with Him. In a higher sense of unification, the ego of a devotee becomes identified with God and his will with God's will.

Devotion has a preparatory stage, called *aparā bhakti*, and a mature stage of subjective experience, known as *parā bhakti*. The transcendental nature of the mature divine love is non-communicable. It is the experience of unsurpassed bliss and is equated with God-realisation; it is also called liberation in life. When that realisation expresses through moods, thoughts, words, etc. this is called the objective aspect of *parā bhakti*. *Parā bhakti* is extolled as superior to all spiritual disciplines, and it brings liberation. On the other hand, *aparā bhakti* is the stage before the attainment of that maturity. It involves effort and the process is gradual. The advanced stage of *aparā bhakti* is known as exclusive devotion, *ekānta bhakti*, or Supreme Devotion, *mukhya bhakti*. It is the stage of fulfilment of the duties on the disciplinary path of devotion. This results in divine grace, which then flows into the devotee's heart on its own. In this stage, the devotee is perfectly prepared for the final realisation, and God blesses him with divine illumination instantaneously.

The highest spiritual realisation alone is the goal for the permanent release from all bondage. Nārada views that spiritual practices are essential for a devotee, because natural perfection of the human soul is manifested only when all the faculties of the mind are purified and co-ordinated harmoniously. Spiritual practices are meant to effect this through the cultivation of the various faculties of the mind purifying the emotions.

Difference in opinion is admissible regarding the highest realisation,

> which is indescribable. For that matter, it is not proper for one to enter into a controversy about God or other spiritual truths or about comparative merits of different devotees.[109]

Further, he advises to develop certain virtues: non-violence, truth, purity, compassion, faith in higher spiritual realities and the like.[110]

Devotion (*bhakti*), though in itself one only, manifests in the following eleven different forms:

1. Love of the glorification of Lord's blessed qualities,
2. Love of His enchanting beauty,
3. Love of worship,
4. Love of constant remembrance,
5. Love of service,
6. Love of Him as that of a wife for her husband,
7. Love of Him as a friend,
8. Love of Him as a son,
9. Love of self-surrender to Him,
10. Love of complete absorption in Him, and
11. Love of the pain of separation from Him.[111]

When glorified this way, He manifests Himself and blesses His devotees with realisation.[112] Only love of the absolute, eternal Truth is the greatest, this love indeed is the greatest.[113]

Thus, Nārada upholds love that is heightened and directed towards God. He suggests that the attainment of supreme bliss is not something which comes by mere self-effort; but it is a gift

---

109. *Nārada Bhakti Sūtra*, 15.74.
110. *Nārada Bhakti Sūtra*, 78.
111. *Nārada Bhakti Sūtra*, 82.
112. *Nārada Bhakti Sūtra*, 80.
113. *Nārada Bhakti Sūtra*, 81.

from God, when an aspirant trains himself to acquire it. This points to the element of Divine grace in spiritual realisation. Devotion works up to the highest spiritual realisation, which consists in seeing God in everything and loving and serving Him in all beings. Every activity that proceeds from him will emit the sweetness of love. At this stage, devotion (*bhakti*) will express in complete peace of mind and in supreme joy.

The supreme love expressed by Nārada is different from what is generally understood by the term devotion to God. It is the culmination of all Yoga or "methods of realisation", ending in a complete ego-free love of God for the sake of love alone and a realisation of God in all creatures, expressing itself in the form of unselfish service to God and his creatures in the spirit of worship. "The universe is a tree instinct with life, the Lord is its foundation, and so service to all creatures is worship to God."[114]

Nārada's greatness as a seer of the Vedic *mantra*s, as a minstrel, as a great ascetic, as one, who rose from a low position to the highest spiritual glory through divine grace and self-effort, shows how he lived according to the truths taught in the *sūtra*. Nārada is a typical *jñānin*,[115] *yogin* and *bhakta*[116] in one, yet he preferred *bhakti*, being the easiest and the most efficient of all paths.

Once Sri Ramakrishna said to Swami Vivekananda:

> God is like a sweet liquid (or liquid sweet), would you not dive into this sea? Just think of a vessel with a wide mouth containing syrup of sugar, and suppose you are a fly anxious to drink the sweet liquid. Where would you sit and drink?

Vivekananda replied that he would prefer to sit at the edge of the vessel, for if he came to a point beyond his depth he was sure to be drowned. Thereupon Ramakrishna said,

---

114. *Śrīmad Bhāgavata Purāṇa*, VII.14.36.
115. One who has acquired the right knowledge of the Reality.
116. A *bhakta* is a devotee.

> You forget, my son, that by diving deep into the divine sea, you need not be afraid of death. Remember the sea called *Saccidānanda?*[117] When a diver has realised his own nature, the whole world has vanished for him. The prison of misery has become changed into *sat, cit, ānanda* in the sea of immortality. The water of this sea never causes death. It is the water of everlasting life. Do not think like some foolish persons that you may run to excess in your love of God.

Devotion (*bhakti*) is thus no loss of individuality, but only a supreme transcendence of the limitations of individuality and a regaining of the true status of the Self. Perfect personality is in God alone. A devotee never craves for liberation. He is quite satisfied to enjoy the love of God for love's sake and to serve Him for the sake of service. Still, liberation comes to him by the grace of God. God's grace descends on many always like a breeze, but if they want to take advantage of it, they must do spiritual practices, just as the boatman has to unfurl the sails, before he can catch the breeze. Thus, complete freedom of will and self-effort are assured without any prejudice to the doctrine of *bhakti* and grace of God.

Śrīmad Bhāgavata Purāṇa says about the joy of *bhakti* and the glory of Lord Hari:[118]

> Sages, delighting in their own self, though they are free from fetters, still continue to be devoted to Hari, the personal deity, such is the glory of Hari.[119]

Nārada's View on Bhakti

The great ancient sage, Nārada views devotion (*bhakti*) as the Supreme Love for God. But this love is not of the nature of lust, but a form of indifference towards everything that is opposed

117. Existence, Knowledge and Bliss.
118. Hari is another name of Viṣṇu. One who removes the sins is known as Hari.
119. *Śrīmad Bhāgavata Purāṇa*, I.7.10.

to the love of God. It also means abandoning of all other support except the support of God.

Nārada is of the opinion that the consecration of all activities, complete surrender to Him and extreme anguish, if He were to be forgotten, are the essential characteristics of devotion (*bhakti*).[120] Complete surrender is the prime characteristic of devotion (*bhakti*); and every action done with this attitude has a due place in devotional life. Nārada says that all devotional activities — like rituals, chanting of sacred *mantra*s — should be done with the attitude of devotion towards God. Any work that is selfless, has a place in spiritual life. For a man seeking God-realisation it is impossible to forget Him at any time. If a devotee were to forget Him, then pangs of separation should bring anguish in him. But considering from the right perspective, there is no possibility of forgetting Him, as the devotee's mind is automatically prevented from such forgetfulness.

Citing the perfect expression of devotion (*bhakti*) from the example of *gopī*s of Vrindavan[121] and their love for Kṛṣṇa,[122] Nārada says, the *gopī*s knew Kṛṣṇa as God. At no time, did they ever ignore the divinity in Him. They loved Kṛṣṇa with the highest love. Without the knowledge of divinity in Kṛṣṇa, it would not have been possible for them to worship Him or to offer devotion to Him. "Had they lacked this knowledge of Divinity of the object of their love, their love would have been similar to the base passion of a mistress for her paramour."[123] For, the mistress is utterly selfish. She does not care for the happiness of her lover. In pure love and devotion (*bhakti*) there cannot be any trace of selfishness. The lover does not at all care for his own happiness. The *gopī*s did not love Kṛṣṇa out of a selfish motive. They were ready to give up everything to make

120. *Nārada Bhakti Sūtra*, I.19.

121. A village near Mathurā on the banks of Yamunā.

122. A situation in the *Mahābhārata*.

123. *Nārada Bhakti Sūtra*, 23.

Him happy. Their happiness depended only on His happiness.

The supreme love is something more than *karma*, *jñāna* and *yoga*. Spiritual realisation is the fruit of devotion (*bhakti*) and the highest spiritual realisation alone brings release from all bondage. "The taste of devotion (*bhakti*) is like the experience of joy, which a dumb man has when he tastes something sweet" says Nārada.[124] The dumb man too has the sense of taste. His vocal defects prevent him from describing his delight. Yet, he can feel the joy by himself. Likewise, the experience of the Love of God can be felt within and cannot be described. According to Nārada, devotion eludes description. The experience of devotion is one and indivisible. All the powers of the mind are so unified and integrated that it is not possible for the mind to work partially. Devotion is a subjective experience, which cannot be observed by another person.

The highest love for God is always enjoyable, and it is expanding all the time. The devotee thinks, sees, and hears nothing else except God. He feels great joy in serving the world, for he sees the whole world as a manifestation of God. At the same time, Nārada particularly points out that God does not stand in need of any help from His devotees. The work performed by a devotee is consciously done with a definite purpose; it is not aimless. However, the purpose kept in view of the work is not at all selfish. Nārada brings out the dynamic character of devotion (*bhakti*) in the following way:

> On attainment of devotion (*bhakti*) or even for the attainment of it, life in society need not be shunned, but only fruits of all social activities are surrendered to the Lord, while all such activities naturally righteous and so bearing noble fruit, may be continued.

A devotee's life is an intensely dynamic one. At no stage does he give up his spiritual practice or his social service, neither before nor after realisation.

---

124. *Nārada Bhakti Sūtra*, 52.

A devotee, according to Nārada, considers all the creatures in the universe as the children of God; and as such, he sees them with an eye of equanimity. He has so much love for God and His creatures that his heart will under no circumstances and conditions agree to harm or dupe others, because it would mean that God dupes Himself.

Those who have attained the stage of Supreme devotion, that is the stage after attainment of realisation, never care to enter into a controversy about God, His devotees or other spiritual matters. They have wiped out their egoism so much that it is impossible for them to hanker after name or fame by scoring victory over an opponent in a religious controversy. They are only interested in practising the Highest Truth of the presence of God as the one underlying Reality of the universe, knowing that everything else is not true. To Nārada, the devotee's mind has reached a stage, where it can tolerate nothing but intense love for God. He avoids everything that goes against the spirit of love.

A devotee does not have any other desire except to serve God. He does not generally seek for the knowledge of the Absolute,[125] but accepts if God blesses him with it. But even after the realisation of this oneness with God, the devotee likes to retain his individuality and makes himself an instrument for God's work of love.

The state of a devotee after final realisation is called *jīvan-mukti*. This highest state of devotion is also known as "oneness" (*ekatva* or *sāyujya*) with God. At this stage, even the difference between the lover and the beloved vanishes. Treatises on devotion say that this state is recognised only by those who have had the experience of oneness. In this stage, the devotee finds out to be one with his own Higher Self.

According to Nārada, there are as many types of devotion (*bhakti*) as there are human relationships. Nārada points out that

---

125. *Brahma jñāna*.

even if they appear externally as different; they are all manifestations of love which in itself is only one. Nārada and Vyāsa[126] are always found delighting themselves in singing the glories of the Lord and helping to convert others to a life of spirituality and love. The *gopīs* of Vrindavan were naturally attracted by Kṛṣṇa's enchanting personal beauty; and they took delight in it. Each type of devotion (*bhakti*) is characterised by a prominent attitude. A difference in attitudes may also be found in the same person at different times. But the very nature of intense love is that one cannot bear the separation from God. The anxiety to maintain the union with God is supreme devotion; and this is the highest expression of love. The goal to be attained by everyone is Supreme Bliss through the realisation of oneness with the Absolute. This is the same as being near to Him and being in constant contact with Him. The immediate and the final means to achieve this is devotion (*bhakti*) or the love of God.

Nārada views that the experience of love is the highest experience of Bliss to a devotee and devotional practices are also superior to all other spiritual practices. To achieve this highest experience, a devotee undertakes only such practices as enable him to love, to serve and to see God in all his activities. He is interested only in the purity of his mind.

It is the ego that pollutes the mind because of *rajas* and *tamas* influencing the mental nature. The devotee eagerly adopts any method that helps to keep the mind free from ego. Non-attachment is another practice that leads to the purity of the mind. But in the eyes of a devotee, the most purifying agency is God Himself. Constant remembrance of God and service to Him clear all the impurities of the mind. Devotion manifests itself in the one, who has made himself fit for such manifestation, by constant practice and by uninterrupted loving service to God in any form.

Nārada also says that the attainment of the Supreme Bliss does not come from mere self-effort, but it is a gift from God.

---

126. Author of the *Mahābhārata*.

This points out the element of Divine Grace in the spiritual realisation.

Āñjaneya's Devotion[127]

Āñjaneya's devotion to Rāma is unique. His God, his heaven, his joy lay in serving Rāma. This was his objective. He viewed that clinging to the enjoyments of lower worlds, no doubt, produces all kinds of sufferings, binding the soul to these worlds. They are not confined to the lower worlds alone. In its subtler forms, it even exists in the higher worlds. The attachment to the highest object not only removes the lower desires but also brings the devotee to the highest level of enlightenment, which is possible, even while living on the earth. Āñjaneya did not want anything else but serving Rāma on earth as His devotee. When Rāma held out heavens to him as a gift for his achievements, he stepped back from accepting it. He politely refused — saying that he preferred to stay and to live on earth as long as this world exists, where Rāma was born, where Rāma gave the signet ring to him to be delivered to the Divine Mother Sītā,[128] and that he preferred playing the part of a messenger. He wished to stay on the same earth where he carried Rāma on his shoulders to fight with the demon King Rāvaṇa. He preferred the earth where he undertook the mission of searching for Sītā as the real service to Rāma and achieved success. He felt the earth to be a real paradise because it was on this earth that Rāma embraced him wholeheartedly as a token of love for his services, though Āñjaneya never expected anything in return from Rāma for his services. At the coronation ceremony, Rāma tactically honoured him (Āñjaneya) with a garland of gems from the hands of the Divine Mother Sītā, a sign of deep appreciation in front of the gathered audience. Āñjaneya's contentment of joy lay in serving Rāma down on the earth alone and not living with Him in the high heavens.

---

127. A very important character in the epic *Rāmāyaṇa*.

128. Lord Rāma's wife.

In his epic the *Rāmāyaṇa,* sage Vālmīki has beautifuly brought out the superiority of the devotion in Āñjaneya's services to Rāma. Āñjaneya's sincere devotion attracted Rāma so much that, ever since the day Hanumān[129] came to him on the slopes of the Ṛṣyamūka peak,[130] Rāma had been greatly impressed by the wisdom of Āñjaneya, his humility and valour. Rāma felt as though he had already achieved the purpose of getting Sītā back. He felt a deep sense of contentment, which had been absent from his mind ever since he had lost Sītā. This was the reason for removing the signet ring from his finger to entrust it to Āñjaneya, to convince Sītā that he had been sent by Him and none else.

If Āñjaneya had not had this highest devotion to Rāma, this great entrustment could not have arisen in Rāma's mind. As a sign of respect, Āñjaneya received the signet ring with his palms cupped together; and holding it above his head he prostrated before Rāma. Āñjaneya knew that without the grace of Rāma his mission of searching Sītā would be a failure. Therefore, as a true devotee, he surrendered himself to Rāma and prayed for His grace and love. His devotional services to Rāma are revealed in perfection in all his actions: like his valour in the battlefield, his enduring abilities to face every situation, his special skills in all his acts, his strong will in carrying out duties assigned by Rama, his effective methods in fighting with enemies so on and so forth. He earned absolute enjoyment in his services to Rāma. His joy was in listening to Rāma's story, the songs on Rāma, listening to Rāma's name in the form of rosary called *rāma nāma japa,* etc. Āñjaneya mastered the yogic power of presenting himself, wherever the story of Rāma's life was told, read or sung — while living on the earth, but not in the heavens. He was blessed with the power of leaving this world according to his own will. This blessing helped him to fulfil his joy of living on the earth, as long as Rāma's name exists on this planet.

129. Another name for Āñjaneya.

130. One of the mountains of India.

Āñjaneya, being the best among Rāma's devotees, was very cautious in upholding Rāma's honour to the highest degree. As it is the inherent quality of a devotee, he never tolerated any disrespect to his Lord Rāma. His devotion to Rāma was continuous, without any break. His only desire remained in the true worship of Rāma in the form of physical and mental service, staying constantly near His feet to taking orders from Him — his Lord. His services were not for gaining any benefits but for their own sake. This service of devotion is said to go on as long as Lord Rāma and his devotee Āñjaneya coexist on earth. It is an end in itself.

In the rosary of Āñjaneya's name, he is praised as very astute. He was very intelligent and brave. His skilful tactics even saved Sītā from committing suicide.

It is a time-old custom in India, to meditate with reverence on this heroic Āñjaneya, who played the part of the messenger of Rāma to console Sītā and quenched her grief. When Sītā was about to hang herself with her long braid of hair round her neck, Hanumān, knowing very well that uttering Rāma's name will surely work wonders, started singing the story of Rāma with a sweet and gentle voice, hiding by the branches of the tree in the garden of *aśoka* trees (*Aśoka Vāṭikā*), where she was held captive by the demon king Rāvaṇa. His sweet words in an exquisite language and filled with deep devotion to Rāma become very effective in saving Sītā's life. To Sītā, the Divine Mother, his visit was a great comfort, because she was convinced that Rāma was in search of her, but equally pained to know the grief of Rāma.

Āñjaneya is one of the legendary characters we come across in the holy texts. His intense will-power made him cross all the hurdles to reach his goal. In India, it is believed that by offering prayers to Āñjaneya, the Supreme Lord Rāma will be pleased and shall grace the humanity.

Devotion in Patañjali's Yoga-Sūtra

The word *praṇidhāna* has different meanings: meditation, devotion (when the object of *praṇidhāna* is *Īśvara*, the highest among the

Puruṣa), or Self-surrender to God. Patañjali uses this term, both as meditation on *Īśvara* and as Self-surrender to *Īśvara*. He defines *Īśvara* as "a particular *Puruṣa,* who is untouched by the afflictions of life, actions and the results and the impressions produced by these actions".[131] The act of *Īśvara praṇidhāna* helps in the progressive merging of the individual's will in that of *Īśvara,* thus destroying the very root of misery.

The practice of *Īśvara praṇidhāna* takes a different form, when the person who follows this principle, is of a highly emotional temperament. Then the path becomes a path of devotion, *bhakti yoga*. Here, the person earns the ability to keep constant contact with *Īśvara* through an uninterrupted flow of love. The emotional love of the devotee naturally expresses itself in the subordination of personal desires to the will of *Īśvara*. The path of devotion leads indirectly to the dissolution of the 'I-sense'.

Īśvara praṇidhāna is the essence of *bhakti yoga*. The practice of all actions prescribed in the scripture is meant to lead an aspirant to the stage, where he is able to renounce all external aids and to surrender himself completely to *Īśvara*. According to Patañjali, the final result of *Īśvara praṇidhāna* is that "from devotion to *Īśvara, samādhi* (spiritual absorption) is attained".[132]

Devotion Without Religious Convictions

In a sense, devotion is both, religious as well as non-religious. Religion is the result of man's inner urge for freedom. Different religions represent different aspects of this struggle. Devotion is the supreme love to God who is considered as the Creator and Ruler of this universe: infinite, all-knowing, all-powerful, Supreme Being. It is the human nature to seek what he does not have, even if he is satisfied with what he already has. He yearns for something more, which is beyond his means. By

131. Patañjali, *Yoga Sūtra,* I.24.
132. Patañjali, *Yoga Sūtra,* II.45.

discrimination, when this feeling of continuous desires changes into uninterrupted love for God, this love is called devotion.

> This love is not to be had by the power of speech, not by the highest intellect, nor by the study of various sciences. He who desired God will get this love, unto him. He reveals himself. This love is just devotion and it does not require any religion to be followed always.[133]

Devotion is the highest ideal. It is already in man's heart. With or without religion, man can work through the senses to reach God. Religion is any system of faith and worship, involving a code of ethics and a philosophy. It prescribes certain teachings and principles to be followed. However these codes may not suit all minds, or some people may not even have enough time and opportunity to follow them, regarding the circumstances they live in. It is also possible to develop devotion without following any religious codes. It is the earnest desire to develop devotion that is more important than the principles to be followed.

Theoretically as well as practically, it is possible for a man to be a devotee without any commitment to religious convictions. It is an easier path with the assurance of success. Loyalty in love would be the only condition.

In *Īśvara praṇidhāna*, a devotee need not bring any mental action into play deliberately. He simply surrenders himself and his will to God and acts according to the will of God.

Even Lord Kṛṣṇa suggests this method, "Completely relinquishing all *dharma*, seek Me alone for refuge. I will release you from all sins. Grieve not."

Here, relinquishment does not mean to give up all devotional attitudes, but only the sense of religious agony and fruits. So, in order to develop devotion, it is sufficient to seek after God. God

133. *Kaṭha Upaniṣad*, I.2.23.

is compassionate, He is the refuge of all and is an ocean of tenderness for those dependent on Him. The intense desire to love God alone is fundamental; all other actions are subsidiary to this intense desire.

One can follow any method that makes his mind steady on God. If the method adopted suits the temperament of the practising devotee, his mind is further helped to acquire natural attraction and affection towards God. A little experimentation is sufficient to select a method of approach. If the mind acquires tranquillity in the method followed, that method can be adopted. Yet it should be noted that a ceaseless trial of methods should not be undertaken, as this attitude will only affect one's mental peace, resulting in an increasing mental agitation.

The Hindu idea is that God is the goal of life and there is nothing beyond God.

2

Way to Develop Devotion

Let all beings — whether gods, demons, men or non-humans — worship with heart and soul Śrī Rāma, who is God in human form, who comprehends the good deeds of all and who gave salvation to all the inhabitants of Uttara Kosala.

Neither noble birth nor great fortune, neither power of speech, nor intelligence, nor beautiful appearance — none of these can enable one to obtain the grace of Rāma, the Supreme Being incarnate as man. For, see how He entered into friendship with us, monkeys, who are without any of the above-mentioned qualifications and who are mere inhabitants of the wilds!

— *Śrīmad Bhāgavata*, V.19.7-8

Neither the status of a brāhmaṇa, nor of a god, nor of a *ṛṣi;* neither good conduct, nor learning, nor charity, nor mortification, nor sacrificial rites, nor purificatory observances, nor austere vows can please Śrī Hari (another name of Viṣṇu, the Supreme Being). He is satisfied only with pure loving devotion. All other disciplines are but show or a mockery (if they are not accompanied by devotion). — *Śrīmad Bhāgavata*, VII.7.51-52

MAN should, with one-pointed mind, hear about, praise, worship and contemplate upon the Supreme Being, the master of all devotees. The constant contemplation of His deeds is a veritable sword for cutting asunder the bondages of self-centred tendencies of work which only go to strengthen the knot of egoism in man. By resorting to sacred precincts, one gets an opportunity to associate oneself with, and serve holy men. Such service strengthens one's faith in spiritual matters, increases the desire to hear more and more about the Lord, and gradually generates an instinctive delight in such hearings. Kṛṣṇa, the Lord, the friend of devotees, purifies the hearts of those who take His name. He manifests in the hearts of those who hear the accounts of His deeds, and erases all the evil tendencies blocking their spiritual development. When the obstructing evil hindering are mitigated through constant application to the service of holy men, and the study of scriptures, one develops a steady and unshakable love of the Lord of abounding glory and grace. With the growth of devotion, the mind is freed from the agitations of instinctive passions, like greed and sexuality, and gets settled in the peace and poise of *sattva*. In the aspirant, who has, through the practice of devotion, attained the purity and poise of mind as also freedom from every form of worldly attachments, is generated the intuition of the Supreme Being as an absolute Reality. When the Supreme Soul is felt within oneself, the knots of the heart that make one feel oneself as an ego are severed, the doubts of the mind are dispelled, and all the accumulated *karma*s of the past and the future are erased.[1]

Wise people should cultivate the devotional mode of life from boyhood itself. For, human birth, in which alone God-realisation — the supreme end of man's existence — can be had, is rare and difficult to get, and besides life is short and precarious.[2]

Man's Need to Develop Devotion

One of the principle features of Vedānta is the cyclic view of time and man's involvement in it. What is man? Where has he come from? What is the real reason for his existence here? Man is a soul (*jīva*) endowed with a body and mind, undergoing a cyclic process of birth and death, because he is caught in the cyclic movement of time. This state is called *saṁsāra* or bondage of life, the repetitive process of life and death. This process starts

1. Sūta's message of *bhakti*. Sūta is the son of Vyāsa who composed the Purāṇas and taught to his son. *Śrīmad Bhāgavata*, I.2.14-22, 24.
2. *Śrīmad Bhāgavata*, VII.6.19.

with the beginning of a creation. It always depends on God, who is eternal. Even at the end of the created cycle, the embodied soul exists in a subtle form in His nature. The souls come into manifestation at the beginning of a cycle of time, and finally, they dissolve in Him, remaining in their casual conditions, only to come into manifestation again when a new cycle of time starts. If the soul is liberated from this bondage, it gets absorbed in the Supreme and will not come back again in any creation.

Accumulated in earlier lives out of one's own actions, the true nature of soul is hidden, but never destroyed. The purpose of this cycle of creation is to extract the purity of the *jīva* and bring it into the higher states of perfection. The repeated embodiments are the results of actions during earlier phases of the soul's involvement in *saṁsāra*. All actions committed leave some tendencies in the mind and according to the nature of these actions, they provide enjoyments or sufferings. This is an essential theory for the conception of a just and righteous God. In the cyclic theory of creation, there is no first creation; and hence no beginning for the *jīva*. Therefore, it has to be accepted that an original quantum of *karma* goes with the creation of the *jīva*. *Jīva's* entanglement in the cycle of creation is his association with the body and mind regulated by *karma*, which is the effect of past actions. It is only in human birth that the *jīva* gets an opportunity to acquire new *karma* through good and bad actions and to overcome the bondage of *karma* as a whole and attain Liberation through devotion to God. Man has to use his human birth in a proper manner so that it becomes helpful to the higher evolution of moral and spiritual values. While he might have legitimate pleasures and possessions in life, he will debase his human heritage if he makes these his be all and the end of all of his life, but he can rise again in his evolutionary scale.

Hinduism believes in an immanent God and in the ultimate realisation of all people. It offers to show the way to permanent happiness. It teaches that immortal souls cannot be satisfied with impermanent objects of experience. Therefore, it urges men not to put faith in the fleeting pleasures of the world but in the joy of the soul. This faith creates a virtuous disposition and increases the human spiritual powers. Every act is virtuous, if the outcome is pure love, which increases the hidden strength of the soul. This power should be evoked from within. God is the perfection of purity, and by loving him the joy of the soul will be expanded. The love to God is *bhakti*. It is a pure, selfless, subtle, unbroken and ever-expanding experience. One who loves God has no wants. Through *bhakti* he is moved to great joy, attains peace, and his soul is in happiness.

Viśiṣṭādvaita Vedānta Point of View

Creation is a manifestation of *Brahman*, the creator of both, the sentient (*cit*) and the non-sentient (*acit*). The potentiality of matter and souls existed in *Brahman* even before the creation of this world of names and forms. The *cit* and *acit* existed as a part of Reality in the casual state; and they continue to exist as a part of Reality in the effective state. In the creation, only matter and the finite Self undergo any change but never the cosmic principle, the Absolute Reality. These two entities, namely *cit* and *acit*, are adjectival in nature; they characterise *Brahman* in the primordial as well as the consequent stages. That is why Reality is declared as the One Absolute, characterised by *cit* and *acit*.

The finite selves labour under the handicap of *avidyā*[3] and are subject to a state of degradation from which they have to extricate themselves to attain their original status. The finite self has lost its native state of consciousness due to its own beginningless *karma* by which it has tied itself down to the mundane life, *saṁsāra*. The state of bondage is a state of reality and involves unhappiness and the misery of rebirth. To get rid of this miserable plight and to attain the state of liberation (*mokṣa*), the finite self has to follow some discipline; then only it can

3. Ignorance or wrong knowledge.

enjoy the infinite joy of divine experience. The goal one has to attain is a perfect or a positive reality, which one achieves only by one's individual effort.

Schools of *bhakti* consider *mokṣa* only in the form of supreme love to God, which is devotion. The *Śrīmad Bhāgavata* declares that the development of devotion destroys the taints of the mind produced by sins, purifies it and consumes the potency of actions under the influence of *avidyā* (nescience). The seeds of sins cannot be entirely destroyed by penances, sense control and mind control, charity, truthfulness, purity of the body and the mind, restraint and observance of morals, even though they can subdue them temporarily. The potencies remain intact and generate other sins. Penances without faith and devotion cannot purify an individual of his sins and their seeds. However, supreme devotion to God can destroy all sins completely, and can burn up *avidyā*, just as fire burns a piece of wood down into ashes. It destroys *avidyā* and purifies the mind, just as fire destroys the dross of gold. It purifies all. Frequent thoughts of God, the Pure and the Holy, gradually destroy the thoughts of impurities and sins. Withdrawal of the mind from all thoughts of impurities and sins and the concentration on the Supreme Being weakens all impurities and finally destroys them.

Remorse is a mode of atonement for sins. When a sinner repents, the best form of atonement for his sins is the constant recollection of God. An act of devotion, like the chanting or recollection of God's name, etc., however little it may be, can destroy great sins. In the path of devotion, all other kinds of atonement are done away with. Thus, devotion is the most powerful atonement for all sins.

Bhagavad-Gītā says that the devotee, who, full of faith and with the inner self-abiding in God, worships Him, is completely united with Him.[4] It is easier to perform all actions for God and

4. *Bhagavad-Gītā*, VI.47.

dedicate them to Him, make Him the supreme goal of life and meditate on Him and pray to Him with an undivided mind, because he is the personal God of love, with whom man can be in communion and have a personal relation. God delivers man from the bondage of the birth and death.

As said earlier, *Śrīmad Bhāgavata* regards the path of devotion as the best of all kinds of spiritual disciplines. It says that meditation, knowledge, religious rites, study of scriptures and renunciation cannot provide God-realisation as intensely as supreme devotion to God does. No spiritual discipline is more efficacious for worldly men than developing devotion to God.[5]

Devotion does not require hard penances, asceticism and renunciation, abstract knowledge, or complete isolation of the soul from the body and the world. It requires unconditional love for God, which is imperfectly reflected in all human relations. Disinterested action purifies the desire, right knowledge purifies the intellect, and true devotion purifies the emotions. Thus, all human emotions are purified, enriched and fulfilled in devotion to God. All works become worship of God, being dedicated to Him; all knowledge is transformed into knowledge of God in its proper perspective. Human life becomes divine and pulsates with divine energy.

Among the three paths, namely the path of action, knowledge, and devotion,[6] that of devotion is undoubtedly the best. It is easier than the other two and is open to all. It is superior to action, knowledge and meditation because it is its own fruit. The cultivation of devotion is necessary for the realisation of God, just as the personal relationship with a king is necessary for pleasing him. Mere knowledge of God is not sufficient for pleasing Him. The personal relationship with Him should be established through devotion and love; then only can He be

5. *Śrīmad Bhāgavata* XI.14-20, II.2-33.

6. *Karma-mārga*, *Jñāna-mārga* and *bhakti-mārga*.

realised. Hence, all persons who are keen to realise the Supreme should adopt the development of devotion.

The way to earn God's grace is the way of love. Love is so powerful that it unites the lover and the loved in the end. Devotion is not just a sterile remembrance of God's name and His qualities, on the contrary, this kind of meditation is of the form of abundant love of God, since every act man performs would become a dedicated act.

Man gets totally submerged in the huge flood of his love towards God, considers Him as the dearest to him, thinks of Him only and engages himself in activities that please Him. He naturally discards the idea of "I" and "mine" and attains a state of Divine realisation. He dedicates his heart and soul to the eternal service of his Lord. He serves God alone in all his actions. Devotion (*bhakti*) is thus an expansion of a special kind of knowledge which is related to Divine being. *Bhakti* draws the devotee towards God, just as a piece of iron is attracted towards a magnet. The aim of devotion is to attain Divine Communion.

Developing Devotion

> That which is infinite is alone happiness. There is no happiness in anything finite. The infinite alone is happiness. But one must desire to understand the infinite.[7]

It is inherent to the human mind that cannot choose anything lesser when something greater is within its reach. Man is not happy with the least, he wants something more than that; he longs for more than what he already owns and until the very limit of expansion is reached, he cannot find contentment. Limitations and limitlessness are relative. The former implies the latter. The common man does not obtain the latter, and hence, he is restless and craves for it through numerous activities. One who has realised the Infinite, who alone

7. *Chāndogya Upaniṣad*, VII, 23.1.

transcends everything, dwells in the infinite bliss that is never reversed.

The *jīva*'s involvement in the recurring process of matter or body-mind is called *saṁsāra*. It takes the form of repeated succession of births and deaths, with a quantum of enjoyment and suffering, determined by the effect of the maturing load of *karmas* called *prārabdha karma*.[8] Until the *jīva* realises its own nature and its relationship with God, it will be subject to this process. Release from this very process is called *mokṣa*.

In the state of bondage, the *jīva* is under the dominance of the I-sense, where the ego is perverted and arising from the association with the body. In a dog's body, the *jīva* has a dog's ego, in an elephant's body, an elephant's ego, and in a man's body, a human ego. What is generally called a sense of independence, is the elimination of the expression of this pseudo-ego which forms the guardian-knot of bondage. According to Rāmānuja, the *jīva* really is a liege of God, the Lord forming His body as it is. So, the *jīva* cannot exist independent of God in the pan-organic system of Rāmānuja. The sense of pseudo-independence is a result of ignorance. This is to be replaced by the natural sense of dependence, which of course is not a deprivation of freedom, but development of spiritual strength leading to *mokṣa*. The procedures that man must adopt for gaining the natural sense of dependence are called the ways of communion. They are generally designated as *karma-yoga, jñāna-yoga* and *bhakti-yoga*. They uproot the load of *karma* persisting from time without beginning.

Cultivating the ways of communion and the practice of the principles mentioned in the path of communion through *bhakti* is the development of devotion.

---

8. Meaning that part of man's accumulated *karmas*, which has begun to bear fruit in the present life. It is pre-determined and cannot be avoided. It results in those conditions of man's existence which he cannot get over, however hard he may try.

All Hindu philosophical schools agree upon the general principles of the ethical conduct — known as *sādhana* — which must be followed for the attainment of Liberation. These universally acknowledged principles are: all passions are to be controlled, no injury to life in any form should be done, all desires for pleasures should be maintained under control, etc. Even after attaining a very high degree of moral greatness, man has to prepare, strengthen, purify and provide a steadiness of his mind to attain of his ideal. Most Hindu philosophical systems are unanimous about the spiritual practices and the means adopted for the purpose. The uniformity of practice in Hindu religion has unity in all its aspirations and strivings. *Bhakti* is a practical aspect without which the emotional feeling is not purified, and without purification of the emotional feeling communion with God is impossible.

Feeling is the most interesting aspect of everyone's consciousness. It is in one's feeling that one thinks of one's thoughts as being a part of oneself. Even in day-to-day life the elements, which precede an act of knowledge, are probably mere feelings, marking the earliest tracks of consciousness — whether feeling is looked at from the evolutionary point of view or from the standpoint of the genesis of consciousness in ordinary life. A close look reveals that what is called matter-complex, becomes at a certain stage, a feeling-complex, and by passage of time, the feeling complex becomes again matter-complex. Feelings are in themselves the ultimate substances of which consciousness and gross matter are the products. There are three types of feelings: sorrowful, pleasurable and those which are neither sorrowful nor pleasurable.

Bhakti is an emotional feeling. It is a pleasurable feeling, the experience of bliss essence. The particularity of this feeling is that it does not give rise to the two other types of feelings. Therefore, it is called pure, because it is devoid of the other two facets. To develop devotion means to obtain frequently a pure emotional feeling. This emotional feeling helps to direct all emotions towards God.

Reflection on the advancing stages of thought and feelings towards God helps in developing devotion. Certain practices of purification should accompany these reflections. These practices and reflections gradually weaken the vicious tendencies and finally make them disappear altogether. For an uninterrupted meditation on God, the mind should be purged of all impurities. The exercises for this are external as well as internal, like keeping the body clean, contentment of mind, remaining silent in speech (meaning speaking only what is essential), etc. Whenever a bad thought comes to the mind, one should divert it towards a good thought, so the bad thought may not find scope for action. One should habituate the mind in keeping itself in good relation with everyone. The practice of kindness towards those who suffer, a feeling of indifference towards the vicious, a feeling of happiness for the good of all beings, a feeling of equanimity, etc. are the disciplines of the mind. When the mind becomes pure by the practice of these disciplines, the chances of its reflecting the disturbances are greatly reduced. At such a stage, it is easy for the devotee to fix his mind on God, in whatever form he wishes. This is known as *dhāraṇā*, that is, grasping or fixing the mind on God. In the beginning, it will be difficult to fix the mind steadily. Therefore, the same thought on God has to be repeated constantly in the mind. This process of repeating is meditation (*dhyāna*). When the mind attains the power of making itself steady, it becomes one with God — there is no consciousness of subject, object or thinking, but the mind becomes steady and one with the thought of God. There is no movement of mind into its passing states. In short, the developing devotion is a way to adopt these means to attain God, the Supreme Being, to be saved from the sorrows of *saṁsāra* (cycle of births and deaths) and to be blessed with divine communion.

God is verily the ever existent. He is the only source and

sustenance of the universe and nothing can be realised without His grace. The entire universe depends upon His mercy. Divine grace is essential for any kind of achievement and one cannot think of attaining anything by any means independent of Him. Therefore, God is the ultimate means of attaining everything, including liberation. He does not offer liberation unless the devotee's quest is constant, determined and continuous. He waits for an opportunity to rush to the rescue of every single soul. Therefore, it is essential that each soul should win divine grace by following one of the means. Developing devotion is one such means to obtain God's grace and to attain Him.

One should reach the spring of water in the vast desert to be relieved from thirst. One has to board a ship to be carried across the huge ocean. One has to hold on firmly to the staff to obtain any support from it. So too, one has to choose the right means to attain Him. A sincere prayer to God is one of the means to develop devotion in Him. Everyone is capable of praying and thereby fit to develop *bhakti* towards God.

Concentration of the mind is essential for devotion. Fixing the mind attentively on one desirable object, namely God and withdrawing the mind from undesirable objects develops devotion. To achieve this, the body and the mind should be directed towards the desired object. By nature, the mind is very restless and distracting. Restlessness is the cause of distraction; self-control is necessary to control the mind. Certain practical exercises should be taken up to control the body as well as the mind, and to make the mind incline towards the desired object, that is, God. These means help to overcome the mental distraction that hinder the development of devotion. The application of practical exercises purifies the mind and makes it transparent and tranquil, which is conducive to concentration. A tranquil mind easily concentrates on a desirable object. Great care should be taken to cultivate a one-pointed mind, because it is necessary to achieve God Realisation. To develop devotion, is to adopt the methods and practice them, until one realises the ultimate aim. *Bhakti* is not a simple meditation upon God but is a multiform ethical, religious and spiritual discipline to be undertaken and applied over a long time.

Developing Devotion in Absence of a Spiritual Education

Evidentally, that religion did not create man but man created religion. Man pursued his inner urge, found out the goal, and the world named the applied means to achieve this goal as religion.

When man becomes helpless, he craves for something, which gives him assurance of hope and makes him partake of a larger, purer and nobler life. This is religion. But, it is difficult to find a uniform religious formula that would satisfy the needs of all minds.

It should be noted that religion is not a matter of external observances alone. It is mainly a matter of conduct, knowledge and experience. Therefore, it is essential that all followers of *bhakti* should understand what lies underneath religious codes. Otherwise, they will fall a prey to superstition, which is the worst enemy of religion.

Each particular culture defines religion in its own way. It is difficult to understand the essence of all the religions. Religion is the outcome of man's inner urge for freedom from the shackles of this life. It is the outer expression of his great hunger for the Infinite. A significant characteristic of the human existence is the longing for something different, the moment man gets hold of one thing. The moment he has obtained what he wanted, even though it gives him joy and happiness, he is dissatisfied and goes in search of something else, superior, for a greater satisfaction. Thus, he goes on, eternally dissatisfied, endlessly struggling for what he himself did not know. This is his life on earth. This eternal dissatisfaction indicates that man wants infinite freedom. That means he wants to reach the Infinite. Religion, without dogma, is a means to reach this goal.

Under the circumstances one lives, one may not be able to follow the religious paths either because they are unsuitable to the mind, or because one could not receive a proper religious education. There is also the aspect of human life, which compels one to think of some existence behind the phenomenal world. Man finds that he is helpless against certain circumstances; sometimes he fails to work against the circumstances. He feels that there is an unseen or an unknown force, which shapes his destiny. He finds he is not free to do whatever he otherwise likes. He also realises that there is an unseen power behind some of his actions and silently prays in his own way for help to get guidance or strength. He feels relieved, when approaching this unseen power for guidance. Gradually, he realises that real happiness lies in identifying himself with this unseen force. At this stage, he learns to be humble and gives up actions that tie him to his ego to taste real freedom. Then he understands that the great power he thinks of is within himself and not outside. The object he prays to is within him, and the act of prayer is a way of developing devotion. Devotion is the earnest desire, an intense motivation to know the truth. The Truth is God Himself. When a person puts forth special efforts and fixes his mind on a strange object he has never seen before, he perceives it as that of a flash of lightning. The pleasure obtained would incite him to repeatedly recall it so he can remember it forever. It would be the same in case of Truth or God, except that in this case it would be considered as developing devotion.

Just as all the rivers, coming from different sources and directions flow into the ocean, so too all human activities do find a culmination in the ultimate goal. Just as the fruits of a tree are not judged by the routines of religious ceremonies that are conducted under it, so too are not the fruits of man's spiritual ascent. It is primarily his character, purity of heart, the spirit of service, etc. that are the food for his spiritual path and not the performance of religious ceremonies. Belief and faith in the existence of a Supreme Power or God is sufficient.

The great sages and saints declare that grace follows the yearning of faith as certainly as the day follows the night. Faith in the Supreme or God and His grace are the basic requirements in the path of devotion. If man worships this Supreme in all his actions with a true heart and mind, He will reveal Himself to him. "To those who are constantly devoted to Me and who worship Me with love, I bestow that particular mental disposition by which they attain me."[9] The only requirement mentioned here is the unceasing love to God. Other virtues such as spiritual backgrounds or religious education are not essential. Everyone is equal before the Ultimate Being.

Absolute Self-surrender to God, Prapatti

The Upaniṣads call this means as *nyāsa vidyā* and can be performed by anyone irrespective of age, gender, caste, etc. Its *modus operandi* is explained in a detailed manner in *Ahirbudhnya Saṁhitā, Lakṣmī Tantra* and other texts. The Purāṇas also have a good number of references to Self-surrender (*prapatti*). Of course, the Āḷvārs recomment *prapatti*. Moreover, the Lord Nārāyaṇa Himself has favoured *prapatti* in His various incarnations.

The final goal of truth is realised by following certain paths like that of love, wisdom, concentration and meditation, or that of desire-less action. All these pathways are like so many rivers, which ultimately flow into the ocean of Truth. The choice of the way of approach depends upon the physical and mental condition of the different individuals. One in whom the feeling of worship is predominant will naturally choose the path of love and devotion. When love awakens in the soul, man rises above all duties and works through love. The intensity of human

9. *Bhagavad-Gītā*, X.10.

love inflames the worshipper, when he sublimates it in throbbing prayers. God is already present in man. He just has to kindle the awareness of God's presence. When His presence is felt, all worries, fears and doubts disappear and sheer bliss replaces them. In this pure delight, man realises the merit of his unfailing conviction in the Supreme. Rāmānuja declares that every devoted man will have the same experience, when he takes refuge in God or the Supreme.

Taking refuge in God means the act of self-surrender. In the *Ṛgveda* God is called a leader, who leads everyone to peace and happiness through the turmoil of life. He is described as a dear friend and near relative of all men.[10] He is called a universal saviour whom nobody can obstruct.[11] None other than Himself is capable of protecting man from the hazardous ocean of life. In *Īśāvāsya Upaniṣad*, man is advised to surrender himself to God with implicit faith, unreservedly to be saved and led to Him.[12] Rāmānuja calls this act of self-surrender *prapatti*.

Unrelenting strength and firm conviction are the essential characteristics of faith. To offer oneself to the Supreme develops devotion: the ever-existent means for the Eternal Bliss of divine communion with the ever-merciful Lord Himself. Without faith in the grace of God, no one can hope to be saved. The merciful Supreme Being has given the soul the freedom of action. He has made man strong enough to withstand the temptations and to march steadily on the path of progress towards spiritual perfection. When the aspirant realises that he cannot get his desire fulfilled, neither by himself nor with the help of some other method, he takes refuge (with unshakable faith) in God to attain his goal. He chooses God directly as the means of attaining his aspirations. He who runs into innumerable

---

10. *Ṛgveda*, III.20.4 and I.75, 4.

11. *Ṛgveda*, V.7.7.

12. *Īśāvāsya Upaniṣad*, 18.

difficulties in developing his religious or spiritual background, or who cannot get any religious education, surrenders himself to God and prays to Him to lead him safely on the path of devotion and enable him reach his goal. Though *bhakti* is the best means for this type of man, he surrenders to God for the perfection of his chosen means, namely divine communion. This type of self-offering to God — called *prapatti* — is open to all.

Self-offering is a direct means to attain liberation. It is capable of perfecting all other means. It is an independent means to liberation, because there are no other means involved. In all other approaches, man needs to follow the disciplines of one or the other means.[13] Self-surrender is a means, which is within the competency of everyone without any restrictions. Not only that it is not necessary to have a religious education or background but also it frees man from the shackles of religious dogma. Even the weak and the infirm can attain the goal of Divine communion through self-surrender to God. Unlike the *bhakti-yoga*, which requires a rigorous training that is not possible for many and those who are incapable of adopting these means, self-surrender is the means that brings many mental transformations. In fact, even the *bhakti-yoga* ultimately leads to self-offering. It starts as a substitute to devotion, preserving in itself the essentials of the *bhakti-yoga* without its hard-and-fast rules. Moreover, it has a universal appeal, as there is no restriction attached to it. Taking refuge in God or the Supreme is so powerful that it averts all hindrances. It is a means for achieving all aspirations and producing results very soon.

Self-offering directly stands in the place of *parā bhakti*[14] and the performance of any other act is not necessary. In the act of self-offering, the devotee intuits the will of God and submits

13. *Bhakti-yoga* needs *karma-yoga*, *karma-yoga* needs *jñāna-yoga*, *jñāna-yoga* needs *karma-yoga*, etc.

14. The perfected stage of meditation serving as direct means to liberation.

himself without any reserve to His will. He gets his will emptied of egoism and attunes it to the redemptive will of God.

The conditions required to be fulfilled for the self-offering to God are:

- Attune oneself to the will of God by keeping away from transgressing the Divine laws,
- Have confidence that there is no means of redemption available other than the Supreme,
- Have the firmness of mind to maintain an unswerving faith in God,
- Be convinced of the redemptive will of God, and
- Entrust the Supreme with the burden of one's protection with a feeling of thorough subservience to Him, etc.

Śrī Kṛṣṇa says, "Completely relinquishing all *dharma*,[15] seek me alone for refuge. I will release you from all sins, grieve not."[16] The *bhakti* path is not within the competency of everyone whereas *prapatti* has a universal appeal. Even Buddhists find the need of it. They are required to take refuge in *Buddha*, *Saṁgha* and *Dharma*.[17]

Taking refuge in God is inevitable to attain steadfast devotion. Lord Kṛṣṇa says, "My devotee never gets destroyed".[18] The devotee whose mind is specially attuned to God's worship quickly becomes one with Him and enjoys enduring peace. He

15. Relinquishing *dharma* means the complete relinquishment of the sense of agency, possessiveness, fruits, etc. of action in the practising of *karma, jñāna* and *bhakti-yoga* in the way instructed.

16. *Bhagavad-Gītā*, XVIII.66.

17. *Buddham śaraṇam gacchāmi,*
saṁgham śaraṇam gacchāmi,
dharmam śaraṇam gacchāmi.

18. *Bhagavad-Gītā*, IX.31.

attains an eternal state of freedom from obstacles and quickly obtains perfect *bhakti*.

Śrī Kṛṣṇa says,

> Neither by Vedas, nor by austerities, nor by gifts, nor by sacrifice can I be seen as thou has seen Me. But by devotion, exclusive, I may in this form be known as seen in true form, Arjuna, and also be attained.[19]

Only the unconditional, deep-rooted love for God serves as a means to know God in His true form, to have His vision and eventually to attain Him. The Upaniṣads say,

> This Self (the Supreme Self or God) cannot be obtained by instruction, not by intellect nor by much hearing. Whomsoever He chooses, by Him alone is He obtained. To such a one He reveals His own form.[20]

Nārada says,

> Devotion is like the experience of joy, which a dumb man has, when he tastes something sweet.[21]

Vedāntadeśikam explains that Self-surrender (*prapatti*) is neither a mere faith in the saving grace of Lord Nārāyaṇa nor a mere prayer to Him for protection. *Prapatti* does not mean merely a surrendered life in this world, centred around serving Lord Nārāyaṇa. *Prapatti* encompasses all of this and is much more. Though *śaraṇāgati*[22] is in general used for denoting surrender, what all things that needs to be fulfilled in that surrender which is performed only once for obtaining *mokṣa*, is very important.

---

19. *Bhagavad-Gītā*, XI.53-54.
20. *Kaṭha Upaniṣad* II.2.23 and *Muṇḍaka Upaniṣad*, III.2.3.
21. *Nārada Bhakti Sūtra*, 52.
22. *Śaraṇāgati* seeking refuge, particularly, seeking refuge at the feet of God.

Two main qualifications for one who is desirous of release from bondage (*mumukṣu*) to adopt *prapatti* are:

(a) Destituteness, which may result either because of one's lack of mental and physical strength to adopt *bhakti-yoga*, or lack of the requisite knowledge of sacred texts or any inability to put up with any delay in attaining *mokṣa*.[23]

(b) Seeking the Lord Nārāyaṇa as the sole refuge with complete aversion to all fruits other than *mokṣa*.[24]

Prapatti has the following five accessories:

1. Determination to perform whatever is pleasing to the Lord. Since the traditional texts are His divine commands, one should be firm in following one's religious duties.[25]
2. Avoidance of such acts that are displeasing to the Lord. So, one should abstain from acts that are prohibited in the sacred texts.
3. Feeling of utter helplessness. One should sincerely feel helpless in order to attain *mokṣa*.[26]
4. Intense faith in oneself that the Supreme Lord will certainly grant *mokṣa* for the *prapatti* performed, even though one has committed countless sins. This complete faith and conviction is *mahā-viśvāsa*.
5. Begging the Lord for eternal protection. This is the prayer to obtain *mokṣa*.

Performance of *prapatti* is always accompanied by a threefold pure renunciation (*sāttvika tyāga*):

---

23. *Akiñcanyam*.
24. *Ananyagatitvam*.
25. *Anukūlasya saṁkalpam*.
26. *Kārpanyam*.

- One should shed the attitude of doership and realise that the Lord is the actual doer.
- One should give up the thought of "I" and "mine" while performing *prapatti*. It is also done for the pleasure of the Supreme Lord.
- One should give up the thought that the fruits of Self-surrender belong to him or her and realise that they too belong to the Lord.

The most important thing to understand, while performing *prapatti*, is that it itself is not the reason for one's *mokṣa*. It is the mercy of the Lord which is responsible for one's Liberation. Since the one who is desirous of release (*mumukṣu*) has the proper *karma* due to various pious deeds and has the divine blessings, to him, the Lord, out of His mercy grants liberation, using the devotee's past virtuous deeds as a means.[27]

In *Viśiṣṭādvaita* philosophy, the Lord and His consort Śrī, is both the means and the end.[28] *Vedāntadeśikam* beautifully portrays the state of a *prapanna*[29] while performing *prapatti* in the best and unparalleled heart-melting poem:

> With no refuge other than Your grace, abandoning my ageless erroneous ways, committing to the way that will please you, resolving that your lotus feet are the only means, I surrender unto your lotus feet with the hope that you will save me from the darkness that has stood by me, and deliver me the life of eternal angels, with your beautiful grace, release me from the burden for salvation, accept me as your ward, the consort of Śrī.[30]

The actual performance of *prapatti* is composed of the following three acts:

---

27. Technically, *sādhya upāya*.
28. *Upāya* and *upeya*.
29. A *prapanna* is one who seeks refuge with God.
30. *Amṛta Svadhini* of *Vedāntadeśikam* 31.

1. A bound soul thinks that he is independent on its own. This is the greatest mistake since all souls are the most precious properties of Lord Nārāyaṇa. One should recognise, accept and meditate on the fact that one completely belongs only to Lord Nārāyaṇa. In the same way, one should recognise, accept and meditate on the fact that all the souls and the created world in which the souls enjoy their lifetime are also the precious properties of the Lord.[31]

2. Recognition and contemplation of the fact that the Lord protects not only the embodied souls but also the whole world with which the souls are associated. This type of surrender is unique in *prapatti*.[32]

3. Recognition, acceptation and contemplation that the fruit of one's protection also belongs only to the Lord.[33]

It is however very important to understand that *prapatti* is not some mechanical process that fulfils some conditions. It is the fully blossomed stage of complete understanding of the principles.

Spiritual truth is to be felt by direct experience. One has to feel it, realise it in the depth of one's heart. The essential characteristics of devotion are the consecration of all activities by complete self-surrender to Him and an extreme anguish if he were to be forgotten. For, self-surrender is only another name for the effacement of the ego and any work that is selfless has a place in spiritual life.

---

31. *Ātma samarpaṇam.*

32. *Bhara samarpaṇam.*

33. *Phala samarpaṇam.*

3

Concept of Bhakti in Vedānta

It (meditation) has to be performed till death, for here also scriptural authority is seen. — *Brahma-Sūtra*, IV.1.12

There is no return (for the released souls), because scriptures say so. There is no return. — *Brahma-Sūtra*, IV.4.22

Living indeed thus throughout the length of life, he reaches the world of *Brahman*. — *Chāndogya Upaniṣad*, VIII.15.1

Bhakti in Vedānta

In the scriptural traditions of India, it is said that there are two kinds of knowledge: the lower and the higher. The lower knowledge (*aparā*) consists of the four Vedas, namely *Ṛg*, *Yajur*, *Sāma* and *Atharva*, the Brāhmaṇas, Āraṇyakas, Upaniṣads, the Purāṇas, grammar, etymology, prosody, astrology and so forth. The higher knowledge (*parā*) is invisible, ungraspable by the ordinary intellect, without origin and indescribable. Vedic philosophy in Vedānta (and in Vedas) opens the door for gaining the knowledge of *parā*, the higher knowledge. This is the knowledge of *Brahman*, the Highest Reality, as designated by Vedānta.

The philosophy in *Vedānta Sūtra* (also known as *Brahma-Sūtra*) constitutes the one unity in the inquiry of *karma* and Brahma. After being dissatisfied with the objectives of *karma*, the inquiry into *Brahman* is undertaken to gain His knowledge. This is not a mere intellectual understanding but an extremely devoted and intense meditation on *Brahman*. The process is known as *bhakti*, the loving meditation.

While affirming *Brahman*, Vedānta does not deny the reality of the world. It does not identify the individual soul with the Absolute. The way to bliss is knowledge. Knowledge springs from *karma-yoga*, which matures into *upāsanā* (worship). *Upāsanā* is a devout meditation, which in turn produces a strong current of love. In search of *Brahman*, the knowledge that arises from *karma-yoga* matures into devotion (*bhakti*). Vedānta significantly describes *Brahman* as the Supreme Person, who transcends all imperfections and abounds with auspicious qualities of unsurpassed excellence.

The word *Brahman* stands for the Highest Person, who is by nature devoid of all evils and is possessed of all the auspicious qualities — innumerable and unsurpassed in excellence. He who possesses all greatness is alone the Lord of all.

He alone has to be desired and known by all, who are affected with the three types of miseries: *ādi ātmika* (those which are due to one's self), *ādi daivika* (those which arise out of supernatural origin) and *ādi bhautika* (those that come from natural causes and beings). Ignorance of *Brahman* is the essence of human bondage. On the other hand, to know *Brahman* is a source of joy. Influenced by this joy, the seeker pursues further knowledge through the discipline of devotion. Through God's grace, the seeker's effort is crowned with the joyous triumph of the full attainment (experience of God). The pathway to the final goal in life is the blissful contact with *Brahman* by devout and loving contemplation. This way also reminds of a life of virtue founded on philosophical understanding. The objective attained through this means is the everlasting experience of *Brahman*. This is the state of supreme joy of being with *Brahman*, the experience of final freedom (or final release).

Brahman is the highest reality. There is nothing beyond or superior to It. Expressions, which apparently imply something else as existing, are only metaphorical. "By that Being, the whole universe is filled"[1] and "Just as the world obtained by works perishes here, so also there, (in heaven) the world obtained by merit perishes."[2] "He who knows *Brahman* attains the Highest."[3] "Knowing the individual self and the Impeller (*Brahman*) to be separate and being therefore blessed by Him, He attains immortality."[4] In short, "Scriptures are the only source to lead man to the path of *Brahman*."[5]

The scriptural traditions that are the source of right knowledge with respect of *Brahman*, suggest that one should follow the principles of hearing (*śravaṇa*), reflection[6] (*manana*), and steady meditation (*nididhyāsana*). *Śrīmad Bhāgavata* gives importance to *śravaṇa*:

> For men caught between afflictions of the forest fire of worldly miseries and the dangers of the sea of *saṁsāra*, there is no other means to go across that sea than the boat of absorbing accounts of the Lord's excellences as displayed in His sportive manifestations.[7]

Hearing (*śravaṇa*) is to receive the ideal from the spiritual teacher (*guru*), who has perceived the knowledge of the nature of the Self. When one takes to spiritual life and makes sincere efforts, God responds and helps by appearing in the form of the *guru* at the right time. The spiritual bond between the *guru* and the disciple is neither emotional nor sentimental. The *guru*'s grace helps the aspirant along, until he realises the end, that is, he is released from bondage. The disciple should repose total faith in his *guru*. *Manana* is fixing of the mind in one's Self. *Nididhyāsana* is

1. *Śvetāśvatara Upaniṣad*, III.9.
2. *Chāndogya Upaniṣad*, VIII.1.6.
3. *Taittirīya Upaniṣad*, II.1.1.
4. *Śvetāśvatara Upaniṣad*, 16.
5. *Vedānta-Sūtra*, I.1.3.
6. *Manana* is recollection, constant remembrance, logical reflection.
7. *Śrīmad Bhāgavata*, XII.4.40.

the continuous contemplation on this very idea for destroying the beginningless innate impression (*vāsanā*) of distinctions, which is hostile to this knowledge of understanding the Self.

Bondage has its origin in *avidyā* that veils the true nature of one's Self. This bondage is an obstacle in gaining the knowledge of *Brahman*. Knowledge alone can destroy bondage. This knowledge differs from the syntactical understanding of the scriptures.

Combining work with knowledge is essential for the final release. This view is stressed in the spiritual traditions of India. Mere knowledge cannot bring release from the bondage. So, work should never be given up. When work is combined with knowledge, final release is yielded by removing the bondage. Release, while living, is nothing but the detained attitude towards one's life; this again means being detached to the results of actions performed, or to renounce the fruits of actions performed.[8] Therefore, a combination of work and knowledge is prescribed as the stepping stone for *bhakti*.

For the practice of devotion, all works as they are prescribed by the scriptures, are essential.[9] It is said, Lord Brahmā is pleased with the performance of such devout meditation and guarantees His grace to the devotee. "It is devotion to Lord alone that leads to release, since he who is devoted to the Self is dear to the Self and is therefore chosen."[10] "Self is here referred to as individual soul as well as *Brahman*."[11]

Devout meditation, *upāsanā* is a mental action. It is the constant remembrance of the object of worship. *Upāsanā* and *dhyāna*, both refer to meditation, for which another name is *bhakti*. Divine grace and *bhakti* are the chief means to release. Knowledge from work influences the attitude of *bhakti* in the mind, which in turn

8. *Īśāvāsya Upaniṣad*, 11.

9. *Bṛhadāraṇyaka Upaniṣad*, IV.4.22.

10. *Muṇḍaka Upaniṣad*, III.2.3.

11. *Kaṭha Upaniṣad*, II.23.

liberates the soul from its bondage. On its release, the soul manifests its true nature. It attains all the auspicious qualities of *Brahman*, but does not identify with Him. It continues to have a separate existence, so that it can constantly serve Him.

> The two that have entered into the cavity (of the heart) are indeed the two selves. The individual and the Supreme, because it is so seen.[12]
>
> The wise, who, by meditation on the Self has realised the Ancient one, who is difficult to be seen, who has entered into everything, who is seated in the heart, and who dwells in the abyss — he indeed transcends joy and sorrow.[13]

The "ancient" refers to *Brahman* and the realisation of *Brahman* through *bhakti* makes the devotee transcend joy and sorrow. The mental state of a devotee is in equipoise in this stage.

The individual Self is not produced, but is projected from *Brahman* Himself. This is how the traditional Hindu scriptures express it. Because of this, the individual soul is also eternal. But the Self, in its activity, is dependent on *Brahman*, because it is issued from the Highest Lord. This aspect of *Brahman* is present in all individual souls, beginning with Brahmā and ending with a clump of grass, each having its own *karma* to undergo experiences. The Highest person is *Brahman*. He is that omniscient, omnipotent, all-merciful Being. "*Brahman* is that from whom proceed the creation, etc. of this universe."[14]

Brahman has a twofold characteristic: the subtle and the gross. As He is extremely subtle, "He is the self of all, residing within all souls, controls them as their inner self."[15] So, "Let him (the devotee) worship the Self alone, as the object to be attained."[16] The attainment of Highest Knowledge is in the worship of the

12. *Brahma-Sūtra*, 1.2.11.
13. *Kaṭha Upaniṣad*, I.11.12.
14. *Vedānta-Sūtra*, I.1.2.
15. *Bṛhadāraṇyaka Upaniṣad*, III.7.22.
16. *Bṛhadāraṇyaka Upaniṣad*, I.4.15.

Self (*Brahman*) who is in the Self. This Self "has to be seen, heard, reflected upon, and has to be steadily meditated upon".[17]

Bhakti alone induces the strong desire to know *Brahman*. This knowing of *Brahman* is the same as experiencing Him. Perception is like seeing; it is of two kinds. One which is born of the senses and the other which is born of Yoga (the realisation of *Brahman* through concentration). The former is external and the latter internal. The internal perception is to be gained through meditation. Devotion is a form of internal perception. "And moreover *Brahman* is experienced in perfect meditation according to Śruti or Smṛti."[18] Śruti is the knowledge that is revealed by or heard from the sages. Smṛti is the knowledge based on scriptures.

Based on spiritual traditions concerned with the knowledge of *Brahman*, worship (*upāsanā*) and meditation (*dhyāna*) are the most important means to keep in constant contact with God. Both are modes of *bhakti*. *Brahman* can only be sought after, when the desire to know Him is intense.

Dhyāna is not mere remembrance but deep and continued remembrance: a succession of memories, which is unbroken like a stream of oil. It denotes the uninterrupted series of mental thoughts, which is the one-pointed concentration.

> The meditation of His form is one continued stream without attachment to any other object. Meditation of Him is thus generated by the six limbs of Yoga;[19] then comes *dhyāna* that takes the mind to establish in *samādhi*.[20, 21]

---

17. *Bṛhadāraṇyaka Upaniṣad*, I.4.15.
18. *Bṛhadāraṇyaka Upaniṣad*, III.2.23.
19. Six limbs of Yoga are *yama*, *niyama*, *āsana*, *prāṇāyāma*, *pratyāhāra*, and *dhāraṇā*.
20. *Samādhi* is the concentrated attention and mental realisation. The last stage of mental concentration of the *aṣṭāṅga* scheme in Patañjali's *Yoga-Sūtra*. It is a stage in which the practionner gets so fully absorbed in Self-awareness that he remains unaware of the external world.
21. *Viṣṇu Purāṇa*, VI.6.99.

Meditation has to be practised repeatedly. *Upāsanā* also means "firm memory". Firm memory has the same meaning as *bhakti*; in other words, *bhakti* is synonymous with *upāsanā*. It is possible to know *Brahman* through *dhyāna* and *upāsanā* that are forms of *bhakti* and of its nature. "That Highest person (*Brahman*), O Son of Pārtha is attainable exclusively by *bhakti*."[22] *Taittirīya Āraṇyaka* declares,

> He who knows Him thus, becomes immortal here. There is no other path except *bhakti* for the attainment of final release.[23]

Brahma-Sūtra, speaking of *bhakti* states:

> Wherever there is concentration of mind (there meditation is to be practised) there being no specification.[24]

The only requirement is that the place and the time should be conducive to meditation.

As "*Brahman*'s form does not exist within the range of vision, nobody sees Him with (normal) eyes."[25]

Brahman has two forms: gross and subtle. When these two forms are experienced through meditation, one finds them as *Brahman*'s modes or attributes, just as one finds knowledge and bliss being *Brahman*'s essential nature.

The ways of meditation are the same in all Vedānta texts. The prescribed meditations are on OṀ — *praṇava*, a part of *udgīta*[26] (speech), *prāṇa*, the light and so forth. They are the aspects of the Self, and so meditation on them is given importance. *Brahman* is one, although related with different aspects. For example, Vedānta speaks of *Brahman* as Truth; that, which is Truth, is the

22. *Bhagavad-Gītā*, VIII.22.
23. *Taittirīya Āraṇyaka*, III.12.7 and III.13.1.
24. *Brahma-Sūtra*, IV.1.11.
25. *Kaṭha Upaniṣad*, II.3.9.
26. One of the techniques of reciting *Yajurveda*.

Sun. The Sun is an orb and also the person in the right eye. Special methods of meditation are introduced; they have been connected with different centres in the human body. They will all, in the end, relate to *Brahman*. The heart (*hṛdaya*) is their locus. The object of meditation is glorified thus:

> *Brahman* is greater than the earth, that the ether within the heart (*hṛdaya*) is as great as the universal ether.[27]

Meditating upon the heart reveals the universal Truth, that is, *Brahman*. All the devotees engaged in various meditations attain *Brahman* and go by the path of knowledge. Without restrictions, one will reach *Brahman* through the path of *bhakti*, which consists in the culmination of knowledge of *Brahman*.

Meditation is practised to know the Supreme Self as distinct from the individual Self. As *Brahman* is the Inner Self of all, meditation on any attribute of *Brahman* gives the experience of *Brahman* to the one who meditates.

Vedānta-Sūtra does not speak of special places and times for meditation. Meditation is the deep concentration of mind on a particular object. The only thing required is that the place and time should be conducive to meditation. But the constant, uninterrupted devotion to Lord *Brahman* is stressed. "It (meditation) has to be performed until death, for here also scriptural authority is seen."[28]

Meditation has to be performed until death. All our works should be accomplished along with meditation (and worship) too. Work should never be abandoned until death. "Living indeed thus throughout the length of life, he reaches the world of *Brahman*."[29] Meditation, worship along with work, should be a process of continuation without obstruction.

---

27. *Chāndogya Upaniṣad*, VIII.1.6.
28. *Brahma-Sūtra*, IV.1.12.
29. *Chāndogya Upaniṣad*, VIII.15.1.

Bhakti is a means of release while still living in the world. The released souls attain all the powers of the Lord, except cosmic activity. When the veils of ignorance are removed, they experience *Brahman* unconditionally. The fine attributes of the Self — devoid of sin — belong to His essential nature, but this condition itself depends upon the Supreme Self. This eternal state willed by the Supreme Person exists eternally.

Brahma Sūtra confirms a guaranteed non-return for the released souls:

> There is no return (for the released souls), because scriptures say so. There is no return.[30]

As the released soul has cut the bondage of *karma,* has its knowledge expanded, and its nature rooted in the experience of *Brahman*, it cannot possibly desire anything else. The Supreme Person will never cause the devotee to return to the bondage in life (*saṁsāra*).

Śrī Kr̥ṣṇa has Himself said,

> Among the men who do good deeds, I am very dear to the man of knowledge, and he is dear to Me. Certainly, all these are great, but I deem the man of knowledge to be My very Self, for he, integrated, resorts to Me alone, as the highest end. At the end of many births, man of knowledge finds refuge in Me, realising that Vāsudeva is all.[31]

This human form is the city of *Brahman* and inside it is the place like a Lotus, and inside the Lotus resides *Brahman*, smaller than the smallest. He is the great-unborn Self; and He is knowledge. He sleeps inside the heart. He is the controller of all and the Lord of all. "Having approached the Supreme light of knowledge he is manifested in his own form."[32] When revealed in his own form he becomes indeed the fearless *Brahman*.[33]

---

30. *Brahma-Sūtra*, IV.4.22.
31. *Bhagavad-Gītā*, VII.16 to 19.
32. *Chāndogya Upaniṣad*, VIII.3.
33. *Br̥hadāraṇyaka Upaniṣad*, IV.

Brahman consciousness is the highest state of consciousness, because of His greatness. He should be meditated upon. He should be contemplated with love and devotion; and He should be experienced. This is the stage of perfect evolution of man's spiritual consciousness. Having reached this stage, no man wishes to come down spiritually.

Bhakti in Vedānta Schools

ĀDI ŚAṄKARA

The Upaniṣads taught in the Vedānta philosophy and *Brahma-Sūtra* by Bādarāyaṇa summarised the philosophical thoughts. Great philosophers expressed different views on these scriptures and many were held in great esteem. The views expressed by Ādi Śaṅkarācārya on the Vedānta philosophy attained wonderful celebrity stature because of the subtle and deep ideas it contains.

The philosophy propounded by Śaṅkarācārya gained such a great influence that whoever speaks of the Vedānta philosophy, means only the philosophy propounded by Śaṅkara.

Śaṅkara was born around CE 788-820 (There is also the view on his date as between CE 700 and 800), as the son of Śivaguru, a brāhmaṇa of Kerala, south India, in a village called Kaladi. He is believed to have been the incarnation of Lord Śiva and many miracles are related to his birth. His father named the child as Śaṅkara. *Śaṅ* means "happiness" and *kara* means "one, who bestows". Lord Śaṅkara grants happiness. Śivaguru wished and prayed to God for giving his son the opportunity of bringing happiness to mankind. Śaṅkara was born to Śivaguru after his long observance of austerity and prayer to Lord Śaṅkara.

Śaṅkara soon became the master of all learning: the four Vedas with their auxiliary branches of learning, besides literature and the most difficult Indian subjects — logic and sound reasoning.[34] His excellent power of speech silenced all the proud

34. Nyāya and Tarka.

scholars of his period. Śaṅkara took to asceticism in his 8th year and — travelling a long distance — arrived at the forest hermitage of Guru Govinda Pāda on the banks of river Narmadā.[35] Desirous of being initiated into the knowledge of *Brahman*, he approached Sage Govinda's residence, a cave with an entrance only a cubit in width. Śaṅkara served this spiritual *guru* through the spirit of devotion and became the object of his loving affection. Highly pleased with the disciple's service, the sage imparted to him the knowledge of *Brahman* through the four *mahāvākyas*:[36] "*Brahman* is pure consciousness", "I am *Brahman*", "Thou art that" and "This *ātman* is *Brahman*". Then he was taught *Vedānta-Sūtra* of Vyāsa and through them the innermost essence of the Vedānta philosophy. Though Śaṅkara desired to stay all his life serving his teacher, Govinda Pāda sent his dear disciple off to conquer the world. Incidentally, Govinda Pāda was the disciple of Sage Gaudapāda, the renowned commentator on the Upaniṣads, etc.

Though Śaṅkara's philosophy is based more on *jñāna*, Self-knowledge, his way of life reveals his strong inclination to devotion. In *Bhaja Govindam*,[37] he brings out the great advantage of devotion, which is the easiest and the most natural way to reach the great Divine. He has worked out the singleness of attachment to a loved object, Govinda, without which no genuine love can grow. Śaṅkara shows in *Bhaja Govindam* how the love to God leads to the cause of renunciation of everything else and how perfect bliss is attained. To preach devotion as the only source for attaining God's bliss, he starts his composition with the word *bhaja* itself. *Bhaja* is the root word of the word *bhakti*, which means "energetic mental service". To introduce devotion the name of the composition is also kept *Bhaja Govindam*.

35. A river in central India.

36. Great sayings: Consciousness is *Brahman* (*prajñanam brahma*), I am *Brahman* (*aham brahma asmi*), Thou art That (*tat tvam asi*) and This *Ātmā* is *Brahman* (*ayam ātmā brahman*).

37. One of Śaṅkara's writings.

Worship Govinda, worship Govinda
Worship Govinda, Oh! Foolish one.

He considers all those people as fools, who do not worship Govinda, to reach the state of mental tranquillity. He advises further,

Content yourself with what may come,
Through deeds performed in earlier lives,
Devote your mind to righteousness,
And let dispassion be your law.[38]

The highest truth of the Vedānta, so essential for man's mental and spiritual health has been set forth from the verses of this composition. He suggests some simple, yet significant points for practising devotion like:

Good association breeds detachment,
Detachment leads to freedom from delusion
Undiluted, one contacts changeless reality,
Contact with Reality bestows Liberation while alive.[39]

It is beyond an ordinary person's capabilities to describe the culmination of Śaṅkara's devotion, when he humbly says,

Hard to cross is the world's wide ocean,
Lord redeem me through Thy mercy.[40]

His pure attitude of complete mental surrender to Govinda is revealed here. His highest joy in devotion is spoken in the lines,

For the heart that delights ever in *Brahman*.
It is bliss, bliss, bliss — bliss without end.[41]

According to Śaṅkara, meditation is a form of devotion. For people generally say: he is devoted to the parents, he is devoted to his

38. *Bhaja Govindam*, 1.
39. *Bhaja Govindam*, I.9.
40. *Bhaja Govindam*, II.9.
41. *Bhaja Govindam*, II.9.

teacher, he is devoted to the king, he is devoted to his elders and so forth. A person doing so has got that principle in view. People also say like: a loving wife meditates on her loving husband and so forth. It is found here that a sort of continuous remembrance is indicated. According to Śaṅkara, this form of meditation, which is continuous remembrance on the object in focus, is devotion.

Meditation is a constant remembrance of an object or subject meditated upon. It is like the flowing of an unbroken stream of oil poured out from one vessel to another. When this kind of remembrance has been attained in relation to God, all types of bondage will break away. The act of constant remembering, which is the same as devotion, is also a means for liberation.

In his *Vivekacūḍāmaṇi*[42] also Śaṅkara makes salutations to Govinda, the Vāsudeva, whose ardent devotee he was and to his own Guru Govinda Pāda in his absolute aspect.

> There are three things, which are rare indeed and are due to God's grace — namely a human birth, the longing for liberation, and the protected care of a perfect sage.[43]

According to Śaṅkara, without God's awareness no precious thing can be obtained. His philosophy on devotion is expressed as,

> There is no liberation without the realisation of one's identity with *ātman*; not in the lifetime of a hundred Brahmā's put together.[44]

His practical definitions on devotion can be found, when he says,

> Among the things conductive to liberation, devotion alone holds supreme place. The seeking after one's real nature is designated as devotion.[45]

---

42. *Viveka* = discrimination; *cūḍā* = crest; *maṇi* = jewel; Crest Jewel of Discrimination.
43. Śaṅkara's *Vivekacūḍāmaṇi*, 3.
44. Śaṅkara's *Vivekacūḍāmaṇi*, 6.
45. Śaṅkara's *Vivekacūḍāmaṇi*, 31.

> Others maintain that the inquiry into the truth of one's own Self is devotion.[46]

His clear idea of meditation on *Brahman* to be constant is indicated here. Meditation is also a form of worship, which again is devotion itself.

Śaṅkara also stresses the need of a spiritual *guru* — a wise preceptor — who imparts devotion in the mind of the inquirer after the truth of the *ātman*, because only a wise preceptor is capable of removing ignorance that has veiled the truth in man (the identification of the Self with the body is solely due to ignorance).

Śaṅkara, in his composition *Saundaryalaharī* (Waves of Divine Beauty), has described the divine beauty of the divine mother (*devī*). This description enables the devotee, while chanting the hymn, to visualise Her form, which in turn controls the senses and the mind without getting distracted. This experience is spiritual in nature, as she is the very personification of the knowledge that liberates man from bondage.

Śaṅkara laments in one of the hymns that man does not have the element of discrimination that the honeybee has. The six-legged bee is compared to man with his five senses and mind, with which he derives joy in the world. Unlike the flies, which are attracted to all kinds of food, the honeybee is very selective in its food. It gathers honey only from flowers, whereas man wanders from birth to birth, running after sensory pleasures, without seeking the source of infinite joy. Śaṅkara prays that the Divine Mother should grace the devotee with Her glance, so that his devotion will strengthen. In this hymn too, he heightens the idea that divine grace is very essential to develop devotion to seek liberation.

Once Śaṅkara's father, Śivaguru could not go to the Devī temple of the Divine Mother for worship. Instead, he sent his

---

46. Śaṅkara's *Vivekacūḍāmaṇi*, 32.

son Śaṅkara to offer milk to the Goddess. The small boy, with his childlike devotion prayed to Goddess Devī, to drink milk. When he saw that the image of Devī was not drinking the milk, he started weeping uncontrollably for his fate. The compassionate Divine Mother drank all the milk then, in the form of her icon. Now again, the boy Śaṅkara wept, for She did not leave any milk for him in the container, not even a single drop. At that moment, the Divine Mother revealed in her true form and laughed at him. Pleased with his devotion to Her, she blessed him with all aspects of knowledge. Immediately, Śaṅkara chanted the hymn *Saundaryalaharī* in praise of Mother Devī which came pouring out from his heart.

The hundred verses of *Saundaryalaharī* bring out the shining essence of the power of God manifesting through the 100 aspects of Goddess Devī. It is said that each verse in this hymn is composed in such a way that when recited with devotion — singly or completely — it bestows special powers on the one who recites them.

This devotional hymn composed by Śaṅkara describes how the individual soul, graced by the Mother Divine, pierces the six lotuses[47] in the body and their correlated principles, to merge finally with the Supreme.

BHĀSKARA BHAṬṬA[48]

Bhāskara, an ardent admirer of *bhedābheda* theory or "Theory of transcendence and immanence of God", said that the world is a spiritual manifestation and a spiritual transformation of the Supreme and what passes as matter in reality is spiritual. The attachment to *Brahman*, which is an essential condition for attaining liberation, is defined worship or devotion. He defines

47. The six *cakra*s are *mūlādhāra, svādhiṣṭhāna, maṇipūra, anāhata, viśuddhi* and, *ājñā*.

48. Twelfth Century.

devotion as an attendance on God by meditation. Devotion is conceived as *dhyāna* or meditation. The meditation on *Brahman* results in liberation. Bhāskara states that, so long as man lives, he must try to realise the nature of God and attend on Him through meditation without neglecting the duties of life, since these can lead to liberation after death.

RĀMĀNUJA: BHAKTI AND PRAPATTI

A human being is God's most enviable and precious gift to the Universe, as he can act using his intellectual faculty in a proper manner. Every person by his efforts, can either rise to a higher level, where he will be endowed with Divine qualities, or shall acquire traits of beasts, when behaving in a despicable way, resorting to cruel deeds. The choice is purely his, either to conform to the moral order or to violate the glorious norms.

Measures have been laid down for man and woman, which, if adopted, will surely lead him or her to the abode of God. These steps are so marvellous and carefully planned so as to enable everyone to climb up gradually, to reach the ultimate stage, where he or she can enjoy the bliss in this world itself. God has thus granted the power of discrimination and ability to use the intellect. This privilege is given only to human beings. Given flour, sugar and water, man can make a paste, a variety of sweets, each in a different shape. So too, he has the path of devotion in front of him, which he can pursue arduously and reap the fruits. He can worship at home, visit temples, go on a pilgrimage and resort to any type of spiritual exercise. There are many paths one can choose from, but among them the devotional path is the excellent one; easy to follow and the result is surely beneficial. While God knows the past, the present and the future, man has neither the knowledge of the past nor of the future. However, he has the potential, he can elevate himself and reach the stage of no return.

Rāmānuja (also called Ilaya Perumal) was the son of Keshava Yajvan (also known as Asuri Keshava Dikshita). He was born in CE 1017. Rāmānuja lived a very long life of 120 years from CE 1017 to 1137. He received the initial training from his father. When Rāmānuja was 16 years of age, Keshava Yajvan got him married. But about one month later, Keshava Yajvan died, leaving the whole family plunged in grief. To erase the memory of this unfortunate event, as also to provide higher education to Rāmānuja, the family moved from Bhutapuri (Tamil Nadu, south India), his native place, to Kanchipuram (near Chennai, south India). In Kanchipuram, he started studying the advanced philosophy, especially the Vedānta under the tutorage of a celebrated philosopher named Yādava Prakāśa, who was considered an authority on Advaita Vedānta. Rāmānuja observed all the disciplines expected of disciples and did personal services to the teacher. Yādava Prakāśa loved Rāmānuja very much and gave him the first place among his aspirants. The working of many miracles was attributed to Rāmānuja. This irritated Yādava Prakāśa.

As studies continued, there was a difference of opinion between Yādava Prakāśa and Rāmānuja on the interpretation of some Upaniṣads, which Yādava Prakāśa interpreted in a monistic manner, while Rāmānuja argued on the principles of modified dualism. Rāmānuja was also gifted with miraculous powers, which resulted in bringing fame to him. Annoyed with this, Yādava Prakāśa forged a plot to get rid of Rāmānuja by throwing him into the river Ganges, while he was on a pilgrimage to Varanasi (north India). But his cousin Govinda, who was studying with him, divulged the plot to Rāmānuja and thus saved him. Coming back to Kanchipuram, he became associated with a devout person of a lower caste, called Kāñcīpūrṇa. Rāmānuja justified his act on the ground of Kāñcīpūrṇa's mature devotion to the Lord, which was far superior to high birth and learning. As per Kāñcīpūrṇa's instructions, Rāmānuja carried a vessel full of water everyday, from a neighbouring holy well, for the service of Varadarāja[49] to get his devotional aspirations fulfilled.

Yāmunācārya, otherwise called Alavandār, son of Īśvara Muni and grandson of Nātha Muni,[50] once came to Kanchipuram[51] and saw Rāmānuja at a distance among the students of Yādava Prakāśa. From that very moment, he was greatly anxious to have Rāmānuja as one of his pupils. And as Lord's blessing Rāmānuja once again disagreed with his teacher, Yādava Prakāśa on the interpretation of the meaning of a text from *Chāndogya Upaniṣad*. After Yādava Prakāśa drove him out, he became attached to the worship of Nārāyaṇa. From his maternal uncle Mahāpūrṇa, Rāmānuja learnt of Yāmunācārya and accompanied his uncle to Sri Rangam (Tamil Nadu, south India). But before he could reach Sri Rangam, Yāmunācārya died. It is said that at the time of his death three fingers of Yāmunācārya were found twisted and Rāmānuja there and then took the oath that he would fulfil his three unfulfilled desires: (1) To convert the people to the doctrine of *prapatti* (Doctrine of Divine grace) of Śrī Vaiṣṇavism, making them well versed in the works of Āḷvārs,[52] (2) To write a commentary on *Brahma-Sūtra* according to Śrī Vaiṣṇava School and (3) To write many works on Śrī Vaiṣṇavism. Just after Rāmānujas oath the three fingers of Yāmunācārya got untwisted. Rāmānuja decided to execute all these three wishes of Yāmunācārya. He returned to Kanchipuram and became attached to Kāñcīpūrṇa, the disciple of Yāmuna. Mahāpūrṇa later initiated him. Rāmānuja renounced domestic life, when he was just thirty years old. He took to ascetic life (*saṁnyāsa*) and started his teachings on Śrī Vaiṣṇavism. His Advaita Master, Yādava Prakāśa, too later became his disciple.

49. Name of Viṣṇu, the temple in Kanchipuram is dedicated to Varadarāja.

50. The authors are the descendants of Nātha Muni.

51. In south India, near Chennai. A very important pilgrim centre.

52. Āḷvārs are the Vaiṣṇava spiritual and philosophical saints of Tamil Nadu.

Rāmānuja provided the needed intellectual support to the heritage of passionate love of God that the Āḻvārs left for mankind. His teaching of devotion is meant for both: the intelligentsia in search of an intellectual support to their spiritual approach, as also the simple souls who have got natural, unalloyed faith in God, and submission to His will. Devotion to the Lord and total surrender to Him, is the only way to get liberation, as it is a direct pathway to God's kingdom.

Rāmānuja describes devotion as the knowledge of the Ultimate reality as one's highest treasure and the excessive adoration and attachment to Him. It is a continual thinking of God, without which pure knowledge will not provide liberation. The special feature of devotion is that it makes man lose all interest in everything else other than that which is done for the sake of the dearest God. According to Rāmānuja, devotion is not a feeling but a special kind of knowledge (*jñāna viśeṣa*), which seeks to ignore everything, that is not done for the sake of *Īśvara*, the Supreme Lord and the dearest of all. Devotion is the conviction consequent on the knowledge of one's relationship with God that generates love and attachment to Him. Rāmānuja equates devotion with *dhyāna*, that is, concentration of mind on Him, and *upāsanā*, that is, continuous thought of Him.

To obtain this state of mind, Rāmānuja divides devotion into three stages of development in his teachings:

1. *Sādhanā bhakti* (practice of devotional means),
2. *Parā bhakti* (higher devotion), and
3. *Parama bhakti* (supreme devotion).

In Viśiṣṭādvaita Vedānta, devotion is the means to *mokṣa*. This is evident from numerous scriptures.[53]

According to Rāmānuja, *mukti* is a state, which a man can

53. Also, *parā-bhakti*, *parā-jñāna* and *parama bhakti*.

acquire, when he is freed from all *avidyā* and has the natural intuition of the Supreme Soul and his relations with Him.

To come to this stage, the ordinary, obligatory and ceremonial duties have to be performed, all the highest ethical virtues have to be practised and a true knowledge should be obtained from the scriptures. For the understanding of oneself as the *ātman*, *karma-yoga* and *jñāna-yoga* have to be practised together, as they are mutually involved. It is only when a man has thus qualified himself, that he can ultimately attain liberation from all worldly bonds by supreme self-surrender and devotion to the Lord.

Vedāntadeśikam, the most ardent follower of Rāmānuja, says that the performance of *karma* makes a man fit to acquire the true knowledge, which in turn makes a man apt to attain devotion. When a man is fit enough to inquire after true knowledge, he may give up *karma*s. Devotion, according to *Vedāntadeśikam*, is the feeling of joy (*prīti*) in the adorable and not mere knowledge. Liberation, as similarity of quality (*sāyujya*) with *Īśvara*, is the result of such devotion.

Performance of one's duties and rituals should be purely a divine service and not with any expectation of any personal rewards. It is only the unconditional, deep-rooted love for God that serves as a means to know God in His true form, to have His vision and eventually to attain Him. This means that Divine vision is possible only through God's grace which can be obtained by deep devotion to God. Only to such an individual, who loves God and who craves to have His vision, does God shower with His grace and reveal Himself.

Rāmānuja, referring to the *Muṇḍaka Upaniṣad* and the *Bhagavad-Gītā* (XI.53-54), says,

> Without deep devotion to God, the mere study of the scriptures, observance of austerities and performance of rituals will not help to attain God.

The culmination in devotion is known as *prapatti,* taking refuge in God. According to Viśiṣṭādvaita philosophy, besides devotion, *prapatti,* the absolute self-surrender to God is also laid down as a means to liberation. Devotion is a rigorous discipline and for those, who are incapable of undertaking it, *prapatti* is advocated as an alternative easy way to liberation. Taking refuge (*prapatti*) in the devotional attitudes is like:

— Resolving to subordinate one's will always to the Divine will,

— Avoiding all that is contrary to His will,

— Firm faith that God is the saviour of all,

— Acceptance that one always has God's protective grace,

— Feeling of one's pitiable state owing to a realisation of the insufficiency of all self-effort made for one's liberation, and

— Resigning oneself completely to His care and protection.

Prapatti represents the ideal of devotion. As said earlier, this is usually considered as the complete surrender of one's ego to the Divine — the climax in the ultimate stage of devotion is *prapatti.*

Prapatti means to reach the abode of God, through the mind, through spiritual sacrifice and through steady thought of God. This means to make one's ordinary consciousness reach progressively the level of God's consciousness in order to know Him. As the *jīva* is an integral part of God, it always hankers to reach his home, from where it has come down to have the experience of his *karma.*

Prapatti is also called *śaraṇāgati* in Sanskrit. *Śaraṇa* means "abode of protection", *āgata* means "having come" or "having reached". *Śaraṇāgati* means "to reach God's abode for protection". If devotion is the outer protection for the soul, *prapatti* is its inner protection.

In short, *prapatti* portrays the return of *jīva* to its home in God. *Upāsanā* is the steady thought of God, which gains in intensity by constant practice until the end is attained. The philosophy of devotion is the ladder of love from the earth to the heaven; and the philosophy of divine grace (*prapatti*) can be taken as the one from the heaven to the earth. The philosophy of *prapatti* lies in the guarantee of liberation to all souls. It is the call of the redeemer for the whole humanity.

BHEDĀBHEDA, DVAITĀDVAITA OF NIMBĀRKA

A noted teacher of devotion, who came soon after Rāmānuja, was Nimbārka. He has most likely preceded Madhva, the founder of Dvaita (dualism) Philosophy of Vedānta. The doctrine of Dvaitādvaita, or Bheda-abheda or the theory of the "Absolute as unity in difference" was introduced by Nimbārka. He was born in Nimbapur.[54] His time is said to be a little later in the twelfth century CE. Nimbārka was originally named Niyamānanda by his parents. One day he invited an ascetic to take food at his house. It was very late when the meal was ready, and so the ascetic would not partake of it, as it was against the practice of ascetics to take food after sunset. Niyamānanda prayed to God for help in this difficult situation, and God responded by placing His radiant discus (known as *sudarśana*) on the Western horizon. The discus shone like the sun; and the ascetic was shown this sun-like brilliance pouring from the top of a *nimba* tree.[55] Thinking that the brilliance was of the real Sun, the ascetic took his meal. On knowing that this was in reality a miraculous happening, he gave Niyamānanda the new name of Nimbārka for showing the Sun (*arka*) from the top of a *nimba* tree. Nimbārka was a devotee of Śrī Kṛṣṇa. He spent his time mostly in Mathura (north India), the birthplace of Śrī Kṛṣṇa. He had many disciples.

---

54. In Bellary district of Andhra Pradesh, south India.

55. *Nimba* is margos (*Azadirachta indica*).

According to him, the path of liberation is open even to those who have no scriptural education. They can follow the path of devotion to attain liberation. Devotion means, service to God with body, speech and mind. Without any desire for fruits of actions, God should be the Supreme end of life to an aspirant of devotion. Devotion ends in complete self-surrender, which generates knowledge by the grace of God.

Nimbārka brings out two phases in the practice of devotion: (1) preparatory and (2) final. The performance of one's duties without any personal desire and as an offering to God is the principal part of preparatory devotion. The final phase of devotion is the passionate and undeviating love of God. In one who has attained this state, the mind naturally and effortlessly engages itself with the qualities and forms of the Divine. There is an uninterrupted recollection and absorption, which brings the knowledge of the spiritual nature of the Self and its relation with the Divine. Meditation is another essential means. Nimbārka proposes three kinds of meditation:

1. Meditation on *Brahman* as one's own Self, that is, as the inner controller of the sentient,
2. Meditation on *Brahman* as the inner controller of the non-sentient, and
3. Meditation on *Brahman* as different from the sentient and the non-sentient.

A devotee has to commit himself to do only what is liked by God. *Prapatti* has six factors:

(i) Goodwill towards all,

(ii) Absence of ill-will,

(iii) Faith in the protection of God,

(iv) Acceptance of God as Saviour,

(v) A feeling of helplessness, and

(vi) Self-surrender to God.

Thus, love of God means nothing less than love of mankind. Self-surrender to Him means ceaseless effort to follow the right path. He also considers self-surrender to the spiritual *guru* as a separate *sādhanā*. Here, the *guru* will lead the devotee to God and whatever is essential for liberation; it is done by the spiritual teacher for the good of the devotee.

DUALISM, DVAITA OF MADHVA

The great exponent of the Dvaita (Dualism) school of the Vedānta, Madhva, was a born devotee of the Supreme Being, Nārāyaṇa of the Vaiṣṇava-School of Hinduism.

His period is considered to be between CE 1238 and 1317. He lived a ripe old age of 79 years. He was the son of Madhyageha Bhaṭṭa, who was specialised in the learning of Itihāsas[56] and the Purāṇas. Being a Vaiṣṇava, Madhva's ancestors were devotees of Viṣṇu. As a child Madhvācārya was named Vāsudeva by his father, to indicate that he was born to give knowledge to the world and that he would be ever devoted to Lord Nārāyaṇa. One day, Madhva's father took the infant to the temple of Ananteśvara at Udupi (south India) and dedicated him to the Lord, to become a great devotee of Lord Nārāyaṇa. Vāsudeva was put under the care of a preceptor, observing the vow of celibacy as per the order of celibacy (*brahmacarya*). The boy mastered all learning perfectly in a very short time. He was also a master of sports. At the end of his student life, after obtaining benedictions from his Master, he left for his home. At the age of 16, Vāsudeva decided to enter the order of renunciation (*saṁnyāsa*), to teach all aspects of the wholehearted devotion to humanity. His preceptor, in this order of asceticism, was Acyuta Prekṣa, who adored Nārāyaṇa with devotion. Madhvācārya was given the name Pūrṇa Prajña in this order. He travelled to many

56. The two great epics: *Rāmāyaṇa* and *Mahābhārata*.

regions of India to fulfil his life's mission, preaching and working on philosophies and expounding it to groups of devotees. He authored a vast body of 37 works on the philosophy of realism and monotheistic theology, catering for devotion to Nārāyaṇa.

Madhva views that the spiritual fulfilment is ultimately to be obtained through devotion, which alone can attract to oneself the grace of God. Devotion, both as a discipline and as a fulfilment, is described therein as nine-fold:

1. Hearing about God's majesty,
2. Singing His praise collectively,
3. Silent remembrance,
4. Service of His aspect as society,
5. Worship of His holy images,
6. Salutation of His presence in all beings,
7. Cultivating the attitude of His servantship,
8. Entertaining intimacy with Him, and
9. Making a wholehearted and unreserved offering of oneself to God.

He defined devotion as the continuous flow of the heart that has been liquefied by the love towards God. This is preceded by a deep understanding of His Majesty, the omnipotence and omniscience of the one Independent Entity, on whom the whole universe depends. From Him the universe has its being, which is unshakeably rooted in the object of love and which cherishes Him as the most Supreme Value.

In the Dvaita doctrine, devotion is a means and an end in itself. Knowledge generates love and love strengthens knowledge. Knowledge and love form mutual constituents.

The practice of *nididhyāsana* can be done in three ways, according to the competence of the aspirant. The very ordinary person can meditate on Him externally in an image, the average aspirant as within himself and the best aspirants as everywhere. Liberation according to Madhva is an enjoyment of intense bliss, while retaining individuality.

Even the accomplishment of all religious duties cannot save a man from the hell, but devotion can save a man even if he commits the worst sin. Without devotion, even the best religious performances turn into sin, and with devotion even the worst sins do not affect a man. God is pleased only with devotion and nothing else, and He alone can give Liberation. According to Madhvācārya, in this modern age, devotion to God is the only way to peace, bliss and liberation.

ŚUDDHĀDVAITA, PURE NON-DUALISM OF VALLABHA

Vallabha,[57] the son of Lakṣmaṇa Bhaṭṭa, belonged to a family of learned devoted Vaiṣṇavas from a town Kakarvad, on the southern bank of the river Kṛṣṇa (south India). Lakṣmaṇa Bhaṭṭa, along with his family, migrated to Varanasi, a city noted for its holiness and its learned scholars. Vallabha, as he grew up, showed himself to be an extraordinary prodigy. He mastered the four Vedas, their auxiliaries, the six systems of philosophy and scriptural texts like the *Bhagavad-Gītā*, the *Śrīmad Bhāgavata* and the *Pañcarātra*[58] under the guidance of his *guru* Viṣṇu Citta. His father passed away when he was eleven years of age. From that time, though tender in age, he undertook a pilgrimage of the whole of India; which he travelled three times, taking a period of about 20 years. After living his life as a householder with his mother, wife and two children, he entered into the order of ascetics (*saṁnyāsa*) at the age of 53.

Vallabha's philosophy is known as Śuddhādvaita. The term *śuddhādvaita* means "Pure Non-Dualism". Its purity lies in the

57. His period is said to be 1479-1532.

58. Religious treatises dealing with the modes of worship of God and matters relating to temples.

fact that it does not accept the *māyā*-doctrine, the principle of illusion that necessarily has to be conceived as outside *Brahman*. *Brahman*, who is unalloyed Truth, cannot have a touch of illusion or falsity in Him. Vallabha accepts the scriptures as the sole authority in spiritual matters.

Vallabha defines devotion as an action of service (*bhaja sevayam*). Service (*sevā*) is a bodily affair. Service, in order to be complete, implies love, and without love, service would be troublesome. Also, for its contemplation love requires the practice of *sevā*, in its physical as well as in its mental aspects; and it brings devotion to maturity when it takes the form of intense attachment to God. It creates proportionate detachment from worldly objects and worldly relations.

The different stages of development of devotion are: inclination (*bhāva)*, attachment (*rāga*) and intense attachment (*anurāga*).

God is loved for His own sake, and the soul values itself solely as it exists in and for God. The climax is reached when the soul attains the stage of seeing God in everything. The devotee is in unison with the heart and spirit of God. He is a part of Divine life. The light and joy of God passes through him and upon things. At this stage, the soul is one with God, not in the sense of losing his individuality in *Brahman* as in Śaṅkara's school, but in the sense that the lover becomes absolutely united with the beloved without losing his individuality. It is absorption in God.

Vallabha in his *Bhakti Vardhinī*[59] says that the seed of devotion exists as *prema,* "affection" due to the grace of God and when it is firm, it increases by listening to devotional scriptures and chanting God's name. Even when engaged in one's duties, one should always fix one's mind on God, so that love for God grows and develops into everlasting attachment. The firm seed of

59. One of the works of Vallabhācārya.

devotion can never be destroyed. Devotion sometimes rises spontaneously, sometimes in association with other devotees and sometimes through following favourable practices. Obstacles to devotion can be removed by comprehending the false nature of the causes that give rise to them. It consists in the conviction that God gives everything, and everything is *Brahman*. He who tries to enjoy the blessed nature of God, easily removes the obstacles.

Vallabha says that the seed of the love of God exists in all. Only thing is that it is obstructed by various causes. When it manifests itself, one begins to love all beings in the world. When it grows in intensity, it becomes impossible for one to be attached to worldly things. When love of God grows to this high intensity, it cannot be destroyed.

Vallabha was also known as Śrī Kṛṣṇa Caitanya.

CAITANYA MAHĀPRABHU

Caitanya Mahāprabhu was a junior contemporary of Vallabha. He came from Navadvīpa.[60] His school was named Bengal School. The Bengal School of Vaiṣṇavism propounds the doctrine of *acintya-bhedābheda,* "Inconceivable Identity in difference". This School was inspired by Kṛṣṇa Caitanya. Vaiṣṇavism did exist in Bengal in a rudimentary form even before him. Compositions on Divine Love by devotee-singers like Caṇḍīdās, Vidyāpati and Jayadeva and famous musical compositions, dealing with the spiritual romance of the Rādhā-Kṛṣṇa mysticism, thrilled the devotees. Caitanya gave a boost to this group of devotees, though he did not directly take part in its philosophical activity. He was too full of God to undertake such a work. His time was spent in Divine ecstasies, in singing God's name and excellence and in conversing with devotees, who went to him for the attainment of spiritual insight, on the love of God. The object of his love

60. Near Kolkatta, north-east of India.

was Kṛṣṇa, who is the supreme Godhead. What he failed to pass on in writing, he made up for that by the impact his grand and ecstatic personality made on his talented disciples. The system of Śrī Caitanya is predominantly devotional.

Śrī Kṛṣṇa is the Supreme Self. He is the essence (*rasa*), which denotes that He is astonishingly enjoyable and at the same time the best enjoyer (*rasika*) too — the transcendental *rasika*. He is the embodiment of infinite varieties of *rasa*, which find their eternal expressions in His infinite manifestations. It is He, who appears as so many in His very same Self. Śrī Kṛṣṇa's *rasa* concept has two main aspects: relishable *rasa* (denoting "astonishingly enjoyable bliss") and relishing *rasa* or *rasika* (the one, who enjoys the bliss). The relishing *rasa* is Śrī Kṛṣṇa Himself, and so he is the Supreme *rasika*.

The Bengal School holds that the only effective means of Liberation and realisation of *Brahman*, as Śrī Kṛṣṇa, is devotion. Devotion at the level of practice is graced by inherent energy (*svarūpa śakti*) and is ultimately ripened into love (*prema*).

Devotion is virtuous independently of *jñāna* and Yoga. Unaided by devotion even *jñāna* and Yoga cannot produce their desired effect. It is only devotion that leads the *jīva* to *Brahman*; it is only devotion that shows *Brahman* to the *jīva*. In the practice of *jñāna*, associated with devotion, the inherent energy (*svarūpa śakti*) appears as knowledge of the Self (*ātma-vidyā*) and in the practice of pure devotion, it becomes a mystic experience.

Devotional practices include worship of God, chanting His names and attributes, singing songs about the sweetness and beauty of God, etc. This is known as *sādhanā bhakti*. It is called unalloyed devotion (*kevala* or *śuddha*), because it aims exclusively at the loving service of Śrī Kṛṣṇa as the dearest and nearest one, for His happiness only. The attainment of the dearest Ultimate Reality is known as *prapatti*.

Rādhā, Śrī Kṛṣṇa's consort, who is engaged in His eternal service and is His inherent energy; being His foremost servitor, she expands herself into thousands of *gopīs*, who form the highest expression of perfect self-effacement through their loving service of Kṛṣṇa. The *jīva*, who adores Kṛṣṇa through pure devotion, is graced by His *svarūpa śakti*.

A devotee of the Bengal School worships both: Śrī Kṛṣṇa and Śrī Caitanya. Service as a slave (*dāsya*), friendship (*sakhya*), tender love (*vātsalya*) and bridal feeling (*kānta bhāva*) are their modes of worship.

Progress of devotion is divided into seven stages:

1. Natural attachment and absorption in God without the need of any external stimuli,
2. The indissoluble attachment, binding the devotee to God by the sense of "my-ness",
3. The end-product of love, when the heart melts in love,
4. Sensitiveness due to excessive love,
5. Longing for the object of love, associated with the enjoyable pain,
6. The experience of unceasing novelty in the object of love, and
7. The most ecstatic expression of love, which is called divine madness (*divyonmāda*).

THE ĀḺVĀRS (SOUTH INDIAN VAIṢṆAVA SAINTS)

In the *Śrīmad Bhāgavata Purāṇa* (XI.5.38-40), it is said that the great devotees of Viṣṇu will appear in the south[61] on the banks of Tāmraparṇī, Kṛtamātā (Vaigai), Payasvinī (Palar), Kāverī and Mahānadī (Periar). Tradition holds this view to be right and some of the great devotees were considered as incarnations of God.

61. South India.

The *Śrīmad Bhāgavata Māhātmya* describes devotion as a distressed woman, who was born in the Draviḍian country (south of India); she had reached womanhood in Karnataka and Maharashtra (both in India) and had travelled in great misery through Gujarat and north India with her two sons Jñāna and Vairāgya (knowledge and renunciation) to Vrindavan (Mathura in north India). Owing to the hard conditions, through which she had to pass, her two sons had died.

The Āḷvārs are the most ancient Vaiṣṇava saints of south India. The traditional date ascribed to the earliest Āḷvār is 4203 BCE, the latest Āḷvār is dated 2706 BCE.[62] But modern researches bring down their dates to a period not earlier than the seventh or eighth century CE. The Āḷvārs were of all castes. There are about 10 important Āḷvārs.[63] Āṇḍāl is the only female devotee, who has obtained a status equal to an Āḷvār.

The word Āḷvār means "one" who has a deep intuitive knowledge of "God" and "one", who is immersed in the contemplation of "God". The works of Āḷvārs are full of intense and devoted love for Viṣṇu. This love is the foundation of the doctrine of *prapatti*.

The Āḷvārs were saints who devoted their entire life to the worship of Viṣṇu as the Supreme Deity. Blessed with spiritual insight and intense love for God, they sang the glory of Viṣṇu and spent their active life in the Divine service. They left to mankind a rich heritage of sublime, poetical compositions (hymns) known as *prabandha*. These hymns are not merely intended to promote devotion, but they also aim at spreading the knowledge of the Vedānta Philosophy in Tamil language among the common people. There are 24 *prabandhas* with a total

62. *History of Vaiṣṇavism in South India*, S.K. Aiyangar.

63. Pongai Āḷvār, Putathāḷvār, Peyāḷār, Tirumalisai Āḷvār, Nammāḷvār, Kulashekarāḷvār, Periyāḷvār, Tondardippodi Āḷvār, Pānāḷvār, Thirumangai Āḷvār. To these are added Āṇḍāl and Madhurakavi. Between CE 713 and 800.

of 4,000 hymns called *Nālāyira Divya Prabandham*, "Collection of 4,000 Divine Hymns". They are the laudatory Tamil songs composed in the glory of God in all His diverse aspects.

The Āḷvārs are said to be of divine origin. The hymns they composed reveal that Āḷvārs were all saints by birth, gifted with extraordinary spiritual insight into the glory of God.

Though many Āḷvār hymns describe the experiences of the emotion of Love for God, yet some passages in their works exhibit the nature of the soul. The soul is described as a pure subtle essence unassociated with the impurities of any kind and not cognisable in the same manner as all ordinary things. The Supreme Being abides in everything as invisible, in the same way as the soul abides in the body. The Supreme Being is all that exists in the Universe.[64]

The Āḷvārs very vividly manifest their mystic experience of God. Mysticism is the expression of an intense, loving devotion to God. It is the deep longing of the soul to see God directly in His full splendour.

The collection of 4,000 Divine Hymns covers mysticism of a unique type, providing a deep insight into the most important aspect of devotion, as a superbly loving relation between the human soul and God.

Their way of life involved the intense devotional love to God and strict observance of the prescribed religious disciplines, such as *dhyāna* and other methods of *upāsanā*, which presupposed the preliminary requisites, like the acquisition of *jñāna*, the development of the attitude of *vairāgya* and the cultivation of *dharma*.

The mysticism of Āḷvārs has been qualified as theistic and is distinguished from other types of mysticism, such as nature mysticism, spiritual mysticism, religious mysticism,

64. The very statement is also found in *Īśāvāsya Upaniṣad*, I.

transcendental mysticism, etc. Their theistic mysticism is connected closely with devotion. The love, generated in devotion, is of different types, assuming the form of unceasing meditation on God. The element of sincere devotion on the part of an individual is a major factor in promoting a close relationship between God and the longing soul. It is this type of devotion, which constitutes the seed of mysticism.

As Nammāḷvar, a born *yogī*, brings out, theistic mysticism comprises four phases:

1. *Bhakti,* loving devotion to God,
2. *Parā-bhakti,* perfected devotion, causing mental perception of God,
3. *Parā-jñāna,* occasional clear glimpses of God, followed by joy during communion with Him and anguish during separation from Him,
4. *Parama bhakti,* climax of devotion leading to the direct, comprehensive, everlasting communion with God.

The last three phases are, in an ascending order, the states of devotion. It is the *parā-bhakti* state that brings liberation from bondage.

The Āḷvārs revealed that the devotee conceives his soul as a spiritual essence, which has no independence by itself and is in every respect dependent on God. The devotee's mind is always exhilarated by the Divine presence of the Lord, who animates all his senses, his inclinations, emotions and experiences. The fullness of his realisation of God in all his own actions, thoughts and everything else in the universe, naturally transports him to the sphere of being, in which all mundane passions — antipathy, greed, jealousy, hatred — become impossible with the Divine presence of God. He becomes infused with the spirit of friendship and charity towards all beings on the earth. Then, he will always be ingrained with the consciousness that all his actions are under the complete sway of the Lord. The service of the servant is for God alone; it is of no personal interest for the devotee.

The two important states of devotion are: (1) union with God (*saṁśleṣa*) and (2) separation from Him (*viśleṣa*).

The Āḻvārs conceive the soul as intimately related to God; it (the soul) has the intrinsic capacity to be reunited with God, after overcoming the obstacles in the form of bondage; but it has to make every endeavour to attain it, by following spiritual disciplines laid down by the sacred texts for this purpose.

The Āḻvārs sang their songs in an inspired manner and often believed that they themselves had no hand in their compositions, but that it was God, who spoke through them. The devotional songs of the Āḻvārs show an intense familiarity with the various parts of the legendary life of God in His different incarnations. The emotions that stirred them were primarily similar to parental affection, affection for friends and companions, affection of servants towards their masters, sons towards their fathers, or a female lover towards her beloved.

ĀṆḌĀL'S CONCEPT OF DEVOTION

The impurities, which are accumulated within the mind of a person, are chiefly responsible for preventing him from easily approaching God. Instead of devoting his attention to being released from the worldly bondage, he allows himself to be immersed in affection, attachment and similar factors.

The dross and grime of the mind cannot be removed so easily, but Hindu scriptures have depicted the brush with which they can be cleaned; and that is broadly called devotion, which has many facets like service to God by worship, by chanting His names, through meditation and so forth.

The methods of seeking Divine grace through the observance of rituals and taking a firm vow to do certain acts, which are considered as pleasing to God, have been mentioned in the traditional scriptures.

These steps generate Divine love; God cannot resist the lure of the devotee's love, He is sure to fall into this net. The *Tiruppāvai*, a devotional composition of Āṇḍāl establishes the relation between the God and His devotee.

Āṇḍāl, also known as Godhā, is the only female Vaiṣṇava mystic among Āḷvārs; she imagines herself as a milkmaid in love with Lord Kṛṣṇa of Vrindavan[65] and expresses her love and devotion to God. Placing herself in the position of a bride, she craves for a spiritual marriage with the Lord. This is generally described as bridal mysticism. But the word bridal is not the appropriate epithet, because she was not aspiring for material union with God, like in the ordinary sense of marriage. According to tradition, she was an incarnation of one of the consorts of Viṣṇu. Āṇḍāl manifested herself as an infant in the flower garden of Periyāḷvār.[66] She was God-intoxicated right from her infancy. She, as an incarnation of *bhūdevī*,[67] represents the individual soul (*jīvātmā*) which is inseparably related to God (*paramātmā*). It is apparently separated from God, and therefore, longs for reunion with Him. She yearned for the reunion or the spiritual marriage with her beloved Lord. She directed all her deeds and words towards God. Further, as her biography shows, she developed a craving to marry only Lord Raṅganātha, the *arca* (iconic form) Deity at Srirangam (a pilgrimage centre in south India).

She poured out her intense love to Lord Kṛṣṇa of Vrindavan (Mathura, north India) in her twin-poetical compositions: *Tiruppāvai* and *Nacchiyār Thirumoḷi*. *Tiruppāvai* is considered as the quintessence of the Upaniṣads. *Nacchiyār Thirumoḷi* exhibits the predominant mysticism of Āṇḍāl, adding philosophical and theological ideas. In *Tiruppāvai*, Āṇḍāl as a milkmaid, in love with Lord of Vrindavan (Kṛṣṇa), implores the grace of God to fulfil

65. Mathura — north India.

66. One of the Āḷvārs.

67. Goddess of Earth. With Śrī Devī, the Goddess of Auspiciousness and Prosperity, she is revered as one of the two feminine forces of Lord Viṣṇu. They are also His consorts.

her cherished desire. In *Nacchiyār Thirumoḷi*, she manifests her craving for a spiritual union with God and passes through various mental states of a mystic. Referring to the ritualistic ceremony undertaken by her in order to achieve her goal of spiritual union with God, she appeals to the God of Love, named Kāma Deva (Kṛṣṇa is also named as Kāma Deva), to make use of her soul as an arrow, write her name on it and then shoot it with his bow towards God as the final target. She says that she has been only thinking of Kṛṣṇa right from the childhood and that all her possessions have already been surrendered to Him.

She thus sings,

> Lo Govinda ! This day not the drum alone is gotten!
> For seven and seven more births
> Related to Thy bond will be near
> Only unto thee, we serve sincere
> Converse our passions to vanish,
> Listen and consider, our damsel.[68]

The relation between the Supreme and the individual is permanent and everlasting. It can never be put to an end. Āṇḍāl brings out this point in:

> Among tribe pastoral, sans any intellect, Thou art born,
> This the only virtue we own, our acquaintance is a bond
> The intimacy hither, could never be torn.[69]

She considers non-violence, control of senses, compassion towards all beings, forgiveness, peace, penance, meditation and truth as the fundamental means to devotion.

Āṇḍāl represents the ultimate in devotion; it is Supreme devotion to the Lord without any trace of self-consciousness. Devotion is the churning rod through which the butter of Divinity is realised from the universe of our daily lives.

---

68. *Tiruppāvai*, 29.
69. *Tiruppāvai*, 28.

4

Bhakti in Śaivism

fig. 2: Lord Śiva and Pārvatī
(Courtesy: Claire Sribhashyam, France)

There is nothing greater than meditation (*dhyāna*).
Those who perform *dhyāna* are dear to Śiva, not those who only perform rituals. — *Śiva Mahāpurāṇa*, VII.2.39.28

The Śiva in grace exceeding made me His;
The balm for all my pain, the deathless Bliss.
— *Tiruvācakam* of Mānikka Vācakar

Introduction

THE origin of Śaivism is lost in obscurity, more so because it seems to have had its origin in the pre-Āryan periods. Śaivism has shown a close alliance with Yoga. Śaivism is a blend of allied beliefs and customs. Its hold extends throughout India and wherever Indian population migrated from time to time.[1]

1. The worship of Śiva seems to date back to second century BCE. In the early Christian era, there were already coins with the emblems of Śiva.

The characteristics of Śaivism are the exaltation of Śiva above all other gods, the highly concrete conception of the deity, and the intensely personal nature of the relation between God (Śiva) and His devotees. Just as the *Bhagavad-Gītā* upholds the theism of Vaiṣṇavism, the *Śvetāśvatara Upaniṣad* seems to expound the supremacy of Śiva. "There is no form for Him whose name is supreme celebrity."[2] He is God of all gods, potent for good and evil. He is Gīrīśa. He is the Master (Īśāṇa), the giver of boon, He is Rudra. He is the supreme Lord.[3]

The Purāṇas like *Vāyu Purāṇa, Liṅga Purāṇa, Skanda Purāṇa* and *Śiva Purāṇa* deal exhaustively with Śaivism. Śaivism upsurged in South India mainly with the devotional poems of Nāyanmār (Śaiva saints), written in Tamil. These are divided into eleven collections, which, together with the Tamil Purāṇa called *Peria Purāṇa* constitute the sacred literature of Śaivism. *Devāram* of Sambandar, Appar and Sundarar;[4] *Tiruvācakam* of Mānikka Vācakar; and *Tirumandiram* of Tirumular are some of the works that form part of the Tamil Veda. Their works, in a way, correspond to the *Nālāyira Divya Prabandham* of the Śrī Vaiṣṇavas. An influential Śaiva movement, known as Liṅgāyata or Vīraśaiva, rose in Karnataka and Maharashtra regions of south-west of India. Vīraśaivism was attributed to Basava[5] who is considered as the incarnation of Nandī, the vehicle of Śiva.

Devotion in Śaivism

Both, Vaiṣṇavism and Śaivism, would regard devotion to God as the criterion of the faith.

The Śaivism of south India flourished more or less at the same time as the Āḷvārs. The hymns of saints are full of deep and noble sentiments of devotion which can hardly be excelled

2. *Śvetāśvatara Upaniṣad*, IV.
3. *Śvetāśvatara Upaniṣad*, II.
4. All the three lived around seventh century.
5. Around 1157-67.

by any literature; but their main emphasis is on the majesty and the greatness of God and the feeling of submission, self-surrender to God. The spirit of self-surrender and a feeling of clinging to God as one's all is equally dominant among the Āḷvārs, but among them it melts into the sweetness of passive love. The Śaiva hymns are indeed pregnant with the Divine fire of devotion, but more in the spirit of submissive service.

In one of the 96 *prabhandhas* of Śaivism, a saint enumerates the different sources of pearls in a prayer to Lord Muruga[6] as:

> The pearls born out of the conches, whose spirals turn to the right at the coast, have a price, the pearls evolved from the crescent-shaped tusks of musty elephants have a price; the pearls, emanated from the cluster of ripened paddy and those showered by the clouds have a price. Nevertheless, O Muruga! The pearl of your Kovai-fruit like mouth is priceless. O Lord, girt by the pearl-scattering sea, pray, give me your pearl (of kiss).

Experiences of God of Śaiva devotees melt the hearts of all, who go through them, and make the readers surrender to God, unconditionally.

The Śaiva tradition has also been blessed with a galaxy of saints. They left a rich legacy in the form of their works and hymns. The philosophy of Śaiva Siddhānta was systematised in the thirteenth century CE by Meykanda Devar. The composition, called *Thirumurai*, contains nearly 20,000 verses in 12 sections from 26 mystic saints and the 63 Nayannars.[7]

The 11th *Thirumurai* is a collection of hymns of a motley group of saints; among them, Pattinathor stands out, as his songs have become popular, because of their literary merit and simplicity which appeal everyone; and above all, they are from a God-intoxicated mystic.

6. Tamil name for Kārttikeya, son of Lord Śiva and leader of the celestial army.
7. Śaiva devotional saints.

Thirumurai stresses the unity of the diverse forms of the Supreme Being through the analogy of gold, taking on different shapes when made into ornaments. It also teaches to remain detached in life, without becoming dejected, when beset with problems, and elated when blessed with worldly attainments. All mundane relationships are temporary, only the Lord remains one's permanent friend.

Śaiva Āgama

The Śaiva Āgama discusses the concept of creation, maintenance, destruction, veiling up of the truth and liberation. Lord Śiva is the instrumental cause of these activities. Even if the creation of the world, its maintenance and destruction are designed by the Supreme Lord, yet the things unfold in the natural course, not entirely dependent on human actions. Yet, the attainment of liberation cannot take place without individual effort.

Consciousness is of the nature of intuitive knowledge and spontaneous action. The consciousness abides in the soul.

According to Śaiva Āgama, Śiva is bodiless. But one can conceive the body of Śiva as being constituted of certain *mantra*. When anyone is to be liberated, the quality of *tamas,* as veiling the consciousness of the individual, is removed by God.

The source of all bondage is Māheśvarī Śakti which helps all people to develop and grow in their own pattern. Lord Śiva directs the *śakti* for people's good — to make them wise and get them purged of their impurities (*mala*).

The individual souls are all-pervasive and they possess eternal power by the Power of God. The souls are not conscious of their own nature owing to the veiling of the impurities (*mala*). It is through the action of Śiva that these veils are removed.

Śiva, the Supreme

Just as Śaṅkara, Rāmānuja and Madhva commented upon the

Vedānta-Sūtra to bring forward their own concept of the Vedānta,[8] Śrīkānta[9] expounded the philosophy of Śaivism in his commentary on *Brahma-Sūtra*. In his interpretation, Śiva is regarded as the highest Deity, equated with *Brahman*. According to Appaya Dīkṣita (CE 1550), who commented on Śrīkānta's commentary, Śiva, the Lord, is of the nature of pure ego and that His will is always directed towards good and happiness of all beings. This ego is *sat* (pure being), *cit* (pure consciousness) *ānanda* (pure bliss).

Lord Śiva is the supreme and transcendent Deity and the material cause of the universe just as milk is the material cause of curd. God Himself is not transformed into the form of the material universe, but the energy of God which manifests itself as the material universe is a part and parcel of the entire personality of God. Just as a tree has leaves and flowers, but still in spite of the variety is regarded as one tree, so too God is One, though He has diversified energies as his qualities. The word *Brahman* means not only unlimitedness, it also means that He serves all possible purposes. He creates the world at the time of creation and leading the souls through many kinds of enjoyment and sorrow, ultimately expands them into His own nature at liberation.

Śrīkānta considers *Brahman* as being endowed with omniscience, eternally self-satisfied, independent, and possesses omnipotence. He is externally self-efficient and never depends on any external thing for the execution of his power. Lord Śiva, thus being omniscient, knows the deeds of all living beings and the fruits of those deeds to which they are entitled. He also knows the forms of bodies that these souls should have in accordance with their past deeds. He has the direct knowledge of the collocation of the materials with which these bodies are to be built up.[10]

---

8. Advaita, Viśiṣṭādvaita and Dvaita.

9. Eleventh century.

10. Śrīkānta's commentary on *Brahma-Sūtra* I.1.2.

The Supreme Lord is called by different names: *sarva* because all things are finally absorbed in Him, Īśāṇa, because He lords over all. For the same reason, He is also called Paśupati.[11]

God is called the Lord, *pati*, because He is always associated with the highest powers. These powers abide in Him permanently. For this reason, He can, by His will, produce any action which stands before us as creation and it is for this reason that the creation of the world is considered as a sort of play by Him. This is what distinguishes Him from all other animate beings. This is His greatness.

Umāpati[12] while interpreting *Tiruvācakam* of Mānikka Vācakar says that Śiva is the Supreme Being, neither permanently manifesed nor unmanifested. He is without qualities, free from all impurities, absolute and eternal, the source of wisdom to all souls. He is of the nature of Pure Bliss. He is the final goal of those that truly worship Him. He creates, preserves and consigns all to the power of *māyā*, but He is the ultimate refuge who never leaves us. He dwells everywhere and pervades all things as fire pervades all wood. He offers His boon only to those who approach Him for it.

The Concept of Śakti in Kāśmīr Śaivism

Reality is indefinable and beyond any description. It is conceived both as transcendent and immanent. As transcendent, it is described as Śiva, as immanent as Śakti. Śiva and Śakti are not two separate realities, but two phases of the same Reality. Like fire and its burning power, Śakti is always in perfect identity with Śiva. The Lord and His lordliness, the *Īśvara* and the Aiśvarya (which is another name of Śakti) are one and the same. Śakti is the heart (*hṛdaya*) and essence (*sāra*) of Śiva.

Pure consciousness (*cit*) cannot be without self-illumination

11. *Paśupati* = Lord of all souls.

12. Considered as a successor of Meyakandadeva, lived around CE 1300.

(*caitanya*). The self-illumination of pure consciousness is Śakti. Śakti is possessed of fivefold modes:

1. The power of self-awareness, *cit,*
2. The power of absolute bliss, *ānanda,*
3. The power of absolute will to manifest the universe out of Himself, *icchā,*
4. The power of knowledge of creation, *jñāna,* and
5. The power to assume any form, *kriyā.*

Śakti's fivefold modes come into play at the time of creation of the universe.

The Concept of Śakti in Śiva Mahāpurāṇa

According to great masters of Śaivism, the *Śiva Mahāpurāṇa* is a massive work of 100,000 verses written by Śiva himself. It was condensed by Sage Vyāsa, who is the author of many Purāṇas.

In the section named *Rudra Saṁhitā,* it is said that at the time of the great dissolution, when all things were destroyed, there was only darkness, no sun, no planets, no stars, no moon, and no day and night. It was a state when there was neither being nor non-being; it was beyond all mind and speech, beyond all name and form. Yet, in this state existed only the pure being, the pure consciousness, infinite and pure bliss. It had no form and was devoid of all qualities.[13] Gradually, there arose a desire or will by which the formless was changed into some form. This is the all-creating pure energy. The form created by this energy is called Sadāśiva. He is also called *Īśvara,* or God. This energy created the universe from its own eternal body.

While the state of neither being nor non-being is neuter in gender, its illuminating nature being *sat-cit-ānanda* (pure being, the pure consciousness, infinite and pure bliss) is its female

13. *Śiva Mahāpurāṇa,* II.1.6.

counter-part.[14] This illumination is sometimes impeded, as the flame of a wick is impeded by the smoke and other impurities. These impurities do not belong to Śiva, but are seen in the illumination of pure consciousness. It is for this reason that the energy of pure consciousness is seen in an impure state in human souls. It is to remove all the impurities (*mala*) that the all-encompassing energy, *śakti* exists in creation. Śakti is the symbol of strength (*bala*). In the Supreme Soul there is both Śiva aspect and the Śakti aspect. It is the union of Śiva and Śakti that provides bliss (*ānanda*).

The Śakti is also called *spanda* (vibration). Knowledge, movement and will are like the three sides of Śiva. Human beings get their inspiration from between these three. The first category of vibration is called Śiva *tattva*. Śiva and Śakti combined gives the supreme *śakti* called *parā-śakti*. From *parā-śakti* evolves the power of consciousness. From this comes the bliss, *ānanda-śakti* from which is born the will-power, *icchā-śakti*. From the will-power comes power of knowledge, *jñāna-śakti*, from which comes the power of motivation, *kriyā-śakti*.

Moral Responsibilities

According to Śaivism, God intervenes in the creation and destruction of the world in accordance with the diversity of human deeds and their results. Since God in His omniscience knows the various kinds of deeds that the individual would perform, He arranges suitable bodies and circumstances for the enjoyment or suffering of such deeds already anticipated by Him. The time of destruction comes when the souls become tired by the process of births and deaths, and require some rest in dreamless sleep.

---

14. Since all living beings are constituted of a male and a female part, the original cause must also be represented by a male and a female principle united.

The law of *karma* depends upon the will of God and it does not operate in an autonomous manner, nor does it curb the independence of God. Yet, God extends His grace to all who exhaust their enjoyment or suffering and whose mind is purified and who are woken up by self-knowledge. God's grace is an extension of justice in accordance with the deeds of persons. God does not on His own will make one do bad or good deeds, but the persons themselves perform good or bad actions according to their inclinations.[15]

Man is born with impurities (*mala*). His bondage lies in the veil that covers his wisdom and action, and God, who possesses infinite and manifold powers, is always trying to make man act in such a manner that he may ultimately purify himself and reach Him. According to Śrīkānta, the individual soul is the cause of man's action, either to act or to desist from acting, corresponding to the fruits of his past deeds. Man is ultimately responsible for his own volition. Man performs his actions in accordance with the way in which he can best satisfy his interests. He is therefore, responsible for his action, though in the actual carrying out of the will, he depends on God.[16]

Śrīkānta holds that the individual souls have not emanated from God, but they are coexistent with Him. The souls are the conscious knowers, both by way of senses and by the mind (*manas*). He explains this *manas* as a special quality of knowledge which the soul possesses and by virtue of which it is a knower. This *manas* is differentiated from that which is a product of *prakṛti* associating with the soul in the process of births and deaths. This association gives the *manas* a special character as a knower, by which it can enjoy or suffer pleasure and pain and which is limited to the body and the egoism. This soul is called *jīva*. The difference between the individual soul and God is that the latter

15. *Śivārkamani Dīpikā*, Appaya Dīkṣita's commentary on Śrīkānta's commentary on *Brahma-Sūtra*, vol II.

16. Śrīkānta on *Brahma-Sūtra*, II.3.41.

is omniscient and the former knows things only particularly during the process of birth and death. In the actual state of liberation, the soul becomes omniscient.[17]

In the state of liberation the liberated soul does not become one with *Brahman*, yet shares with God all His excellent qualities but it never becomes divested of all qualities. A lotus flower can be white, big and fragrant, but it cannot be both white and blue at the same time.[18]

Śrīkānta holds that only that *karma* which is ripe for producing fruits will continue to give fruits and will do so until the present body falls. No amount of knowledge can save man from enjoying or suffering the fruits of *karma* that he has earned. If man attains true knowledge by continuing his meditation on the nature of Śiva, he shall not have to suffer birth and rebirth of the accumulated *karma*s which are not yet ripened.[19]

When all impurities are removed and a person is liberated, he can then enjoy all blissful experiences, except the power of creating the universe. He remains free within himself in tune with Lord Śiva. His experiences would no longer be of the type of the experiences of normal persons. His experience of the world would be a vision of it as being of the nature of *Brahman*.[20]

Concept of Bhakti

According to Śaivism, pure knowledge is devotion. At the same time, there can be no knowledge without devotion. Where there is devotion, there is no distinction in the way of attaining the grace of God.

---

17. Śrīkānta on *Brahma-Sūtra*, II.3.19.
18. Śrīkānta on *Brahma-Sūtra*, III.3.40.
19. Śrīkānta on *Brahma-Sūtra*, IV.1.19.
20. Śrīkānta on *Brahma-Sūtra*, IV.3.14-22.

In Śaivism, devotion is listening to the name of Śiva, considering oneself as servant of Śiva, developing the spirit of friendship through which one can surrender oneself to Lord Śiva, chanting the name of Śiva and listening to the legends on Śiva as described in the Purāṇa.

The meditation on Śiva develops the idea that Śiva is all-pervasive and is omnipresent. This makes the devotee fearless. It is through devotion that true knowledge and disinclination to worldly things can occur.

The *Śiva Mahāpurāṇa* describes four types of liberation: *sārūpya*, *sālokya*, *sānnidhya* and *sāyujya*. These four types of liberation are almost identical to the Rāmānuja's point of view.[21] As fire, which exists in the wood, can be kindled by the constant rubbing of the wood, so by the various processes of devotion one can attain Śiva. Just as the ocean, or a piece of gold may appear in various shapes, though actually they remain the same, so it is only by various conditions through which one looks at things that they appear so different, though they are actually nothing but Śiva. From the seed comes the shoot, appearing as different from the seed, but ultimately, the shoot grows into a tree and fructifies and thereby reduces itself into fruit and seed. The true seer is like the seed from which there are many transformations, and when these have ceased, the true seer is perceived again. With the removal of ignorance (*avidyā*), a person is disassociated from egoism and becomes pure and then through the grace of Lord Śiva he becomes what he really is, that is Śiva.

Śaiva Philosophy in Vāyavīya Saṁhitā

Vāyavīya Saṁhitā is the seventh Saṁhitā of the *Śiva Mahāpurāṇa*. According to this Purāṇa, the ultimate God is regarded as being the original cause, the cause of maintenance and also as the

21. According to Rāmānuja, the four stages of *bhakti* are: *sālokya*, entering the abode of God, *sāmīpya*, remaining near God, *sārūpya*, attaining likeness of God, and *sāyujya*, total merger with God.

cause of destruction. The ultimate God is called Puruṣa, the *Brahman*, or the *Paramātman*. *Prakṛti* or *pradhāna* is considered His body. Though the world has been created and maintained by the Supreme Lord, yet people do not know him as they are under the delusion of *māyā*, illusion or ignorance.

The Supreme Lord stands silent and rooted in one place and yet He pervades the whole universe. Everything else in the universe is moving excepting the final cause, the *Brahman*. He alone is the inner controller of all beings, but yet He Himself cannot be recognised as such. All that is destructible (*kṣara*) and indestructible (*akṣara*) have sprung from the Supreme Lord. In the end of the *māyā*, the universe will vanish with the disappearance of the individual souls.[22] Every being is under His control and He can be realised only through devotion (*bhakti*). Devotion to God is due to the extension of grace of God and the grace is produced out of devotion.

When the devotee invokes the nature of the Supreme Lord, then he receives God's grace which increases his merit attenuating his sins. When sins decrease, devotion to God increases opening the door for His grace. With His grace, the devotee gets rid of all desires for the fruits of his actions, although he may live in this world of actions.

The two main steps to achieve liberation according to *Vāyavīya Saṁhitā* are:

1. By the renunciation of the fruits of *karma*, one becomes associated with the faith in Śiva,
2. Through the knowledge of Śiva one begins to discover the sorrows of the cycles of birth and death,

According to this Saṁhitā, the real knowledge of the individual soul (*paśu*), the bondage (*pāśa*), and the Supreme Lord (*pati*) is the ultimate aim of knowledge which leads to happiness.

---

22. *Vāyavīya Saṁhitā*, VII.1.3.13.

All sorrows are born of ignorance and they are removed only through knowledge. The individual souls *paśu* are indestructible (called *akṣara*); the *pāśa* is destructible (called *kṣara*). That which is beyond these two is the Supreme Lord.

The Supreme Soul

The Supreme Soul pervades all things, yet it manifests itself under certain circumstances and is itself unperceivable. It cannot be seen by the eye or by any of the senses. It is only by the right wisdom of the mind that this Great Soul can be realised. It is different from the body and the senses. It is by being associated with the body that it undergoes all impurities and sufferings and is drawn to the cycle of births. As a field that is flooded with water soon generates new shoots, so in the field of ignorance the *karma* begins to shoot up and produce bodies. All beings from the plants to Brahmā are the *paśu*, manifestations of this Supreme Soul (*puruṣa*).

The *pāśa* is the energy, Śakti of Śiva manifesting itself as *prakṛti*. It evolves the material world, the subjective world as well as pleasure and pain. All these fetter the universal soul, the *paśu*, appearing as many under different conditions.

The Supreme Lord is the creator of both the *paśu* and the *pāśa*. Without Him, there would not be any creation of the universe.

Though the soul is the same, yet some of the souls are in bondage while others are in a state of liberation. The impurities associated with the bound souls can be either unripe or ripe and in these two forms, they are responsible for the commission of all actions leading to birth and rebirth. Though all souls are associated with the impurities (*mala*), they are pervaded in and through by Śiva. As the impurities are purged, the nearness of Śiva becomes manifest, the devotee becomes more and more pure, until he becomes like Śiva.

Bondage and Liberation

Śiva as Śakti manifests Himself as a correlated order of knowers, knowables and means of knowledge. The self-limited Śiva is designated as *paśu, jīva,* etc. The signs of *paśu* are false identification of the self with the non-self, ascribing the non-self to the self, having limited authorship, knowledge, interest, pervasion and duration and being subject to causality. The goal of the *jīva* is to realise the unfettered condition, to recognise oneself as equal to everything or everything as equal to oneself, to be free from and independent of causality or destiny and to be oneself as Śiva.

The Four Means to Attain the Supreme

There are four means of attaining the Supreme: *anupāya* or *ānandopāya, śāmbhava, śākta,* and *āṇava upāya.*

1. *Anupāya* (no-means) or *ānandopāya* (blissful means) does not really involve any process, since by the grace of Lord Śiva everything needed for the realisation may be achieved by the devotee.
2. *Śāmbhava upāya* is the means which awakens the limitless knowledge of the soul. It is obtained through initiation. Initiation is given by a realised soul. Initiation destroys all the limitations that surround the soul.
3. *Śākta upāya* is the means by which the limitations are purified through the study of Āgama and other sacred scriptures under a teacher. This presupposes mental and physical discipline. This means includes the practice of rituals, sacrifices, solemn vows, repetition of *mantra* (*japa*) and similar spiritual disciplines as directed by the teacher.
4. *Āṇava upāya* is the personal effort including *dhyāna, ucchāra, varṇa* and observances of external injunctions.

Dhyāna means meditation in the heart (*hṛdayākāśa*) on the Supreme Reality inherent in all the elemental principles (*mahā-*

bhūta and *tanmātra*) and also on the unification, in the Supreme Consciousness of the knower, the means of knowledge, and the knowables.[23] *Uccāra* is directing the *prāṇa* upwards. This is obtained through the practice of *prāṇāyāma*.[24] During this practice, the devotee hears an undifferentiated sound, *dhvani* which emerges spontaneously which is called *varṇa*. Meditating on this spontaneous sound is also *varṇa*. It also includes the repetition and listening to *bīja mantra*.[25] Constant repetition of *bīja mantra* results in the attainment of the Supreme.

Through these means, the limited soul attains the rich treasure of his true Self.

Specificity in the Vīraśaiva Practice of Devotion

By the middle of the twelfth century, there appeared in Karnataka (south-west India) a great revolutionary in Śaivism by the name Basava. His revolutionary Śaivism is called Vīraśaivism or Liṅgāyata. Among the great personalities of this movement are about 60 women of whom Akkā Mahādevī is the most prominent.

All their teachings named *vacana*, are in Kannada literature, which is the spoken language of Karnataka. Later, Vīraśaivism extended to the neighbouring northern state of Maharashtra.

The devotional practices of a Vīraśaiva devotee comprise five codes of conduct (*pañca ācāra*) and eight protective armours (*aṣṭa āvaraṇa*).

The five codes of conduct are:

1. Daily worship of *liṅga*, the representation of the Divine,

---

23. Technically called *vahni*, *arka* and *soma*.
24. For technique of *prāṇāyāma*, see Chapter on "Practical Approach to Devotion".
25. *Bīja mantra* is a one lettered *mantra*. *Bīja* means seed. *Bīja mantras* are the seeds to the manifested sounds and matter.

2. Assuming a professional responsibility and strictly leading a moral and virtuous life. To earn money by honest work and utilise the savings for the needy,
3. Equality of view non-differentiation between one devotee and another,
4. Practice of complete humility towards Śiva and His devotees, and
5. Intolerance (without being violent) to any adverse remarks against the God, as also ill-treatment of men and animals by others. A devotee should care for the betterment of the community.

The eight protective armours that safeguard the devotee from the onslaught of ignorance, and guide him safely to the final beatitude, are:

1. Spiritual and religious guide who initiates one into Vīraśaivism. It is he who gives the devotee real insight into the principles of Vīraśaivism, explains the inner meaning of the practices and guides him on the path of righteousness.
2. Wearing of *liṅga* from the time of birth until one's death. A *liṅga* is a divine representation. It is given by the *guru* at the very birth. Wearing of the *liṅga* entails the devotee to worship *liṅga* everyday.
3. Respect the itinerant liberated soul. An itinerant liberated soul is one who has the knowledge of God. He is equal to the spiritual teacher and the *liṅga* itself. *Liṅga* is a great mass of light and fire which, when it is worn on the body, burns all the impurities of a devotee.
4. Receive with respect the holy water from the feet of the *guru* or an itinerant liberated soul.
5. Share the consecrated food, that is the food or fruits

offered to Śiva during a prayer, with all. Both the holy water and the consecrated food create divine essence in the devotees.

6. Coating the body with the holy ashes. The holy ashes[26] (*bhasma*) symbolise the burning into ashes of the world of illusion and the revelation of the pure soul.

7. Wearing of *rudrākṣa*.[27] *Rudrākṣa* means "eye of Rudra, or Śiva". The devotee should try to perceive the Divine in all events and movements of his life. This is called internal *rudrākṣa*. As an outward symbol of this, the devotee should wear a rosary of *rudrākṣa* beads.

8. Repetition of the *pañcākṣara mantra*[28] and meditation on the sound of *mantra*.

These eight protective armours keep a Vīraśaiva devotee pure in body and mind.

RIGHTEOUSNESS IN ŚAIVISM, ŚAIVA DHARMA

The Śaiva Dharma consists of knowledge, action, right conduct, and *yoga*. The knowledge is the knowledge of the nature of souls, the objects and the Supreme Lord. Action is the purification in accordance with the instruction of the teacher. Right conduct is the proper worshipping of Śiva. Yoga means the arresting of all mental states, excluding the constant thinking of God. Universal charity, non-injury, truthfulness, abstention from

---

26. The Holy Ash is very closely associated with Lord Śiva. As the God appeared as the column of fire, It was adorned by the Ash from that fire.

27. *Rudrākṣa* is a large evergreen broad-leaved tree which grows in the area from the Gangetic Plain to the foothills of great Himalaya and middle area of Nepal. The *rudrākṣa* stands for the eyes of Lord Śiva or Rudra implying thereby that it was pleasant to the eyes of Lord Śiva, and hence so named in His honour.

28. The *Śiva Mantra* is *oṁ namaḥ śivāya*. It is also called *pañcākṣara*, because it contains five Sanskrit letters.

stealing, absolute faith, performing sacrifices, meditation on Śiva are accessories to right conduct.

Purity of mind is more important than purity of body, because without the purity of mind nobody can be pure. God accepts only the internal states of man, the one who is sincere in his devotion. Devotion to God must be spontaneous, without expecting any material advantage.

MORAL VIRTUES OF A DEVOTEE

The *Pāśupata-Sūtra*, one of the most important texts of Śaivism, lays great stress on moral virtues. They are called *yama* and *niyama*. The *yama*s are non-injury, sense-control, truthfulness, and non-stealing. The *niyama*s are non-anger, service to teachers, purity, lightness of diet, and carefulness. Of these, non-injury (*ahiṁsā*) is considered the most important. Non-anger includes absence of jealousy, enmity, vanity and absence of desire for the evil of others. When a devotee is firm in *yama* and *niyama* practices and meekly suffers the indignities and abuses showered on him by other people, he is considered well established in devotional path.

DHYĀNA

When the mind is steadily attached to some object, it is *dhāraṇā*. This object should be Śiva. In this state, the mind should not be disassociated from its object. By constant and continuous practice of *dhāraṇā*, the object of one's meditation is constantly repeated in the same form without the association of any other idea. This is *dhyāna* (meditation). *Japa* (repetition of *mantra*) is a prerequisite to *dhyāna*. When *dhyāna* is practised uninterruptedly for a long time, then the devotee's mind would be illuminated with intuitive wisdom. This is *samādhi*. It is a mental state in which the object alone shines like a limitless, waveless ocean.[29]

29. *Śiva Mahāpurāṇa*, VII.2.37.53.

The devotee should be vigilant to avoid obstacles coming in the way of his practice. Some of them are indolence (bodily and mental laziness), troublesome diseases, carelessness and doubt as to the object of meditation, inconsistency of mind, absence of faith, illusory notions, pain, melancholia, and attachment to wordly objects. When these obstacles are overcome then other obstacles come in the way of appearance of miraculous powers which should also be carefully avoided.

Meditation (*dhyāna*) should first begin with an object, and later it can become objectless. Meditation on a form of Śiva is highly recommended, even if meditation on a formless Śiva is not excluded. Śaivism gives importance to practice of *prāṇāyāma* in the practice of meditation. The practice of *prāṇāyāma* and meditation provides a transparent mind and this allows the thoughts of Śiva to occur continuously. This continuous thought of Śiva is considered the object of *dhyāna*. Both happiness and liberation come from *dhyāna*. That is why one should always try to practise *dhyāna*.

The union of the soul with Śiva must be so intimate that no physical or sensory disturbances should lead the devotee away from the Divine. In the preliminary stages of *dhyāna*, the attachment with Śiva takes place by the withdrawal of the mind from all other objects, making the mind settle on the Lord. Subsequently, the association with Śiva becomes continuous.

To the extent possible, God should be meditated upon in His aspect as formless, because God is unassociated with anything else that can be expressed by speech.[30] To arrive at this, the devotee should disassociate himself from the impurities. The impurities are caused by the various sensations of sound, touch, taste, etc., which feed the devotee's mind with desire, anger, greed, fear, sleep, attachment, antipathy and delusion. These causes are like the fruits of a poisoned tree which taste sweet,

30. *Pāśupata-Sūtra*, V.27.

but in the end will produce much suffering. So one should refrain from enjoyment of all sense objects and be satisfied with whatever one gets.

The Doctrine of Ṣaṭ-sthala

The concept of *sthala* is a particularity of Śaivism, especially in Vīraśaivism. Very often, the Reality is called *sthala*. While the letter *stha* denotes the source from which the phenomenal world emerges and draws its sustenance; the letter *la* denotes the goal to which it tends and in which it ultimately loses itself. Hence, *sthala* represents the Divine (called *Parāśiva*). *Sthala* is defined as one *Brahman* identically the same with *sat, cit* and *ānanda*, which is the ultimate category of Śiva. It is the source of all energies, and all beings have come from it, and shall return into it. This one *sthala* may be divided into *liṅga sthala* and *aṅga sthala*. As the empty space can be distinctively qualified as the space inside the content and outside, so too Śiva remaining unchanged in Himself appears as pure consciousness and also as part of *liṅga*. The part of *liṅga* (*liṅgāṅga*) is also called *jīva,* individual souls.

As *sthala* is of two parts (Brahmā and *jīva*), so too is His *śakti*: *pravṛtti* and *nivṛtti*. When the energy moves forward for creation, it is *śakti* as *pravṛtti*, and when the energy recedes to its original state, it is *nivṛtti*. *Nivṛtti* is also called *bhakti*.

The *liṅga* is the worship (*upāsya*) and *aṅga* the worshipper (*upāsaka*). *Ṣaṭ-sthala* is a hierarchy where the *upāsanā* develops progressively gaining in content until the apparent duality between *aṅga* and *liṅga* vanishes and unity is achieved.

On the practical aspect, the one *sthala* becomes divided into *aṅga* and *liṅga*, each of which again undergoes a threefold modification. The three forms of *aṅga* are: *tyāgāṅga, bhogāṅga* and *yogāṅga*. The three forms of *liṅga* are *bhāva liṅga, prāṇa liṅga* and *iṣṭa liṅga*. They are respectively the manifestation of Śiva's Being (*sat*), Consciousness (*cit*), and Bliss (*ānanda*).

1. The *jīva* gives up attachment to worldly objects and so is called *tyāgāṅga*, because renouncement becomes the means through which the devotee realises his divine nature.

2. *Iṣṭa liṅga* becomes the object of worship of a renounced devotee (*tyāgāṅgin*), and he realises that the individual Divine (*iṣṭa liṅga*) is manifesting itself in the devotees' day-to-day life. It is how a devotee invokes Śiva in the beginning of his devotional path.

3. The subtle body (*sūkṣma śarīra*) is the means through which the soul experiences pleasure and pain from sensuous objects. The devotee having given up carnal objects and taken to the realisation of the Self, takes delight only in what is conducive to spiritual growth. He is a *bhogāṅgin* and *prāṇa liṅga* becomes the object of his worship. *Prāṇa liṅga* is the universal Divine present in every action. In his progressive approach, the devotee becomes conscious of the universal Divine.

4. In the next step, the mind and senses are no more entangled in the ignorance and desires (the matrix of the causal body) which separated the devotee from Śiva. Now, the mind and the senses change their natural course and the devotee realises the divine peace and presence in everything. This state is called *yogāṅga*, as this state leads to the union of *aṅga* with *liṅga*. The object of worship in this state is the infinite Divine. It is called *bhāva liṅga*.

To reach at these four stages, the devotee has to meditate on the following six *liṅga*s:

1. The aspect in which by its action, it upholds the universe and holds them in the mind, it is *ācāra liṅga*.

2. When, by its own knowledge, power and omnipotence,

the *Liṅga* assumes the role of a *guru* (one who leads every being beyond the range of all pleasures), it is *guru liṅga.*

3. The manifestation of *cara liṅga* as ego, it is *Śiva-liṅga.*[31]
4. The pure luminous *puruṣa,* which is without inward or outward, without any form called *ātman* (*cara liṅga*).
5. That in which one finds the seed of development as consciousness beyond the senses (*prasāda ghana liṅga*).
6. That which is completely full in itself, subtle, having no beginning nor end, and is indefinable, which can be grasped only by intuition of the heart (*mahātma ghana liṅga*).

Each of the above meditations make the devotee realise the following six truths, also called *sthala*:

1. The devotee worships the Lord with firm faith. All his activities are energised by love of God. All enjoyments are considered as grace of God. All his daily activities including his physical, sensorial and mental as well as his intentions are transformed into a spiritual reality. This stage is called *bhakta sthala* or *bhakti sthala.*
2. The devotee seeking perfection progresses from devotion to firm faith[32] in God and eventually becomes a Maheśvara. He receives and accepts everything wholeheartedly as a gift from God, whether it is pleasant or unpleasant. This stage is called *maheśvara sthala.*
3. In the next stage, the devotee considers everything as

31. *Śiva-liṅga* is the holy symbol of Lord Śiva that is considered very sacred and worshipped with devotion by the devotees. The Sanskrit word *liṅga* means symbol, so *Śiva-liṅga* means symbol of Śiva. It is considered the foremost sacred symbol for Śaivaites and has been worshiped for ages. *Śiva-liṅga* resembles the infinite column of flame.
32. Faith is a constant love for God; one loves God to the extent of firmly believing in Him and placing his entire trust in Him.

God's gift. He becomes like a child, trusting completely in his mother and placing himself under her protection with full confidence. God, in turn, showers His grace. The devotee recognises Lord Śiva's presence in all aspects of life, including his own senses. The world of experience is thus a gift from God. This stage of devotion is called *prasādi sthala*.

4. The devotee enters a new relation with God which enriches his spiritual progress. He realises that all his progress is due to *cara liṅga* (a manifestation of Śiva). This relation becomes by itself, a sort of prayer and the devotee realises that this new relation cleanses his soul. This stage is called *cara sthala*.

5. As a next phase, the devotee finds delight and confidence in the service of God. He wins intimacy with God and becomes a faithful servant of God. Anything and everything he hears is the sweet voice of God. Life is no more a burden but a delight. With great delight, he surrenders himself to Lord Śiva. This stage is called *śaraṇa sthala*.

6. In the final stage of his devotion, the devotee's mind and heart move in unison with the Supreme. His desires, affections, and thoughts become the echoes of God's desire, affection, and thoughts. The created and the Creator (*paśu* and *pati*) are in perfect harmony. The devotee's soul becomes one (*aikya*) with the Great Lord. This final stage is called *aikya sthala*.

According to Śaivism, devotion (*bhakti*) is the revelation of pure oneness or identity with God.

5

Chosen Deity, Iṣṭa Devatā

I, the devotee, am standing in the midst of deep water,
yet I feel thirsty.
O Blissful Lord, have mercy, slake my thirst
And bless me with happiness and contentment.
— *R̥gveda*, 7.89.4

Spiritual Ideal

EVERY human experience confirms that life in the relative world cannot be unalloyed joy all the time. Joys and sorrows are the two sides of the ever-spinning coin of our life. Instinctively, everyone seeks only happiness and avoids sorrows. Man acts with the objective or motive of finding happiness. There are many things that bring happiness to man. But his mind dwells on a particular object of his liking and craves to find happiness through it. If he is dissatisfied, his mind becomes extremely restless.

Why is this restlessness of mind in man? Because his mind is weak. A man's desires are like wild horses, each trying to run wild and leading him to a dangerous end. If a man is weak, he runs a great risk of life. But if he is an expert charioteer, he controls his desires and reaches the destination of his life safely. In order to strengthen the mind, the most secure and probably the only way is to adopt a Spiritual Ideal.

According to their prominent behaviour, men can be classified under three heads:

1. Those who are constantly unkind,
2. Those who act with some sense of discrimination between kindness, and unkindness, and
3. Those who follow only the path of kindness.

There is the animal nature in man which prompts him to seek sensual pleasures only. To some people joy comes mainly through sensual pleasures. They are no better than animals and beasts in their nature, though they appear as human beings. This is the first type.

There is a higher class of men. They have got the awakened sense of discrimination between right and wrong, between things which have descriptive appearance and those which are really good. They reject the bad and try to follow the good. They lead a life of constant struggle, because they have to be constantly vigilant. They try to follow a noble ideal instead of streaming with the flow of many desires. They are said to belong to the human plane. The sense of discrimination and the constant effort to follow what is good distinguishes them from the first type.

Finally, there are those who are fortunate enough to have succeeded in their attempt to have full mastery over themselves. Their mind is no longer astray. They always follow the right path. These men are said to have become divine, though belonging to the earthly existence. Man's goal in life should be to reach this stage of divine nature.

The human inclination is to hanker restlessly for new things, new ideas, new experiences and new knowledge. Out of these, the desire for knowledge is a sign of effort for a spiritual ideal. So long as there is this desire, there is the hope that, at some time in future, the essence of the spiritual ideal is surely enjoyed.

Human birth is of supreme importance. It is the only embodiment in which the soul (*jīva*) can evolve into perfection. Indian scriptures repeatedly advise to take advantage of the human birth to acquire higher spiritual evolutions. Human birth is a very good fortune in this universe with its countless species. If man utilises the brief lifetime for the sensual pleasures of life only, he will be debasing his human heritage, and consequently, his moral and spiritual evolution will be jeopardised.

The right course of human evolution lies in directing the senses towards noble views. Through this comes the raise in the scale of spiritual evolution. Man should transform his self-centredness to selflessness and expand his consciousness spiritually by introducing a spiritual ideal in his life. This is the way to experience the unalloyed joy in life.

A spiritual ideal consists in the conception of something in its perfect form, a principle of especially noble character, a visionary image, or an object of noble thought in the mind. The highest possibility that mind can conceive is the conception of a spiritual ideal. This ideal illuminates the mind, allows its full expansion. Embracing that noble conception with will and pleasure is devotion.

Something can be noble and spiritual, when it is distinguishable and exalted from the mental view in every respect. In the language of devotion, a spiritual view means a godly view. To be devoted to the spiritual ideal stands for being devoted to God. Constant pondering on the spiritual ideal gives man mental strength, he ascends to the higher stages of spiritual evolution and also gets the direct experience of the joy of his spiritual ideal. Ultimately, whatever spiritual ideal man takes up, it leads him to God.

It is possible for man to accept a spiritual ideal, only if it has some special qualities that give him peace and joy. As spiritual ideals are many, an individual can take up anyone of these. All spiritual ideals are noble in nature, because they enable man to have the experience of God.

Steadfast devotion to the spiritual ideal changes man's attitude towards life completely and transforms him to the perfect form of the ideal, illuminating his mind. Though spiritual ideals are always of high and noble qualities, man will constantly feel that he has to keep on ascending mentally in order to reach perfection. This prompts man to go further and further till he tastes the little joy of divine. This joy induces him to strive for more joy. If during the mental elevation, he comes in touch with the Divine, he finds everything.

As long as man lives, he must use his life as a fight to serve his spiritual ideal, namely God, with a pure unselfish love. Self-dedication to this ideal is necessary if he is keen on the experience of divine joy in life. Of course, difficulties are unavoidable on his path of realisation. But the results of intense and constant efforts will bring purity and strength to his character. This enables him to face the obstacles fearlessly and to reach the goal. When the mighty ideal holds the mind, nothing will dare to disturb the mental peace.

Perception of the ultimate reality, the Truth (*sat*), is the ideal in life. Man has many ways to realise this Truth. While at times there is a transcendental evolution in man, at other times he is content with his mundane existence and his soul, being bound by human desires and motivation, blindly follows his ideals. When man's ideas are clear and systematic, his soul will stimulate him to follow the transcendental way. It is the only situation when the soul can act independently of man's desires. In all other situations, the soul would be, as it were, a slave to man's carnal desires and motivations.

To find his relation to the Supreme, man has to modify the concept of duty. In his day-to-day relations, he should not act out of right but out of duty. This would inculcate in him the habit of keeping his heart free from contempt, selfishness, hatred, desire to hurt the other, and so on. This way of purifying his heart and mind would reduce restlessness, impatience, anger and such other behaviour. He would then see and realise that there is something more valuable, something superior, something that is not in man's hand. Another human tendency is to have what others do not have; he would incline to find ways of finding the transcendental. This impatience is the hunger of the soul, which can be satisfied only in a calm and spiritual mind. Mind serves as an instrument of the soul. While the human relation with other humans and other species that surround him undergoes changes, that with the Cosmic Being remains always unchanged.

To understand the relation between man and God, man must have a spiritual attitude within himself. Only then can he establish a proper relationship between him and the Divine. When it is established, he can extend the same relationship to humanity as a whole.

God is one, but the approaches to reach Him are many. God is the highest truth. It is natural that man has to step to this highest truth from lower ones. To attain this, ideals must be assimilated and applied in life. These ideals should always be of a higher type and their conception should be clearer. To realise these ideals, the feeling, willing and knowing must be coordinated. They must be transcended through prayer, meditation, carrying out the duties of life and self-control. The goal of man is to realise his (soul's) relation with the Divine. Noble ideals have a great spiritual value. If faith is added to this, they take man nearer to God. Devotion is the dominant factor in this.

Love is always the highest ideal. Love knows no rival. Love should be man's highest ideal too. Identifying all the highest ideals of beauty, love, power, etc. to "Love of God", man experiences the feeling of bliss. To every human being, whether he is ignorant or wise, saint or sinner, man or woman, literate or illiterate, civilised or uncivilised, the highest ideal should be Love of God, which is the best spiritual ideal. This is *bhakti*.

Ideals exist in some form or the other in every mind. They are part and parcel of the human mind. The active struggle in human nature is to realise the ideals in life. It is very difficult to mould the inner ideals through the external conditions of the world. So ideals should be worshipped from within and from the highest standpoint of love. One should choose devotion to God as one's highest ideal.

Devatā

The Sanskrit word *devatā* means "one who is possessed of spiritual glow". *Deva* means "the shining ones" or "to shine". When something shines with spiritual glow, that one is called *devatā*. *Devatā* with its own spiritual glow makes its worshippers glow with its special powers.

Hindu spiritual masters give much importance to the conception of the Deity. They do so, because they realised that these deities have special powers, and the human mind can perceive only as much as it can grasp, just as a man, going to the river, can only take as much of water as his jug can contain. Hinduism speaks of various conceptions of deity. All these conceptions are true because they are parts of the Infinite, as it were. So long as man has a body and a mind, he can only have such a conception of God. But if he can transcend his mind, then he can apprehend God in his fullness.

Deity is not a Supreme Being. It is the manifestation of the one or more aspects of the Supreme.

> All the Gods, all Manus, the seven seers, as well as the sons of Manus, and Indra, the chief of the Gods — all these are special manifestation or glories of Lord Viṣṇu.[1]

The concept of deity and the worship of deity play an important role in Hindu cultural, philosophic and religious systems.

---

1. *Viṣṇu Purāṇa*, III.1.46.

The universe, consisting of an infinite number of objects and an infinite variety of creatures, is divided into broad divisions. Each division has been placed under the control of a supervisor called deity, so that the maintenance may be carried on strictly according to the law. These deities have both, an embodied and unembodied form. All of them represent the glories of God.

The status of a deity is acquired by the practice of the principles of self-dedication, austerity, good deeds, etc. when they were born as human beings. This, of course, is a long and hard process of continued efforts extending to many lives. Deities earn the status of divinity by the power of *mantra*. So, *mantra*s are to be recited to invoke them. It is the power of *mantra* that makes them shine, and so they are called shining or the deity. The significance in deity worship is that the worshipper will also become illumined by the power of the deity, whom he worships. Hindu Tantra scriptures provide the details regarding rituals to be practised and the *mantra*s to be recited for invoking different deities.

Deities are many, and along with their subsidiary deity (*gauṇa devatā*), they become numerous. Very often, and mistakenly, the deities are identified with the Supreme God.

Deity in Vedic Religion

> What God shall we adore with our oblation? The Divine being that existed in the beginning who was the one lord of creation, who fixed and upholds this earth and sky?[2]

God is the Creator and Ultimate Being. He is the Lord of all existence and so sustains the universe. He is the source of all strength, spiritual as well as physical. In him, man has his ultimate refuge. It is typical of Vedic worship that the worshipper seeks the knowledge of the object to be worshipped. The worshipper loves enlightenment.

---

2. *Ṛgveda*, X.121.1.

While describing the creation of man's body in the beginning *Atharvaveda* says,

> When they had fused the mortal man complete, the Gods entered into him.[3]

Man is constantly in search of the Supreme Being. Finding it difficult to grasp all the aspects of the Supreme, he started worshipping certain aspects of God, naming them as deity. Man's eagerness, yearning of love for the vision of God and enlightenment are expressed as:

> In my heart thoughts and feelings agitate; love yearnings proceed; they fly to all the regions. No comforter exists other than these, in the Gods are my highest longings fixed.[4]

The deity conception of the orthodox school can be found right from the Vedic period. In the Vedas, each vision of divinity carries some aesthetic values. For, it is a vision of beauty and splendour that attracts man. All Vedic Gods and Goddesses are beautiful and noble with no taint. The typical form of splendour is light; it is glory, greatness, as well as loveliness, beauty, wonder, etc. According to this outlook, the divinity is *deva*, the "shining one" or "the glorious one". The conception of divinity becomes a general idea, and also an idea of an individual deity. As long as this general idea remains, there is no essential contradiction in identifying one specific deity to another. Deity symbolises certain ideals. But all deities do not stand in the place of the Eternal Supreme Being or the Absolute of philosophy.

The Supreme Being is that which is not animated by anyone. Deities are different divinities, being different aspects of the one Supreme Being and remain under His control. From the spiritual point of view, in the Vedas there is no difference between

3. *Atharvaveda*, XI.8.13.

4. *Ṛgveda*, X.64.2.

singular, dual or plural numbers, or between the masculine, feminine and neuter gender in which the name of the divinity may appear. They are all protectors of human beings and so considered as "shining ones".

> I saw the protector,
> who never rests, who moves forward and backward over the earth,
> He, wearing splendour that gathers together and spreads out,
> travels constantly within the world.[5]

The practice of spiritual ideals for life and character was followed by generations of sages and saints, kings and leaders, as well as by the masses of people. Their practices gave them certain divine visions, which were worshipped later by others. The worships were in the form of poetry, which represented prayers. Each Vedic prayer is born in a spiritual mood, a praying attitude, in which the mind responds to the vision of the deity. This attitude and feeling remained constant, though the contents of the vision varied.

The Vedic view of a deity is very subtle and deeper in spiritual content. There were also proper adjustments, made from age to age, to meet the needs of the time. Vedic deities do not have conflicting qualities like virtue and vice, goodness and evil, love and hatred, etc. Unlike humans, they are all good, representing the highest moral values. Besides all of them (male or female deities) are beauty and nobility personified. Vedas adopted all the five elements,[6] namely earth, water, fire, air and space (ether) as the most important deities and worshipped them devotedly.

The divinity in Vedic prayers represented by the expressions, is the supreme hero, the supreme beneficent, the supreme Father, the supreme Mother, the supreme poet, etc. God is supreme, because He represents all goodness, all virtue and all nobility. Vedic Gods also represent the beauty and the splendour

---

5. *Ṛgveda*, I.164.31.

6. Called *pañca mahābhūta*: *pṛthvī*, *āp*, *tejas*, *vāyu* and *ākāśa*.

of nature. The "one being, the wise call by many names."[7] The divinity is supreme, all-pervading and all reality becomes unified in Him. "In whom all find one nest."[8]

Vedas contemplate deity in masculine, feminine and neuter genders as well as singular, dual and plural. For example, One is *Agni* (m), kindled in many a place. One is *Sūrya* (m), shining all over. One is *Uṣas* (f) the dawn, illumining all this. That which is one has become this all. "This all" (n) refers to the Supreme Being.[9]

Some of the Vedic deities are formless. They have received embodiment only in the poetry of Vedas. Some of the images in Vedic poetry cannot be reduced to definite forms, e.g. the famous description of *puruṣa*.[10] The cosmic person as thousand-headed (*sahasra śīrṣa*), thousand-eyed (*sahasrākṣa*), thousand-footed (*sahasra pāda*) is not the description of a figure, as Vedas do not entertain the grotesque — all Gods are beautiful. *Sahasra* means innumerable. Hence, there is no arithmetical coherence between head and hands. Thousand-headed, thousand-footed and so on imply the manifestation of divinity through the vastness of creation. Similarly, there is a reference to *puruṣa* as occupying a space of ten-fingers (*daśāṅgula*). The ten fingers are the 10 directions or regions. The divine as *puruṣa* makes the material universe a means of self-expression. The divine manifests his glory through creation. Vedas also call the deity as a manifestation of *dharma* (the Eternal Law) and *satya* (the Truth). In the Veda, it is said of Viṣṇu, "He upholds the eternal statues".[11] *Agni* has been described as the president of the eternals, *pṛthvī* as "upheld by eternal law"[12] and so on. The *Mahābhārata* says, "Because it

7. *Ṛgveda*, I.164.46.
8. *Yajurveda*, 32.8.
9. *Ṛgveda*, VIII.58.2.
10. Hymn to *Puruṣa* or Puruṣa-Sūkta (found in all the Vedas).
11. *Ṛgveda*, I.22.18.
12. *Ṛgveda*, VIII.43.24, *Atharvaveda*, XII.1.17.

upholds, it is called *dharma*. *Dharma* upholds the creation".[13]

In Sanskrit, "truth" is referred as *satya*. *Satya* applies to one's conduct. *Sat* is an object of search, of knowledge, or the realisation and vision. There is also the Upaniṣadic prayer:

> Lead me from unreality (*asat*) to reality (*sat*).[14]
>
> The three and thirty deity, the manifestation of truth, saw you two (the *aśvinī* deity, the divine physicians) approach truth.[15]

All verses in Vedas are meant for prayer. In its primary sense, *Brahman* means prayer. One deity in Vedas is called Brahmānaspati, the Lord of prayer. While saying the prayers, the worshipper experiences the divine feeling, when he merges his soul into the prayer. Devotion is a feature, which follows the divine feeling. The prayer reaches its zenith, when said from the soul. When the prayers are said with divine feeling and devotion, the worshipper realises *Paramātmā*, the Supreme Soul.

Deities are differently named ideas of the one Supreme Being. Prayers were offered to Indra, the source of all strength, spiritual as well as physical. In Him, man has his ultimate refuge. He is the saviour and helper, merciful, the most loving; he is the supreme goal of all. Indra lights up darkness. Indra is considered as the Lord of all other deities. Viśvakarmā (the divine architect) is worshipped as the architect of the universe. He is but another aspect of *Puruṣa*. Agni is divine energy. He is the refuge of man. Symbolically, Agni is identified with the inner principle of light whether associated with fire, lightning, or the sun. He is contemplated as the effulgent one, sending his light to earth, to the sky and to water and supplying life-energy to plants. Soma (moon) is worshipped for benevolence. Viṣṇu is worshipped as the supporter of the humble.

---

13. *Mahābhārata*, Karṇa-Parva, 69-59.

14. *Bṛhadāraṇyaka Upaniṣad*, 1.3.28.

15. *R̥gveda*, VIII.57.2.

The ideas of sweetness, peace and joy have been associated with the conception of the divinity as Viṣṇu. He is the source of sweetness.

> Viṣṇu whose three places are filled with sweetness, imperishable places that joy with holy bliss, Viṣṇu the One, who upholds the three — the earth, the sky and the worlds of living creatures.[16]

Sarasvatī[17] is worshipped as Divine mother. The *R̥gveda* (VII.95.5) describes, "As birds seek the shelter of the tree, so we, men seek the shelter of the Divine mother Sarasvatī". Intellectual treasure is her special gift. In the etymological sense Sarasvatī is "the lady of lake".[18] The idea of stream often goes with the conception of the deity, though the association with the higher life of intellect remains unchanged. Savitā symbolises the power of light. The divinity is the power of light beyond darkness. Gāyatrī is considered as the wife of Brahmā and the mother of Veda. All the essence of Veda is in Gāyatrī, who is the manifestation of the Absolute. Gāyatrī is a metre, a rhythm in a verse, what is known as *mantra* in Sanskrit. Gāyatrī is considered as deity, though it is a prayer, because its repetition results in the higher mental power that leads to enlightenment. Gāyatrī is also the name of a *mantra*. One reason why Gāyatrī is considered to be the most representative prayer in Veda, and as mother, is that it is a prayer for the highest power that man is capable of possessing — material and transcendental. The repetition of Gāyatrī *mantra* is said to cleanse one from all one's sins. Suparṇa, a fine-winged bird, is a mystical symbol for the Ultimate Reality in Veda. Sūrya (the sun), is spoken of as the face of all Gods, that is, the symbol of divinity. He is the eye, the seeing faculty and the inner intellectual principle. He is the source of light. His light symbolises the spiritual glory.

---

16. *R̥gveda*, I.154.4.
17. Goddess of knowledge and learning.
18. *Saras* = lake; *vatī* = lady.

The conception of sin is particularly associated with the conception of Varuṇa, whose emissaries detect all the trespasses of man. The prayer for the forgiveness of sins is a typical Vedic form of religion. The typical Vedic spirit is the approach of the all-good through goodness, the all-powerful through power and the all-pure through purity.

The origin of the Purāṇic conception of Durgā with 10 arms lies in Vedas. In the Veda, the 10 arms have the original abstract significance of the 10 directions.

The idea of unity of the divine existence is given in Veda as:

> They speak of Indra, Mitra, Varuṇa, Agni and there is the winged Garutmat. The one existence the wise call by many names as Agni, Yama, Mātariśvan (Vāyu).[19]

Arjuna says,

> Thou art Vāyu, Yama, Agni, Varuṇa and Moon. Lord of creation art Thou and grandsire.[20]

Veda asks for the accomplishment of some essential conditions, like the purity and prayerfulness of mind. Whatever deity the worshipper entertains, it should be conceived as truth, goodness and beauty; it should establish the metaphysical basis of unity in diversity, securely keeping up the rituals with the idea of unity, etc. Unity should not remain a mere abstraction but must find a concrete form in terms of social life.

Śrī Kṛṣṇa declares,

> Even those devotees who worship other gods with faith really worship Me (though) in an irregular way.[21]

All true worship is worship of the Supreme Being.

---

19. *Ṛgveda*, I.164.46.
20. *Bhagavad-Gītā*, XI.39.
21. *Bhagavad-Gītā*, IX.23.

It is the essence of the Vedic outlook to be progressive. Vedas do not contemplate a movement without a purpose, a mere life without content. Man has to grow to the fullest stature of his being, so that he may live in a broad and free world in the joy of the soul.

Deity Worship

The battle of life is a battle between happiness and sorrow, satisfaction and dissatisfaction, good and evil and other opposites. Our survival does not only apply to the mere biological existence but also to our moral and spiritual life. It also implies the acceptance of man's existence on the material plane. Building up of the body, sharpening of the mind, striving to live a full life with health and vigour are required for the joy of living. In order to acquire these, worships, rituals, prayers, etc. are offered to different deities.

Man worships deities, praying to them to keep him on the right path and to take him out of the path of evil and sin. Goodness is divine. So, to tread the path of goodness one should follow the divine. If the will that proceeds from the depth of man's heart were good, his whole conduct would be good. The psychological approach to man's conduct and attainment of his higher spiritual quality are possible through the worship of a deity, for it destroys the wicked thoughts. Different deities are invoked for man's success and worshipped for protection.

Deity worship is also aimed at creating unity. The deities and the method of worshipping them differ from one culture to another. Yet, the reason behind the evocations and the worship are the same: protection against evil, sorrow and dissatisfaction, and grace of happiness, goodness, contentment and spiritual uplift. In each culture, each deity is endowed with some particular powers. These deities are one aspect of the Supreme Being, and are considered as the rulers of certain powers in the universe. When man worships a particular deity, it will bless him with some powers; but the worshipper has to use that power for good purposes only. If the will to do good arouses from the depth of man's heart, then only man will find success in acquiring the powers and will have control over that power. "Foster the Gods through sacrifice and let the Gods be gracious to you." And "Fostered by sacrifice, the Gods will surely bestow on you unasked all the desired enjoyment."[22]

From the very beginning of creation, man has been nourishing and fostering the gods through the performance of sacrifices, and the gods have been providing him with desired enjoyment. This tradition of mutual service between the gods and man has come down from the beginning of time.

Man worships deities for different reasons. Among them remission of sins is one. Man bears on his head a load of sins committed by him in the past lives, and in the course of the current life too he is led to commit sins, that are incidental with the vocation he follows for his livelihood, however honest and lawful it may be. "Even as fire is enveloped in smoke, all undertakings are clouded with demerit."[23] Fire is mixed with smoke; it cannot be completely separated from it. Even so, every undertaking is tainted with fault. Every form of activity does involve, in one way or the other, some sins.

In order to relieve these sins, Hindu traditional scriptures have prescribed various forms of worships to propitiate the deity.[24] The methods of worship are attuned to different types of men with due regard to their positions in society, stage of life, nature and circumstances. These worships also form the spiritual practices. Those who desire to realise God or seek liberation from the binding effects of *karma* should invariably devote themselves to some form of spiritual practice. Worship

---

22. *Bhagavad-Gītā*, III.11-12.
23. *Bhagavad-Gītā*, XVIII.48.
24. Tantra and Āgama scriptures provide the necessary guidelines.

gradually destroys all the latencies of the *karma* stored in the mind and brings Liberation to man.

Deity worship is one of the most striking characteristics of the ancient Hindu tradition, which provides the richest source of mythology, theology and worship available to the worshippers. Deity worship also supplies ideas that underlie the Hindu philosophical visions. They express the nature of devotion and the divine-human relationship.

Many deities are associated with geographical features of the Indian subcontinent. This association suggests to the Hindu thinking about the relationship between a sacred place and spiritual liberation. Many sacred places are specifically associated with or presided over by a god or goddess. The Indian subcontinent is a land of sacred places and revered as a mother.[25] Another significant point is that there are deities of all types: male, female, married, single, bachelor, virgin, etc. All are worshipped by different classes of people according to their needs. There are village deities that are to be worshipped, because they are considered as guardians of that place. Apart from this, the worship of a seasonal deity is also in practice. Strict measures of austerity are followed to worship these deities. Each deity has a particular story attached to it. It is believed that deity-worship will surely protect the masses as a whole.

The central idea with which the deity is associated is the idea of *Brahman*. Ever since the time of the Upaniṣads, *Brahman* has been the most commonly accepted designation for the Ultimate Reality in Hinduism.

In the Upaniṣads and throughout the Hindu tradition, *Brahman* is described as *nirguṇa* — having no qualities — and as *saguṇa* — having qualities. As *nirguṇa, Brahman* is beyond name (*nāma*) and form (*rūpa*). *Nirguṇa* is considered as superior by some

25. Bhārat Mātā or The Mother India, is the Goddess of the Asian sub-continent.

philosophers. *Brahman* as Ultimate Reality transcends all qualities, categories and limitations as the basis of all things and as the fundamental principle of existence. *Brahman* is also spoken of as having qualities, as manifesting itself in a multiplicity of deities, universes and beings. As *saguṇa, Brahman* reveals itself as various deities. The philosophical point asserted in the idea of *Saguṇa Brahman* is that in all different Gods, there is a unifying essence, namely *Brahman*. Each deity is a partial manifestation of *Brahman*, who ultimately is beyond all specifying attributes, functions and qualities.

The Hindu tradition affirms Vedic literature as the sacred source of Hinduism. This literature is of course vast, varied and eternal. God is eternal. Therefore, Veda which embodies His commandments, is also eternal. Veda is classed as Śruti — that which is heard or revealed — because Veda was given to this universe by God at the beginning of creation and gets absorbed into him at the time of final dissolution. Vedic texts are a collection of *mantra*s or hymns offered to celebrate deities and divine powers. The hymns were sung by ancient sages (who did not compose, but heard them directly) in praise of the deity during worship while praying for protection.

It is difficult to say how a particular deity or some deities became popular. But even today, it can be observed that reverence for many deities is being offered constantly. Many sacred places specifically associated with, identified with a deity, or presided over by a deity are visited and worshipped. Many cities, towns, villages are given the names of different deities as a mark of respect. Countless number of small shrines are found scattered throughout India, and those places have become places of worship. In all, deity-worship helps humanity to develop devotion to God.

Chosen Deity, Iṣṭa Devatā

Every religion accepts that God permeates every particle of the universe, directs and knows everything, yet only few know Him.

In fact, all existence is the projection of His All-Intelligent-Self. That is why God realisation is said to make a man perfectly possessed of full knowledge. God, being the essence, the fountainhead and the root cause of all existence, of every branch of knowledge, would fall short of completeness, if He were seperated from spirituality. All manifestations of name and form are objective. The knowledge in that sphere always varies depending on the intelligence of the onlooker.

God is the Supreme, the Self-effulgent and Self-evident. He needs no proof (to a believer in God). He exists as the very stuff and substratum of all phenomena and can be experienced by anyone who practises concentration, meditation and analyses the transformation from one mental state to another in the three stages, namely waking, dream and sleep. The analysis helps him recognise the inner witness of these three states, who remains unchanged even amid changes. The pure consciousness constitutes the real essence of *sat* (a sentient being different from a material object, *asat*), the cause and support of the universe.

Generally, the basic, essential and absolute pure consciousness is described as *Paramātmā, Puruṣottama, Brahman, akṣara, turīya, Bhūman, Īśvara*, etc. It is also known by other names: Kṛṣṇa, Vāsudeva, Nārāyaṇa, Rāma, Hari, Śiva, Mahādeva, etc. It is beyond words and thoughts and also free from all attributes and limitations of time, space and causality.[26] God is the Supreme Being, though named differently according to man's personal views. He can be grasped in different attributes, when all the obstructions in man's passage to reach Him are removed.

The individual consciousness in all intelligent beings springs up from the main source of universal consciousness. Human intellect cannot transcend the limitations inherent in it (that is, an embodied soul is under the limitations of flesh and mind)

---

26. It means that though He possesses countless attributes, yet He is not bound to them, or by them.

and therefore remains imperfect. So, it is said that God is absolutely inexpressible by any thought, word or activity.

God is described as an impersonal "superior person", the creator, maintainer and the final refuge of the whole universe of mind and matter. He is its first and material cause and is present in every aspect of the universe in his completeness and full glory. He regulates every thought, feeling and activity from inside and outside, but remains unaffected by the worldly phenomena. He is the Lord of the Universe wielding infinite power. Yet ever gracious in bestowing upon his devotees, all the fruits of their actions according to their merits, and thereby leading them to the ultimate goal of intimate relationship with Him. He is the embodiment of infinite beauty, love and bliss. He is of the highest good, holiness and truth. He is the source, ground and the goal to be aimed. He remains formless, even if He takes on whatever form his devotees desire to worship him. Therefore, He is described as the Highest. A form is attributed to him for the purpose of worship and sometimes God himself assumes certain forms and reveals them to his devotees. He assumes these forms by His special power in order to bless them. Often, the devotees transcend these forms in their highest spiritual experience and see God in his more distinctive aspects. (Just like the cosmic form Śrī Kṛṣṇa revealed to Arjuna in the *Bhagavad-Gītā*.)

After revealing His form in certain visions and drawing the mind of the devotee to it, the Lord withdraws those forms again. The devotee gets attracted towards it, starts liking it, lets his mind getting absorbed in that form constantly. It is human nature to take as his own what he likes most. He becomes lost in what he likes most. He visualises his chosen deity as the personal god. The pleasure he gets from that form develops fondness and intimacy towards it and it becomes his favourite god too. The conception of certain forms becomes the devotee's personal god, his chosen deity and his favourite god — all in one. The same becomes his spiritual ideal, which shines in his heart. A personal god is more suited to love, devotion and worship. In the particular form, He is not an abstract figment of the imagination, but a concrete being. As said earlier, the Supreme Being viewed through human eyes is named differently like *Īśvara, Pārabrahman* and *Paramātmā*, etc. The devotee may also choose anyone of His aspects for worship. Whatever the form of God may be, when man fixes his mind on a particular form of God, it is He alone that man remembers. The names, virtues, glories and stories on God serve to maintain His thoughts and image in the mind. When the impersonal Absolute of philosophy is viewed in relation to the universe, he is referred to as a personal god.

> When the *yogī* realises the truth of *Brahman*, through the perception of the truth of *ātman* in this body as a self-luminous entity, then knowing the divinity as unborn, eternal and free from modification of *prakṛti*, he is freed from all sins.[27]

The pure spirit in man is identified with the Supreme Spirit which is the cause of the universe, denoted by the word *Brahman*. The true knowledge of God is to be understood only with the perfection of man's soul. The perfection of soul is attained when it is no more under the sway of the sense objects. Yet, owing to the latent tendencies, the soul feels the trace of the sense experience. When this trace becomes inactive by complete detachment, the vision of the Supreme is obtained.

The Absolute is beyond thought and speech, and thus cannot be the object of devotion. Devotion requires the duality of a devotee and God. So, to approach the unity of the Absolute, some perfect form is to be conceived by the intellect. A favourite god responds to the conception, and this is named "chosen deity", *iṣṭa devatā*. "That *Brahman* which is absolutely subtle although not Void, but when thought of it, it is like Void. Him, *bhakta* calls *Bhagavān Vāsudeva*."[28]

---

27. *Śvetāśvatara Upaniṣad*, II.15.
28. *Śrīmad Bhāgavata Purāṇa*, IX.9.49.

Upaniṣads, *Śrīmad Bhāgavata*, *Brahma-Sūtra*, *Bhagavad-Gītā* and many more scriptures use the term *Brahman* for praising the Supreme Being. The word *Brahman* is derived from the root-word *bṛh* meaning "vastness, growth". Because of this sense, *Brahman* is that which is not limited by time, space or causation. The word *Brahman* has its own positive significance and cannot refer to Void. The extreme subtleness of God makes man imagine that he is void, but he can be attained.

According to the needs of each context, the Supreme Being is termed as Lord, God, *Brahman*, *ātman*, *Īśvara*, *puruṣa*, *parama puruṣa*, etc. The individual soul is a part of the Supreme Soul. The *Śvetāśvatara Upaniṣad* describes the individual soul as,

> Individual soul is as subtle as a hair point divided and sub-divided hundreds of times. Yet he is potentially infinite.[29]

God is subtler than ether and the minute atom. So it is possible for Him to be present in everything He created. He is unconditioned and unlimited. He is personal and impersonal, manifest and non-manifest. This experience is only possible through a spiritual awakening, which is obtained by him after a long term of uninterrupted meditation on the Absolute. It is like "the separation of a very subtle stalk of a blade of grass from the fibrous materials adhering to it".[30]

God, the Supreme Being, is called *Paramātmā*, the soul of the entire universe. He is the whole being, who includes in Himself the material cause and the effect of the universe and the individual selves as limbs (*aṅga*). In other words, they are organic parts of His being. The "whole", with the Supreme Being as soul (*ātmā*), as well as matter (*prakṛti*) as his body, is in inseparable union with the whole. His *māyā*[31] comprises that he manifests

---

29. *Śvetāśvatara Upaniṣad*, V.9.

30. *Kaṭha Upaniṣad*, II.iii.17.

31. *Māyā* is a great power whose effects are wonderfully variegated; one →

this universe of living and non-living beings and also dwells in them as their soul. At the same time, they do not contain Him, but He contains them. Being subtler than the subtlest, He can pervade everything without being affected or limited in the least by it. He is the support of the universe just like the string supports the beads of a rosary. He is the Lord of the universe. He is indestructible.

Patañjali describes the Supreme Being as "the special *puruṣa* unaffected by the vehicles of *karma* or actions and their fruition".[32] The Lord *Īśvara* is ever free, unique, without a second and without being a second. No one can restrain him, no one can control him. According to distinctive functions, the power of *Īśvara* has different manifestations and also takes different names such as Brahmā, Viṣṇu, Devī, etc. Each god has His characteristic power and function. One can fulfil all his interests, whether worldly prosperity or liberation, by worshipping these gods.

A man's knowledge of God is necessarily finite, because human vision is inferior to God's vision. When the Almighty is brought into relation with man and the world, the dynamic aspect comes into play. So, the distinction between God, the Supreme and the god of religion, the personal god, the chosen deity, the favourite god, etc. results. Each religion in its own way considers the philosophical Absolute as God and has its personal concept of Him. Likewise, each person has his own idea on God that suits his nature. He takes to that idea on God and proceeds with it because his religion rejects other concepts on God. That god becomes his particular god with his special ideas, his chosen deity. It is natural that this special liking becomes his favourite god, which he will preserve forever.

→ of its effects may be of the nature of illusion. Nature is not an illusion but by virtue of its immense productiveness, it generates all the illusions of mortals.

32. Patañjali *Yoga-Sūtra*, I.24.

Anything man preserves forever is considered as his personal. At first, this appears like a contradiction, but it must be remembered that only the Absolute Truth is One; all relative truths are various, just as each person hears and sees the universe in his own way, though the universe throughout is unchangeable and unchanged. The God of religion is considered as personal god as chosen by each religious group. Often, the God of religion suits to man's choice, but one may select one's favourite god for worshipping. The chosen deity is personal as well as favourite and is man's choice.

The dynamic aspect of reality is more important to man, who is in bondage, even if he has the urge and potential to transcend his state of bondage. The impersonal Absolute, when conceived by human mind, becomes the personal chosen deity, the favourite of a particular human nature. The personal aspect of the Godhead in relation to the triple function of creation, sustenance and dissolution of the universe is also known as trinity — Brahmā, Viṣṇu and Rudra.

The personal god is also *Īśvara*, the Eternal, the Pure, the ever Free, the Almighty; the all-knowing, the all-merciful and the teacher of all teachers. The Lord is indescribable love by his own nature. The personal god of indefinable love is also the Supreme Being. The personal god worshipped by the devotee is neither different nor separate from the Supreme Being, who is *Brahman* of the Upaniṣad or the Absolute of Vedānta. The Supreme Being is one without a second. As unity, it is too much of an abstraction to be loved and worshipped; so, a devotee chooses the relative aspect of the Supreme Being.

Moreover, it is very difficult to realise God in his perfection. If at all He is realised in His perfection, it is only graced through the divine vision. But only a few can accept this vision without any mental agitation or fear.

> Among thousands of men, some strive for perfection. Even among those who strive for perfection, some only know Me. Among those who know Me, only some will know Me in perfection.[33]

Birth as a human being is very difficult to attain. It is obtained through the exceptional grace of God. Everyone belonging to this species is qualified to strive for God realisation by virtue of one's birth. Sub-human creatures, such as birds, beasts, insects and reptiles, neither possess the power nor the capacity to strive for this end.

Though blessed with a human birth as a fruit of divine grace, most of men does not even think of looking at the path of God, due to the excessive attachment to enjoyments caused by the latencies of their past births and through lack of faith and love in God. Barely, one among thousands, whose latencies (*vāsanā*) of previous births are favourable and who possesses some amount of faith and reverence for God, treads the path of God realisation and strives for it. And again, among those who strive to realise, many do not attain the same level — owing to the difference in the latencies of their past lives, and lack of continuous faith, devotion and effort. Obstacles of various kinds continue to come in their way too, in the shape of egotism, mine-ness, desire, attachment, evil association, etc. Therefore, there are only few whose faith, devotion and practice help them to attain a degree of perfection and who, as a result of such perfection, are able to realise God in this very life.

In a spiritual-minded life, one is considered wealthy, if one remembers God all the time. Adversity sets from the moment a person forgets that he belongs to God. The fundamental bond between God and His creation must never be forgotten. As everything belongs to Him ultimately, the feeling of ownership or the claim for possession of material things and relations will only result in anxieties. Thus, even the thought that everything

---

33. *Bhagavad-Gītā*, VII.3.

one enjoys belongs to God is spiritually beneficial. This needs mental alertness of the spiritual aspirant.

A devotee selects an embodied form of God, or a sign, or a sound for his worship. This becomes his favourite aspect of God. He fixes his mind with utmost reverence and devotion. Through worship to his chosen deity, he advances gradually on the path of God.

A devotee who meditates on chosen deity will remain satisfied and earn certain merits too. But realisation is possible only by the realisation of the Supreme. The personal and the impersonal god are not two different beings but God in his two aspects. The realisation of the Supreme Being can only be attained when the devotion to the personal god is mature. The personal form of God is held in high esteem in the scriptures. A prayer runs thus:

> O dweller among the mountains,
> the arrow which thou holdest in thy hand to throw, make kindly,
> O mountain-protector! Injure not man or beast.[34]

Admitting God as higher as a personal god, the *Śvetāśvatara Upaniṣad* says,

> Higher than this personal *Brahman,* who is concealed in all beings according to their bodies and who though remaining single envelops the whole universe, knowing Him to be the Lord, one becomes immortal.[35]

It continues:

> There is not higher than or different from Him, naught greater or more minute than Him. Rooted in His own glory, He stands like a tree, one without a second and immovable. By that being the whole universe is filled.[36]

---

34. *Śvetāśvatara Upaniṣad,* III.6.

35. *Śvetāśvatara Upaniṣad,* III.7.

36. *Śvetāśvatara Upaniṣad,* III.9.

Though there are many forms and signs of God, a spiritual aspirant must devote to one form, according to his preference, with faith for attaining spiritual progress. This can be compared to digging for water at one point instead of frittering away one's energy by trying at different places.

God is one, the Eternal. Scriptures affirm the existence of the Supreme Being as one.

> In the beginning this being was alone, one only without a second. That being willed. May I become many, may I grow forth. It created fire, water, etc. that is "one" evolved and creation took place in names and forms.[37]

A personal god may seem to be different in the beginning, but maturity of devotion reveals the close connection with the Supreme. To justify this statement the *Mahā Nārāyaṇa Upaniṣad* describes the Supreme Being as: "He is the Lord of all creatures". "He who is within the sun is the golden person. The golden person (meaning the shining one) is the Supreme Lord."[38] Āditya means "sun", the Lord who was in the beginning. The chosen deity is the highest possible personal aspect of God that can be grasped by human mind. Where there is liking, there develops love. So, devotion can only be established through God's personal aspect, that which a man likes.

A devotee is one who is possessed of such love. Love is a relative term, which always presupposes an object. A devotee prefers a personal God for his worship, unlike a *jñāna yogī* who prefers and worships the impersonal Absolute as identical with himself. The devotee knows well that the real God exists beyond his personal god.

> Far beyond even this unmanifest, there is yet another unmanifest

---

37. *Chāndogya Upaniṣad*, VI.II.1-3.

38. *Mahā Nārāyaṇa Upaniṣad*, IV.15.

existence, that Supreme divine person who does not perish even though all beings perish.[39]

The word unmanifest existence has a particular meaning in the *Bhagavad-Gītā*. He is named as *ādi yajña*, divine person, or Supreme person, unmanifest aspect of God and so forth. Terming God thus, a decidedly superior, higher and different aspect in the unmanifest existence of God is established. So, the chosen deity, or a personal God, or a favourite God cannot be the highest God. During the deluge, all the gods and deities are absorbed in the dissolution.

As far as the unmanifest principles are concerned, one is sentient and imperishable and the other is insentient and perishable. The former is considered superior, totally different from the later and master of the later, and naturally obtained the status of the Lord. This sentient principle is eternal, as it has neither a beginning nor an end. Sāṁkhya philosophy calls the former *puruṣa* and the later *prakṛti*. The eternal unmanifest exists in his own glory, absorbing within himself all beings together with *prakṛti*. The process of emanation of beings from the unmanifest and their merging into the same has been a cyclic phenomenon.

Just as the elements air, fire, water and earth are integral parts of ether which is their sole cause and substratum, even so, the entire creation consisting of sentient and insentient beings which are inseparable from God.[40] It has emanated from God and on Him alone does it sustain.

The impersonal God, though all-pervading, assumes the form of a personal god under the influence of devotion.

The supreme person, the eternal unmanifest in whom all beings

39. *Bhagavad-Gītā*, VIII.20.

40. According to Sāṁkhya philosophy, from *ākāśa* (space or ether), *vāyu* (wind) is produced; from *ākāśa* and *vāyu*, *tejas* (fire) is produced; from *ākāśa*, *vāyu* and *tejas*, *ap* (water) is produced; and from *ākāśa*, *vāyu*, *tejas* and *ap*, *pṛthvī* (earth) is produced.

abide and by whom all this is pervaded is attainable through exclusive devotion.[41]

Man realises God by worshipping Him with form and attributes. This realisation of the Supreme (the stage of liberation and final beatitude) is the reward for the worship of the Supreme indestructible Absolute.

The Supreme Being rules over all creatures as their very soul; and since He is their ultimate source, they are under His control. The soul is considered as the conscious principle that sustains, actuates and owns a body, which is his means of expression. God is the soul of all; and all beings — sentient and non-sentient — constitute in their whole the divine body. He is the creator, preserver and destroyer of all; and hence He is described as the beginning, the middle and the end. There is no beginning which is independent of God.

> He, the Supreme Being witnesses the birth of the first born, the *Hiraṇyagarbha,* the cosmic soul also the Golden Egg, who projects universe and nourishes him with wisdom.[42]
>
> He is the transcendent adorable master of the universe, who is the supreme Lord over all the minor deities like Indra, Agni, Varuṇa, etc. and rulers (Prajāpati).[43]

All these confirm the supremacy of God.

Contemplation which is free from human emotions and the worship of the deity are essential steps to realise the Supreme Being as the personal God with attribute and as impersonal Absolute.

God is the finest essence, which the whole world has for its Self. Uddālaka Āruṇi clears this point to his son Śvetaketu:

> Just as when some salt is dissolved into water and when sipped

41. *Bhagavad-Gītā,* VIII.22.
42. *Śvetāśvatara Upaniṣad,* IV.12.
43. *Śvetāśvatara Upaniṣad,* VI.6-7.

from the top, the middle and the bottom give the same salty taste in the water, and the salt that is dissolved in water cannot be perceived by sight or touch and it must be known by some other means, so too, the God, the root of this universe, who is in this body, is not perceived by the sense organs, but to be known in some other way.[44]

There are different means to know Him: exclusive devotion to a personal God and surrendering everything to Him, considering that He sustains all and is the inner witness of all, constantly thinking of Him with love in every way, and so on.

There are two classes of devotees: one is born with divine love in him, the other tries to earn it. Those who are born with divine love in them do not give up their devotion to God, even if they come across hundreds of difficulties. They adore God to attain Him. They seek God as their supreme goal, for without Him they find themselves incapable of living. God considers such devotees as His soul, since He finds His life in them. According to Vedānta philosophy, it is through the results of merits, accumulated by countless lives in the past, that an individual comes to understand the nature, attributes and glories of the Supreme. This understanding elevates him to the highest rank. This type of knowledge also accrues as an outcome of a great holiness of character built up through a series of lives. Such a man loves God with all the love his nature is capable of. The other type wavers in his devotion to God and turns to the world again, when he meets the slightest obstacle in his path of devotion. He worships God mainly to earn personal benefits. His devotion is not single-minded, because he is attached to the immediate tangible results, and he is interested in God, mainly for securing these results. His heart is divided and his love for God is not integral.

Generally, people in this world do not conceive a liking for the practice of adoration of God. Even if a man puts forth a

44. *Chāndogya Upaniṣad*, VI.13.1-2.

special effort, owing to lack of faith and devotion, he continues to divert it towards the satisfaction of his desires, with the result that he fails to realise God. Keeping in mind that the entire creation is a manifestation of God and there is nothing apart from God, man should worship Him and establish his relationship with the Supreme.

Why do people fail to recognise God, though he is present everywhere and so near them? Śrī Kṛṣṇa answers:

> The whole of this creation is deluded by the objects evolved from the three modes of *prakṛti* — *sattva, rajas* and *tamas*; that is why the world fails to recognise God, standing apart from these and imperishable.[45]

These modes of *prakṛti* are created by God. *Prakṛti* abides in the senses, which are its particular offshoots. *Prakṛti* is divine in its power. Man fails to recognise God because of the manifestation of divine power in *prakṛti*. There is nothing higher than God. Everything is strung on Him, just as threaded rows of gems.

Man usually tries to see God according to his own nature. He moves in a particular direction according to the effect of the qualities inherent in his nature. These qualities do not originate from the natural condition of the Self. His nature influences him to choose what he likes. The chosen deity is that aspect of God which man's nature likes. Man's nature also depends upon his *karma*. Where there is a liking, love will develop too. Man's liking depends on variations in his nature: he might reflect noble ideas when the *sattva* mode dominates in his nature; he might reflect devilish or beastly ideas when *rajas* dominates him; and he might reflect dullness when *tamas* dominates him. He can reflect a mixed character of two or three of the above-mentioned modes. Only when the *sattva* influences dominate, be it for a short time, an unconditional love towards God emerges, and becomes the main character of man.

---

45. *Bhagavad-Gītā*, VII.13.

Worship of the chosen deity (*iṣṭa devatā*) will also bring a great change in the mind of those who worship God with personal motives. The mind of man is determined by his inborn dispositions which spring from his past conduct. To some, worldly desires blind their vision. So they seek to gratify their desires through the propitiations of lower gods. No doubt, Supreme Lord himself increases the faith of those who are devoted to lower gods (his dynamic manifestations), for they all are his manifestations. The entire universe is considered as his body. Through those gods, the Supreme Himself grants the wishes of the worshippers. But the results obtained are transitory whereas direct worship of the Supreme will result in His everlasting results.

A choice is one's liking. The liking of man and the attitude of devotion, both arise from the cultivation of love for God. To like a thing or an idea means, placing it in the heart and having the pleasure gained through it. The joy thus earned builds up the special effect and the moral strength. Moral strength thus gained, gradually leads man to expect nothing from outside and to turn his thoughts within to worship God. Illumination of thoughts is the greatest effect man gains. The moral strength he attains makes him keep faith in himself. One cannot have faith in God, if one does not have faith in oneself. The consequent mental transformation increases the strength of his devotion to the chosen God. He will also gradually understand that something, offered to a chosen deity, should not be used for personal satisfaction. He realises the real sense of self-sacrifice and thereby experiences the pleasure in the attitude of renunciation. This leads to spiritual progress that is essential for the mind to have the feeling of God.

God is the Supreme Being. Man can visualise God in his chosen deity only as long as the attachment to body and mind exists in him. With the vision of the chosen deity, man not only starts shedding his egoism, but his wisdom also grows and provides guidance to the experience of the Supreme Being. Worship of the chosen deity is nothing but a preliminary step in the way of *bhakti*, which trains the devotee qualified to progress to the further stages that are essential to ultimately obtain the glimpse of the Supreme Being. Upaniṣads declare that the Ultimate Reality is beyond the reach of human words and conception. *Taittirīya Upaniṣad* declares, "That from which words together with the mind fall back without reaching It."[46] A complete comprehension of the Supreme by human mind is therefore impossible. He should aim for the grace of the divine vision through devotion.

The Vedas say that the Supreme Soul cannot be described, because human words are insufficient to bring its description. Moreover, the experience of God cannot remain in that state of union with God forever, because of the latencies that are not yet destroyed.

In the worship of the chosen deity, man's liking predominates. In the chosen — being one's liking — there will always be the presence of "I-ness" and even a certain degree of predominance of "my-liking". This liking is not God's liking, but one's personal liking. Man chooses and loves God in his own way; his love to the chosen God is not universal love, but limited to a special liking. On the other hand, devotion to the Supreme is for pleasing the Supreme only. The question of choice does not arise while offering love to the Supreme. The devotee loves the Supreme for His sake, for the pleasure of God.

Role of Chosen Deity in Devotion

The mind runs through all steps beginning with traceable to untraceable. Mind is the eternal manifestation of *prakṛti*. In one aspect, it becomes the subject and in the other, it becomes the object. It also serves as an instrument of consciousness. All

46. *Taittirīya Upaniṣad*, II.4.

different forms of different states are centred in the mind. Mind can be disciplined through some process. Endowed with the gross as well as the subtle operations it has two stages: the lower in which all kinds of impure thoughts and emotions are entertained and the higher, which responds only to pure thoughts and emotions. The lower mind is affected with afflictions — gross as well as subtle — which are its enemies. Just as the gross impurities of a cloth are removed first by washing and the fine ones are then removed by efforts and means, the afflictions of the mind are destroyed progressively through the practice of spiritual disciplines. These practices gradually replace the impure thoughts and emotions by pure and lofty thoughts, thus bringing the mind to a stage where it becomes difficult for it to entertain any impure thoughts.

When mind wants to be in touch with the external world, the senses begin to function. When the mind decides to withdraw, they are able to withdraw from it, breaking all connections with the external world. Just as the bees follow the queen bee as it flies from one place to another and do not live independently of the queen bee, the senses do not function independent of the mind. When the mind is joined to the sense organs, the perception of objects takes place. As the senses are diverted to the chosen deity, the mind will acquire the capacity of steadiness, which enables it to remove the afflictions, thereby improving the capability for devotion. The more one is aware of a thing, the more one's mind reflects it. If the object has some attraction, it brings pleasure to him, which influences in bringing about steadiness and calmness, which in turn strengthens devotion.

The mind is very restless and nervous due to *vāsanā* (past impressions that exist in the present life). It will not easily stick to a particular object for any length of time. *Iṣṭa devatā* makes the mind fit for meditation by turning it away from external and internal objects. It develops serenity and steadiness of mind.

According to the law of life, man tends to reproduce the ideas in his life which constantly occupy his mind. A beginner who is still trying to acquire steadiness of mind is not likely to derive many benefits from meditation on an abstract virtue. The association with a beloved divine form with virtues helps in developing the devotee's virtues. This accelerates the spiritual progress of the devotee. The object of meditation may be one of the divine incarnations, great masters in spiritual discipline, the seers, etc. the mind becomes automatically transformed and coloured by this kind of support, attains steadiness and assumes the form like that of a pure crystal. When the mind is coloured by the receivable support, that is, chosen deity, it transforms into that support and shines with that form of God's manifestation in the chosen deity. Patañjali says, "Also the mind fixed on those who are free from attachment acquires steadiness."[47]

When one works freely, serving the personal god without selfish motives or desires, that work is the real work. One can attain perfection through it. Such unselfish service to the chosen god will remove all bondage from the heart and will give purity. Purification of the heart is the essence of religion. Outer cleanliness without inner cleanliness would not bring the sense of purity. Inner cleanliness is attained by removing the impurities of the mind. With a pure mind, one obtains a pure heart. When the heart becomes pure, the vision of one's goal is attained. The heart is like a mirror. As long as it is covered with impurities, so long it would not reflect the chosen god. So, purification of the heart is the most essential thing. Devotion to God is the royal road to the purification of heart.

God alone is the ultimate support and substratum of this animate and inanimate creation. It is from Him that everything originates. Therefore, considering the chosen deity as identical to Him and knowing *iṣṭa devatā* as pervaded by Him, one should

---

47. Patañjali *Yoga-Sūtra*, I.37.

think of God alone in whatever form it presents itself before his mind. There is no limit to His manifestations.

The mind also has a tendency to seek after peace, which is its real nature, but it is curtailed by the strong power of the senses. Unless the senses are subjugated, it would be impossible to attain peace of mind. These are gross stains. The spiritual practice washes away subtle dirt which is a major enemy of the mind. Afflictions of the mind are some of these dirty marks. When the mind is filled by the power of the chosen deity, it attains mastery over the senses. Since, the chosen deity (*iṣṭa devatā*) is not a sense object, devotion helps to subjugate the sense activities, thereby reducing all types of the mental distractions. When the distractions are eliminated, the mind acquires strength in concentration. In *iṣṭa devatā* worship, the object of concentration is a chosen deity and this would be an object of special significance to the devotee.

Normally, concentration begins with the controlled movement of the mind and then reaches a state in which all movements stop. In this ultimate stage, the mind becomes one with the essential nature of the object concentrated upon — with no further movement. This type of concentration has two limitations: One is that the mind can never fully realise the essential nature of the object concentrated upon; the other is that consciousness always remains confined to the limitations of intellect from which it cannot be released.

Concentration on the chosen deity enables man to remain in steady concentration, which in turn influences him in the worship and meditation on God, eliminating the intruding thoughts. This kind of worship is the only way to have direct contact with God.

It is to be noted that worshippers of trees and stones as chosen deities do not worship each and every tree or stone, but only particular trees or stones as representatives of God. They are true worshippers. They alone can feel the omnipresence of God and become capable of reaching the highest stage of spirituality.

Full aspiration after God automatically leads a person to study, to acquire knowledge on the distinctive characteristics of the Supreme Being, the soul and the world. This knowledge would incite him to follow the austerities which consist in performing actions accordingly. With the purity of mind comes contentment. The purity of mind leads to the devotion to a personal god, because the worshipper chooses it according to his attraction. The purity of mind too induces the devotee to dedicate all actions to his personal god, who is the aim in all his actions. The purified mind becomes an instrument for the realisation of God.

Worshipping with devotion combines in itself the significations of a number of practices, like purification, self-discipline, austerity, etc. These practices are like the process of subjecting alloyed gold to strong heating, whereby all the dross is burnt and pure gold is left behind. So too fasting, observing vows of various kinds, concentration, study of scriptures, etc. purify the mind and control the mental activities. Worship begins with simple and easy exercises, even though the devotee has to apply his will-power and determination.

In the case of ordinary men, the mind becomes one with the medium through which it works. Worship of God takes man to communion with Him, and prepares the mind to receive the real knowledge and clear insight of God.

The potency of the *mantra* related to the chosen deity harmonises the agitated state of mind, makes the mind sensitive to the subtler vibrations and gradually brings about a fusion of the different states of mind. This progressive devotional worship ultimately leads the worshipper to the stage of constant communion with God by removing the sense of "I-ness" and the "mine-ness" that veils the devotee. The sense of bondage, the limitations and illusions of life are due to the presence of I-consciousness. This is the root of miseries. True devotion to God destroys this "I" content by systematic and progressive union of the worshipper's will with that of God. Love is the driving force that brings about the removal of egoism. The transparency of the mind comes from developing supreme love to God. The transparent mind becomes one-pointed. The worshipper, penetrating through the gross mental ideas, will then reach the subtlest vision. This stage aids in the real understanding of the Supreme Being.

God is the Supreme Reality and attaining Him is the supreme goal. *Īśvara* (God) is the general term frequently used for this infinite reality, which is the object of spiritual aspirations and the central focus. God in His fundamental nature is beyond the reach of the *jīva*, caught up in the complex of *māyā*. But *bhakti* towards the Supreme will make man come out of this *māyā* and will help to develop an uninterrupted union with Him. God is the active principle in the resulting communion and worship. He transcends the realm of the finite real nature and the individual self by His perfection and sustains them from within as their immanent inner soul by virtue of his very infinitude. Śaṅkara, Madhva and Rāmānuja have all brought up solid methods in their philosophies.

According to the Viśiṣṭādvaita philosophy of Rāmānuja, God is the ultimate soul and the finite entities constitute His body. The body is that which is supported, controlled and used by the soul for its own purpose. To be spiritual means to understand that man is not a mere body-mind as he himself feels to be in his natural state, but to understand his relation with the Supreme Being in fullness. If the spiritual value of this world is neglected, then man's effort to improve his life at the material level will only result in making him an animal. The experience of *mokṣa* consists in the preliminary knowledge of God, love of God and the final offering of oneself to the service of God. Realisation and intimate relationship with God in the fullness of experience are the essence of perfection.

The Universal Validity of Choosing a Deity

Every man likes to relish his exercise of judgement in settling upon a course of actions. The freedom to express one's will is no doubt very important, but at the same time, one should be vigilant in using this freedom. The principle in man's life is the will to be free. When he does not find enough scope to be free, he suffers. When he cannot get right guidance in his accomplishment of a deed, then also suffering falls to his lot. So, everyone should be given enough scope for his self-expression, each man should have a maximum of freedom for his growth. The greater the freedom, the better for him.

In the depth of man's mind lie hidden many desires and hankerings. They constantly try to free themselves up to the conscious plane. But, as all these desires do not give him satisfaction, he pushes them down to the lower level of the mind. This ends up in a conflict as a result of which man suffers physically as well as mentally. A small fraction of these desires is visible on the conscious plane too. The rest lies submerged in the unconscious (or subconscious). The unconscious is the storehouse of all thoughts, good or bad. This has great influence in determining man's way of life. The unconscious also is the repository of the impression of the past lives. Yet, the unconscious cannot be ignored for a long time, even if man is helpless in its clutches. It must be faced with care and diligence.

When suitable opportunities are provided, the past impressions take different forms and shapes in man's life. The impressions are both good and bad according to the actions done. It is but natural that one wants to push back the bad ones; but this ends up in his lack of discriminating ability, because reflection on both — the good and the bad impressions — is necessary for a discriminating intellect. By nature, the human mind is oscillating and restless, due to these past impressions. At one time, man projects high ideals, and at another time, he falls a victim to base impulses. This is because of the good and bad impressions anchored in the mind. Unless mind is made strong by personal efforts, its inclination to base impulses will not stop.

One of the greatest sources of disturbance to the mind is man's uncontrolled reaction to the conditions in which he gets involved while living a hectic life. If he has no well-defined principle for the regulation of these reactions, he will be disturbed by all kinds of violent emotions. Ancient Hindu psychologists proposed some remedies to regulate the disturbed mind, like cultivating the feeling of friendship towards all living beings, compassion towards those who suffer, helping the needy, keeping away from bad company, cultivation of virtues like non-violence, kind speech, cultivation of truthfulness, etc. Application of these virtues helps man in regulating his reactions to his surroundings, which results in pleasant emotional reactions to all conditions he has to face.

Patañjali, taking note of the vagaries of the mind, suggested some remedies in the form of positive methods. As the common man is a victim of lust, greed and other passions, Patañjali said that by thinking constantly of the opposite virtues, one could keep his mind in a balanced state. "When the mind is disturbed by improper thoughts, constant pondering over the opposite is the remedy."[48] To replace the wrong habits of thoughts and attitudes, the development of contrary thoughts is required. For example, if one wants a cure for anger, he should think of love. The definite remedy against all maladies of the mind is to strengthen it through meditation. Meditation is an act of deep reflection on sacred subjects as a devotional act. By meditation the modifications of the mind, which are the sources of troubles,

---

48. Patañjali *Yoga-Sūtra*, I.33.

are reduced. Man suffers, because of his weak mind.[49] Meditation is the only way that assures strength to the mind. Regular practice, particularly of meditation, makes man reach a state in which his mind will remain untouched by vagaries, thereby strengthening it.

For meditation man needs a noble ideal. It should suit his mental requirements and should also attract his affections. The object, that is, the noble ideal chosen for meditation, becomes the chosen deity for man. Man is free to choose the ideal. Naturally, the ideal should respond to some noble ethical and moral values. The act of selection is universal, independent of caste, creed, place, time and circumstances. All individuals have the freedom to choose their *iṣṭa devatā*. Everyone can enjoy the pleasure and the peace his chosen deity bestows. Humanity as a whole belongs to God. *Iṣṭa devatā* is that aspect of God that develops faith in Him through his attractions.

God is not linked to any particular cardinal point. People living in any direction can worship Him. The only condition needed is that man should be pure in body and mind, when he wants to contemplate or meditate. Purity is Godliness. The *R̥gveda* says,

> The deity from the westward, the deity from the eastward, the deity from the northward, the deity from the southward may he send us all bliss, may he grant us long life.[50]

Describing the creation of man's body in the beginning, it is said,

> When they had fused mortal man complete, the Gods entered into him.[51]

---

49. Indian psychology defines a weak mind as a mind that has lost control over the sense activities as well as over the process of evocation from memory. There is a degree of anarchy in the interrelation of sense activities, emotional values and recollection.
50. *R̥gveda*, 36.4. Also, in *Sūryopaniṣad*. The deity is Savitā.
51. *Atharvaveda*, XI.8.13.

This shows that God did not select one particular person, but entered into humanity as a whole. So everyone can select a deity as a medium of approach to the Supreme Being to get the joy of the soul, which can be compared to the vessel filled brimful with treasures.

God is equal to all. According to Veda, the beauty and the splendour of the universe and of man are part of the glory of the Divine. The earth does not belong to a single race but to different races, speaking different languages, following different cultures and having different religious beliefs. As a universal outlook, one should recognise the fact that the earth is common to all. The sole aim should be to create unity in variety. The different classes of people living at different places on earth, living under different stages of civilisation, have the freedom to choose their god for offering prayers and worships. *Atharvaveda* declares, "God is of the foreigner as much of our own land".[52]

The foundation of any good action is the goodwill of the mind. If the will that comes from the depths of human heart is good, then man's whole conduct will be good. Goodwill is the source of high knowledge. It is through goodwill alone that man can develop his contact with God.

The principle of unity in diversity covers all human relations. The conception of universality requires of man to establish friendship with the entire universe. One should look at one another with a sentiment of friendship. Then alone will universal peace and serenity exist.

To overcome troubles in life, it is essential to have strength, power and energy. The conception of divinities, perfect beings whose qualities indicate ideal virtues, helps a lot in acquiring these capacities. Very often, divinity becomes an ideal hero for man to conquer life. It is but natural that a man who is mentally

---

52. *Atharvaveda*, IV.16.8.

weak needs a hero as support. As God is the hero of heroes, the conception of God for such a man is God in His heroic aspect. In his need, man chooses that particular aspect of God for worship that gives him the mental strength to face life. The place where he stays does not come as a hindrance to approach God.

The act of creation cannot be compared to the making of a pot out of clay by the potter. The creation is a spiritual act of God. It is His spiritual sacrifice, through which the Absolute reveals His splendours. God is the warp and woof in all created things. "All this is threaded in Me (the divine) as pearls on a string."[53] All beings are creations of "One God". So God can never be partial. Of His own accord, He would never put one in surrounding that help the progress of the soul and another in a situation that would hinder his progress.

Free will is God's gift to humanity, wherever he lives. Man has the liberty to choose what he likes most. Yet, people in this world feel a sense of limit on them. Of course, every act of a person is kept under certain limits to keep up the unity in the circle. The fear of losing this unity is the reason to avoid Liberation. The strength of a society and the strength of a country lie in unity. But man can use his free will without harming the unity of society, without forcing one to follow his choice, without damaging others' progress. This is possible only through the choice of a spiritual ideal that influences unity among the masses. The spiritual ideal has the power of goodness and truth, which are divine. To follow the path of divinity means to tread the path of goodness and truthfulness.

One of the distinctive features of Hinduism is that it is not a simple homogeneous religion. All types of religions can be found in the comprehensive and tolerant fold of Hinduism. It does not force all minds into one groove; it gives freedom to all minds and recognises the various grades of culture. It looks upon the

53. *Bhagavad-Gītā*, VII.7.

whole world as a joint family. It welcomes all religions and people of all countries. It does not make any distinction between its views and that of the other, for God is common to all. *Atharvaveda* declares, "Having fused the mortal man complete, the Gods entered into him". God entered into all that He created human beings, even animals, insects, etc. The whole world is one nest protected by God. So we should not forget that God is but One, but He is contemplated in many ways. The multiple conceptions of God are contained in His Oneness.

All the religions in the world have a common aim, the aim to make man a perfect being so that he can realise God. Hindu scriptures prescribed certain disciplines for practice that support man to become perfect, free and a God-like soul in the end. The principles laid down serve to guide man along the path of ascent by invigorating his intellect and forming his good character.

Spiritual practices prescribed are intended to develop the virtues of devotion to God. A virtuous life purifies and strengthens the soul. God is eternal perfection. To approach Him, the soul must be pure. If man directs all his activities towards God with the idea of communion, that is, relationship with him, he will reach his goal.

Hinduism teaches that God is not only infinitely higher than individuals are but also infinitely closer to the individual selves. He is nearer to man than his hand and feet. He lives in the heart of man. He is the very ground for all beings. He is the Soul of all souls.

God is eternally perfect, the ultimate reality from which all our moral and spiritual values are derived, and there can be nothing outside Him and differentiated from Him. He is the indivisible spirit present in the heart of all persons. Man can realise God as He really is. The embodied soul loses its perfection, as it is incarnated. This natural disqualification of the soul prevents it from understanding God. The soul has to earn the qualifications to communicate with God. To remove the hindrances, the human heart should be cleared of dirty marks like unwanted worldly desires.

The path of divine love is open to all. It is a universal path. Whosoever loves God sincerely can have God's grace. The grace of God is God's response to man's devotion to him. The practice of divine love requires only one qualification, namely the belief in the grace of God. It does not matter where we are, what we are and what age we have. Grace is the awakening of God-consciousness in the heart and soul. It is not something that operates from without. When man is enveloped by the love of God, he is protected against all difficulties of life. The overpowering emotion of love to God makes man forget his difficulties.

Adoration to the chosen deity is also *bhakti*. It is a series of mental efforts, beginning with ordinary worship and ending in a supreme intensity of love for God. "It is the highest love for God."[54] The Sanskrit word often used for this is *anurakti*. The word *anurakti* is derived from *anu* meaning "after" and *rakti* meaning "attachment". The attachment that comes after the knowledge of the nature and glory of God alone is *bhakti*. Blind attachment to wife, children, etc. is not considered as *bhakti*.

Nārada, the great devotee, clearly differentiates devotion from lust, fear, hatred and kinship. Devotion is the enjoyment of the Lord, the Master of the senses, with the senses themselves purified by intense alignment with Him, without laying any condition whatsoever. Spiritual realisation is the fruit. God is attracted by the devotee's constant flow of mind towards Him brimming with love, an unconditioned and uncharted love for the Supreme person. Real devotion is a transcendental experience of bliss, which can never be expressed adequately in words. It is different from ordinary love.

From the point of view of *bhakti*, the relationship between the devotee and God is complete, only where there is absolute merging

54. *Śāṇḍilya Bhakti-Sūtra*, 2.

of the devotee's mind in God. This merging will not take place before the experiencing ego is completely dissolved. "Those who love Hari (name of God), indeed, lose themselves in Hari."[55]

Bhakti is an experience, pure and selfless, subtle, unbroken and ever-expanding. A man, who once experiences it, will see that only, hear that only, and speak that only, for he ever thinks of that only. This experience is the feeling of merging of the devotee's mind in God, or constant communion with God. God takes on the form man has chosen for His worship and adoration. He reveals Himself in that form to the worshipper. The man who loves God has no wants. He neither hates, nor rejoices, nor strives full of zeal for any ends of his own. Through *bhakti,* he attains peace and is ever happy in spirit.

Love of God is like an ocean. There are as many forms of it, as there are gulfs and bays in an ocean. Each devotee has his own form of devotion and likes to choose a form or an aspect of God to offer his love and enjoy the pleasure so obtained. This becomes the worship of *iṣṭa devatā.*

All souls are sprung from God as sparks from a central fire. They inherently seek to reunite with Him, each according to his own suitable way. Though the soul has to accept the limits of the body and act within these restrictions, it should never be unmindful of its own essential purity and eternal freedom. Man should also never forget that every human conception of God is imperfect, because it is impossible for an embodied soul to grasp and understand God fully due to the limitations of his body, mind and intellect. Therefore, man should try to perfect his own conception of God more and more.

Devotion requires the two, the devotee and God. God is not the Absolute, the Unmanifest, but the manifested Lord, also called *Īśvara,* the highest manifestation of the Absolute, which is vouchsafed as the human soul. The different chosen deities are

55. *Śrīmad Bhāgavata Purāṇa,* X.29, 15

like the rays of *Īśvara* to suit the spiritual needs of devotees. When the devotee allows his chosen deity to enter his heart, the peace He brings to him is so great that he gradually yearns to crave for Him always. His presence in his heart is his prosperity, whereas His absence is his great adversity. The true devotee consecrates all his actions to Him alone.

Affection is what dwells in pleasure. It springs from the heart of man. Man will not get pleasure by staying in a particular place. The pleasure is in his own heart. He alone has to understand and feel it. Man can choose any God that attracts his affections to the highest possible degree. God is to be propitiated with extreme affection.

> With their mind wholly in me, with the senses absorbed in me, mutually enlightening and always speaking of me, they are satisfied and delighted. To them ever steadfast and serving me with affection, I give that *buddhi-yoga*[56] by which they come to me.[57]

Iṣṭa devatā, chosen deity worship, enables one to acquire this knowledge of God's greatness. According to the doctrine of *iṣṭa devatā*, anybody can conceive God in his own way as the perfect ideal of his own thinking. But the choice of the chosen deity should suit his nature, and it should respond to his needs and capacities. A symbol, an image, an incarnation of God, a spiritual *guru*, all these stand in the place of the chosen deity, according to the need and the mental state of the worshipper. Naturally, the devotion should always be of *sāttvika* type. Then it is possible to obtain and maintain permanent bliss.

The personal God, or the chosen deity worshipped by a devotee, is only a relative aspect of the Supreme. It is the highest possible understanding of God by man. For the smooth flow of man's love in his life, *bhakti* can only be directed towards the personal aspect of the Supreme Being as chosen by the devotee.

56. A particular mental condition of devotion.

57. *Bhagavad-Gītā*, X.9-10.

The idea of a *iṣṭa devatā* is to realise the Divine Truth. Everyone who wishes to realise this Truth has the freedom to choose his God. The love of God itself is the love of Reality. Spiritual practice begins by investing the chosen deity with all noble qualities attributed to the Supreme, and then worshipping Him. The devotee gradually acquires the fundamental characteristics of his chosen deity. But as an embodied being, a devotee should think of himself as a mere servant of God.

A devotee may love and worship the chosen deity with his whole heart, but he should be liberal enough to give the same freedom of thought and act of worship to others too. An aspirant of devotion should keep in his mind that his chosen deity is his own view of the divine truth from his level of spiritual development. According to the great seers there are different openings to the nature of God they have realised.

An honest study of the principles of devotion reveals that the path of devotion is non-sectarian. Its aim is to hold direct communion with God, who is the Soul of all souls. The seers avoided providing us with the exact definition of God, because they felt that any description of God brings Him down to the mortal level of a finite object of relative knowledge. Every description of God can only be according to the stage of spiritual development of the devotee, and so, each view of God is merely a partial view of Him.

Man can reach God only through love, unbroken love, cultivated at his highest spiritual level. From the love of God ensues the love of everyone in the universe as a sure effect. The nearer man approaches God, the more he begins to see that all things are in Him. When the soul succeeds in earning the bliss of supreme love, it also begins to see Him in everything. Man's heart will thus become an eternal fountain of love.

In the intense state of devotion, worship is offered to every being, being aware that God is in every being.

6

Rāmānuja's Teaching of Bhakti

May my mind be filled with devotion towards the highest *Brahman*, the abode of Lakṣmī;
Who is luminously revealed in the Upaniṣads;
Who in sport produces, sustains and reabsorbs the entire Universe,
Whose only aim is to foster the manifold classes of beings that humbly worship him.
— Śrī Rāmānuja's invocation in his commentary on *Brahma-Sūtra*

A Résumé of the Concept of Viśiṣṭādvaita

GOD, BRAHMĀ AND BRAHMAN

In Viśiṣṭādvaita Vedānta (qualified non-dualism) the words *Īśvara, Nāyaka, Paramātmā, Parameśvara, Sarveśvara* and *Bhagavān* mean the same God. Even the term *Brahman* used in Vedānta bears the same meaning too. The four-faced Brahmā is the first deity of the Hindu trinity,[1] who was brought into existence by the Supreme Lord for the sake of creating the material universe. This Brahmā is different from *Brahman* of the Upaniṣads referred to as the Ultimate Reality or the Supreme Being. In Viśiṣṭādvaita, the Supreme Being is referred to as Nārāyaṇa. Brahmā and Rudra, or Maheśvara, are the creations of Nārāyaṇa, the Supreme Lord. "Nārāyaṇa is the Supreme Deity, from Him was born Brahmā, the four-faced, and from Brahmā arose Rudra."[2] Both Rudra and Brahmā are thus subject to origin and *karma*.

1. Brahmā, Viṣṇu and Maheśvara.
2. *Varāha Purāṇa*, 25-26.

Hence, they cannot be accepted as Ultimate Reality. As regards Viṣṇu, who is included in the Trinity, the Hindu epics say that the Supreme *Brahman* or Nārāyaṇa assumed the form of Viṣṇu for the protection of beings.[3] Brahmā incarnated as Viṣṇu of the Trinity.

THE ABSOLUTE, PARABRAHMAN

In Viśiṣṭādvaita, *Parabrahman,* the Absolute of the Upaniṣads is the personal God under the name of Nārāyaṇa. He is the sole Creator of the universe. He sustains and controls the universe and He is the one, who causes the dissolution of the universe.

> He who dwells in *jīva* (soul) and with *jīva,* whom *jīva* does not know, whose body *jīva* is, and who rules it from within, He is the Self, the Inner Ruler, immortal. He is unseen, unheard, unperceived and unknown but sees, hears, perceives and knows, not like any of us with the help of senses, but directly without their help. There is no other seer like Him, no other hearer like Him, no other perceiver like Him, and no other knower like Him.[4]

Rāmānuja, referring to the *Bhagavad-Gītā* (X.39), says that there is nothing in the universe, which exists without having *Brahman* as the inner controller. Because *Brahman* is the inner Self of the universe, the two are inseparable. "The universe is the body of *Brahman*."[5] Śrī Kṛṣṇa says in *Bhagavad-Gītā*: "An everlasting part of Myself, has become the bound Self in the world of life."[6] Similarly, *Subāla Upaniṣad* declares that matter and soul in all their states constitute the body of the Supreme Self and that *Brahman* is the inner Self of all beings.[7] As *Brahman* is beyond the scope of perceptual experience, Viśiṣṭādvaita seeks to establish the Truth

3. *Rāmāyaṇa*, VII.101.26.
4. *Bṛhadāraṇyaka Upaniṣad*, III.7.22-23.
5. *Viṣṇu Purāṇa*, I.12, 38.
6. *Bhagavad-Gītā*, XV.7.
7. *Subāla Upaniṣad*, VI.I.

on the strength of scriptural testimony. The sensual objects and the living beings are not self-existent and self-maintained but spring from *Brahman*; they are sustained by His pulsating life and exist for His satisfaction.

RĀMĀNUJA'S VIEW

Based on the above statements, Viśiṣṭādvaita considers that the universe has its meaning and motive only in *Brahman* as the life of His life and the Lord of the lords of experience without the imperfections of the body. According to Rāmānuja, the sentient (*cit*) and the insentient (*acit*) are eternal, but not external to *Īśvara*, who is the all-inclusive Infinite. The Infinite enters the finite, evolves the names and forms of the finite and resides in them as their eternal inner Ruler without being tainted by their defects.

Rāmānuja uses several expressive terms to describe this inseparable and integral unity. Some of these are the body and the soul (*śarīra-śārīra*), the subordinate and the principle[8] (*śeṣa-śeṣī*) and the mode and the substance (*prākāra-prākārī*). All these terms unfold the various aspects of the "inseparable union" (*apṛthak siddhi*) of the soul (*jīva*) and the Supreme (*Īśvara*).

The difference between the soul and the body is well illustrated by an analogy of two birds sitting on the same tree, one of which is Self-resplendent and blissful, while the other tastes the sweets and bitters of life.[9] The truth of *Brahman* as the Soul of all beings is clearly indicated by the Āḷvārs and summed up in *Divya Prabandha*.[10] Rāmānuja argues that the fundamental truth of *Brahman* as the Soul, the principle or substance provides the key to the understanding of all philosophical systems.

---

8. Also called the servant and the master.

9. *Śvetāśvatara Upaniṣad*, IV.6.

10. *Divya* denotes divine, Supreme Being, *prabandha* means that which captures Him. *Divya Prabandha* is also called Tamil Veda, compared to the classical Veda which is in Sanskrit.

The philosophy of Viśiṣṭādvaita gives a synthetic view of the spiritual experience of God (*Brahman* of the Upaniṣads). Rāmānuja revived the "qualified non-dualistic" form of the ancient commentators. In expounding the nature of Reality, he harmonises the claims of revelation, intuition and reason. He accepts the scriptural authorities like the Vedas, the Āgamas and the *Bhagavad-Gītā*. *Brahman* is Absolute Truth, Good and Blissful. The scriptural Truth can be verified practically through personal experience. The real proof of the being of God is being in God.

The Āḷvārs are specialists in spiritual experience. In their Tamil writings, namely *Divya Prabandha*, they have recorded their own experiences of the Supreme. Since they are the seers of the truth, their sayings are as trustworthy as the Vedic sayings.

Viśiṣṭādvaita affirms the truth that *Brahman* is the ground of all existence and the goal of all experience, the first and final cause of all things. "The knower of *Brahman* attains the Highest."[11]

Reality has three essential attributes known as the qualities of being the support (*ādhāra*), the supporter (*vidhātru*) and the whole (*śeṣin*). Reality is determinate and can be defined by stating its essential qualities. The Upaniṣads declare *Brahman* to be Truth (*satya*), Knowledge (*jñāna*), Infinite (*ananta*), Sinless (*apahata pāpman*) and Blissful (*ānanda*). *Brahman* is the source and sustenance of all beings and all things; the sentient and the non-sentient (*cit* and *acit*) are existing only for His satisfaction.

Karma, the law of cause and effect of moral experiences, brings to light the inner working of the righteousness of God. Justice consists in the proper sharing of rewards and punishments of each soul (*jīva*) according to the nature of *karma*. In this manner divine virtue realises itself by making the finite Self the cause of its own destiny. Every action must have its effect in the form of

11. *Taittirīya Upaniṣad*, II.1.

saṁskāra or *vāsanā*,[12] whether good or bad. What a man sows, he so reaps. The law of *karma* affirms the freedom of the Self. The *jīva* can control its moral tendencies established in its subtle body (*sūkṣma śarīra*). The individual can make or mar his future. Spiritually the Self is eternal, and it is only *jñāna* that is subject to adventure. The constant urge to do evil and the ever-increasing burden of sin associate the Self in the endless cycle of transmigration. *Avidyā* and *karma* form an endless cycle and their effect cannot be removed by death or divine punishment. The Self or the soul can only attain freedom, when it regains its spiritual consciousness and realises its relation as a mode of God.

THE RELATION BETWEEN GOD AND THE HUMAN BODY

The essential truth of Viśiṣṭādvaita is the concept of God (or *Brahman*) as the "owner of the body", "the sentient" and "the non-sentient" as His body. This is known as the "relation of body and soul".[13] Rāmānuja defines the body as a substance, which is supported completely by a sentient soul or Self, controlled for its own purposes and which is subordinated to the soul. The Self abides in the Absolute; lives, moves and has its being in it. It depends on it for its form and functions and subserves its end. God sustains the soul as its Self and inner ruler and uses it for His satisfaction in the same way, in which the soul animates and sustains the body and uses it for its own satisfaction.

Just as a person is different from his dwelling place, in the same way the subject of experience is different from the object. Owing to the false identification of the Self with the body, it is called empirical Self (*dehin*); and its life is influenced by the three *guṇas* of *prakṛti*, namely *sattva, rajas* and *tamas*. As the body is composed of the principles of *prakṛti*, it is also subject to decomposition and is therefore perishable, while the soul (*ātman*) is indestructible.

---

12. Latent subliminal impressions.

13. *Śarīra-ātmā bhāva*.

> The intelligent Self is neither born nor does it die. It did not originate from anything, nor did anything originate from it. It is without birth, eternal, undecaying and ancient. It is not injured even when the body is killed.[14]

The soul (*ātman*) is eternal and changeless. The changes in the body along with birth, childhood, old age and death are the natural transformations, while the soul is free from the effects of *guṇa*s and so is free from the influence of *guṇa*s (*nirguṇa*[15]). The empirical Self puts on a body at birth and casts it off at death. "Fire does not consume the *ātman*, water does not wet it and air does not dry it. It slays not another *ātman*, nor is slain by any."[16] The nature of *ātman* is difficult to know, as it cannot be proved by logic. Śrī Kṛṣṇa says, "What cannot be logically defined can only be known in terms of experience by direct intuition."[17] Owing to *avidyā* and *karma*, the soul (*ātman*) mistakes itself for non-Self that is engaged in the empirical life of bondage and migrates from body to body.

This soul (*jīva*) is infinitesimal in its monadic existence; its attributive knowledge can be infinite and all-pervasive like the light of the sun. "The Self is infinitely smaller than the hundredth part of the point of a hair, divided a hundred times and yet it is infinite in its range."[18] The *ātman* has more potentiality than the stars. The consciousness of the *jīva* is capable of having a cosmic range and can mirror the whole universe. Like light and luminosity, the centre of a circle and its circumference, the *ātman* and its knowledge are logically distinguishable but physically inseparable. *Jñāna* is the determining quality of *ātman*, but it is also subject to the changes of

14. *Kaṭha Upaniṣad*, I.2.18.
15. Without qualities.
16. *Bhagavad-Gītā*, II.23, 30.
17. *Bhagavad-Gītā*, II.29.
18. *Śvetāśvatara Upaniṣad*, V.9.

contraction and expansion in the empirical state of bondage, because it is enveloped by *avidyā* and *karma*.

In liberation, *jñāna* regains its essential state, being eternal and infinite. Consciousness, which is in the finite and conditioned state, therefore comprises the possibility of becoming infinite. In liberation, when the bondage of *karma* is destroyed, it returns to itself and shines forever as infinite consciousness. The soul as the material Self is imprisoned in its body-mind-complex (*sthūla śarīra* and *sūkṣma śarīra*) and enjoys sense pleasures. When its desires are rationalised by discrimination, it rises to a higher level of Self-feeling and enjoys the happiness of Self-realisation. But when it perceives the Supreme, who is its inner Self, it enjoys Eternal Bliss.

Deeds, good as well as bad, are never lost, and the *jīva* that has done meritorious deeds ascends after the death of the physical body to a higher region and enjoys the pleasures resulting from good acts. But these pleasures too are as fleeting as earthly pleasures and are besides, affected by mental depression due to submissiveness to inferior gods. When the merits are exhausted by enjoyment, the soul returns to the earth to be reborn in a new body, which is determined by the residual *karma* and begins a new life in the new environment.[19]

The *jīva* that has a record of sinfulness is hurled downwards, suffers from pains proportionate to its evil deeds and is reborn in the world with a new opportunity to undo the past. Thus, the Self has the freedom to grow into *sāttvika* goodness or lapse into *tāmasika* wickedness. The Self subjects itself to be caught up in the life cycle. While destiny drags the soul downwards and subjects it to sorrow, the inner divinity in each *jīva* can urge it to choose the way of blessedness. Thus, the soul drifts between destiny and divinity until it decides on *mukti* and becomes a seeker after salvation (*mumukṣu*).

19. *Chāndogya Upaniṣad*, V.10.5-7.

Mukti is the return from the empirical life to the being of *Brahman* and is thus a reversal of the empirical process due to the complexities of *avidyā, kāma* (desire) and *karma*. A seeker after *mumukṣu* longs to go back to his home in the Absolute.

RELIGION AND PHILOSOPHY

Viśiṣṭādvaita sees no difference between the Absolute of philosophy and the God of religion, and reconciles the claims of logic with the needs of religious feelings. It is the supreme merit of this philosophy that it follows the logic of religious intuition, and concludes that *Brahman* of the Upaniṣads, *Brahma-Sūtra*,[20] *Bhagavad-Gītā* and other scriptural texts connotes the same Supreme Self, and insists on Bhakti Yoga as the direct means of knowing *Brahman*. Realisation of *Brahman* (*brahma jñāna*) is immediate as *Brahman* is ever Self-realised.

Brahman as *Īśvara* becomes a redeemer and finally the Lord of Love. To Rāmānuja, *Brahman* as the ruler of the soul, *jīva* is the endeavour as well as the end; and his scheme of *sādhanā saptak* is helpful in the build-up of *bhakti*. Meditation on *Brahman* finally frees the soul from *karma* with its causal chains of merits (*puṇya*) resulting from good deeds and sins (*pāpa*) resulting from wrong deeds.

Rāmānuja's scheme of *sādhanā saptaka* comprises:

1. Purification of the body by consumption of *sāttvika* food, which leads to the purity of mind (*viveka*),
2. Getting rid of sensual attachment or anger for securing mental tranquillity (*vimoka*),
3. Repeated reflection of God, who is immanent in the human souls (*abhyāsa*),
4. Performance of the religious duties, which will provide inner mental strength (*kriyā*),
5. Development of ethical virtues such as honesty, integrity,

20. Also called *Vedānta-Sūtra*.

compassion, benevolence, non-violence, etc. which will give inner purity (*kalyāṇa*),

6. Freedom from despair due to disappointments and unexpected calamities (*anavasāda*), and lastly
7. Not to be overpowered by excessive joy, so that tranquillity of mind is not disturbed (*anuddharṣa*).

The chief aim of *sādhanā saptaka* is the practice of moral and spiritual disciplines by the harmonious development of thought, feeling and will.

JÑĀNA, CONSCIOUSNESS

Consciousness is also an attribute of the soul. There are two types of consciousness: substantive consciousness[21] and attributive consciousness.[22] The former is the inward consciousness, while the latter is outward. Substantive consciousness makes the soul aware of itself but not of the external objects, but still has the knowledge of what is revealed to it. Attributive consciousness reveals itself as well as the external objects, but does not know them. The functional knowledge of the latter is comparable to a light, which reveals the presence of an object, but it does not know it. The *jīva* and the Supreme (*Īśvara*) know their own awareness, but they do not reveal the objects outside them.

God's substance is pure knowledge; and His attributive consciousness covers all existence. It is limitless, because He is unaffected by *karma*, which causes the limitation of knowledge.

When the attributive consciousness of the soul is suppressed, it is as good as any insentient matter; but since it has the potentiality of developing that external awareness, it can reveal itself. That is to say, in the state of ignorance, the *jīva* is almost one with the unconscious

---

21. *Dharma jñāna*.
22. *Dharma bhūta jñāna*.

matter, but owing to the substantive consciousness, it keeps up its individuality and the possibility of developing attributive consciousness, which in turn provides for the knowledge of its real nature. When the *jīva* is liberated, it continues to preserve its individuality, but its attributive consciousness expands and becomes merged in God. But yet the *jīva* never merges in Him. It is like a small wick light kept before a blazing light of intense splendour. The light of the wick lamp continues to have its individuality, but its radiance becomes merged and indistinguishable from the blazing luminosity of the other, yet it does not merge. Just like the luminosity of the stars becomes indistinguishable with the sunlight, yet the stars do not merge in the sun.

JĪVA AND ĀTMĀ

When the *jīva* is called *ātmā*, it means that it is a spiritual ego or I-sense imprisoned in a body. The real nature of the spiritual ego is to be distinguished from the ego of the *jīva* in bondage, when it identifies itself with the nature born body-mind. Basically, the *jīva* is the body of God as His *śeṣa*.[23] The body-bound ego is only a pseudo-ego. One of the central tasks in spiritual endeavour is the liberation of the true spiritual ego — denoted by *ātmatva* — from identification with the pseudo-ego.

A special characteristic of the *jīva* is that it is atomic in nature. The word atomic here does not mean a particle but a monad or attributive consciousness spread everywhere. The atomic nature of *jīva* indicates its indestructible individuality. It is this atomic nature of soul, *jīva* that provides for its separation at the time of death. Souls are countless. They are all of the same nature of consciousness and bliss.

THREE GRADES OF JĪVA

Rāmānuja maintains the gradation in the capacity of the *jīva* to

23. One who exists for the purpose of the Lord. The individual Self.

a limited extent. The three grades of a soul are *nitya sūri* or *nitya mukta*, *mukta jīva* and *baddha jīva*.

Nitya sūri or *nitya mukta* are eternally free souls. They form an inseparable part of the divine nature and have never been in bondage of *karma* and of empirical life. They have always been in attendance at Him, being His principal attendants.

Mukta jīva are liberated souls. They are those, who, evolving through all bodies, come to the stage of human birth at last and eventually attain salvation through spiritual disciplines and surrender to the Divine. By the grace of God, they are liberated from *saṁsāra* and raised to the status of residing in the abode of God, where they get a new spiritual body of transcendental spiritual consciousness.[24] In this abode,[25] they become His instrument of service or remain absorbed in the bliss of *Brahman*. They become one with God in knowledge and bliss, but not in power.

Baddha jīva, the bound souls are not liberated. They evolve gradually in the cycle of life and death according to their *karma* until they eventually get liberated. As long as the body is alive, there is no liberation for the *jīva*, because the cause of embodiment is *karma* and *karma* is only exhausted when the physical body perishes. *Mokṣa* in the fullest sense, is attained only with the death of the present body, after which the released soul is clothed in a body of pure *sattva* (*śuddha sattva*), with which the soul can commune with God and experience His loving presence eternally.

Rāmānuja's main interest was to find unity behind the diversity that exists in Vedānta thoughts. He considered rapturous devotion to a personal deity more important than philosophy. He took every effort to enhance the excellences of Nārāyaṇa. He was aware that an ordinary man required a concrete form or conception of God to attain spiritual insight.

---

24. *Śuddha tattva*.

25. This abode of God is called Vaikuṇṭha.

The practice of concentration on a formless, abstract consciousness endowed with attributes is almost impossible for individuals — except for highly advanced aspirants.

TIME (KĀLA)

Rāmānuja gives a very particular importance to the concept of time. Generally, except *Brahman* and the soul (being sentient called *cit*), all categories are supposed to come under *prakṛti*, which is called *acit* being insentient. *Prakṛti* is the substratum of the three *guṇas*. As *sattva* in *prakṛti* is mixed with *rajas* and *tamas*, it is also described as *aśuddha sattva* (impure *sattva*, non-spiritual consciousness). Outside the bound of *prakṛti*, there is an entity devoid of the three *guṇas*.[26] This entity is called *kāla* (time). Being outside the scope of *prakṛti*, time does not dissolve in the Supreme Being. It resides in Him, and it is through time that the Supreme Being activates *prakṛti*, submerged in Him, to evolve into the various categories. Though called insentient, time is a special and unique glory (*vibhūti*, auspicious manifestation) of God, as the whole creative and dissolutive process of *prakṛti* is regulated by this category.

SPIRITUAL CONSCIOUSNESS (ŚUDDHA SATTVA)

The bodily form assumed by *Īśvara* in his eternal abode is constituted of spiritual consciousness, *śuddha sattva*.[27] It is considered as the non-material, spiritual substance, of which the body of Nārāyaṇa is constituted. *Prakṛti* forms the substance of which all the world systems and the bodies of their residents are formed. Nārāyaṇa and His abode (*Vaikuṇṭha*) are outside the pole of *prakṛti*, and so the substance, of which they are constituted, is also not within the sphere of *prakṛti*. The special feature of *śuddha sattva* is that it is a substance of consciousness,

---

26. *Sattva śūnya* or "devoid of *sattva*" means devoid of the three *guṇas*.
27. There are many valid authorities in Hindu scriptures to uphold the existence of a non-material body of *Īśvara* constituted of *śuddha sattva*.

which reveals other things by itself. Until this spiritual consciousness flashes on the mind of a person, the soul continues to identify itself with material bodies. The light of *śuddha sattva* however enables *jīva* to know his spiritual identity.

Rāmānuja endows the Supreme with names and forms. According to him, the scriptural statement that the Supreme is beyond thought and speech only means that thought and speech can merely give a very partial, segmented aspect of the Supreme. The Supreme transcends the capacity of comprehension of the impure mind. Śrī Kṛṣṇa says,

> Supporting this mighty universe with nothing but one single fragment of Myself, I remain unchanged and transcendent.[28]

His transcendent aspect is supernatural and none of the human means of knowledge, like perception and reasoning, can comprehend Him. It is only through scriptures, which are superhuman in origin that an idea of His name and abode can be obtained. The Supreme Being is indicated by countless names, each name revealing some of His attributes or extolling His exploits in His incarnations. But Rāmānuja indicates Him mostly by four or five names: *Sat, Brahman, Puruṣottama, Bhagavān,* Nārāyaṇa, according to their particularities and personalisation. *Sat* meaning "being" is the most generalised name, indicating that He is the Infinite, out of whom various finite forms come into being, in whom they subsist and in whom they periodically dissolve. *Brahman* is that which has the quality of greatness and is of matchless excellences. His greatness consists in being the cause and the Lord of all. *Bhagavān* indicates that He is the most worshipful. The most intimate name chosen for the Supreme Being is Nārāyaṇa. Nārāyaṇa means "He, who is the dwelling place for the soul". This name of the Supreme Being is established based on the Veda, the *Mahābhārata* and *Mahā Nārāyaṇa Upaniṣad.* Nārāyaṇa is the indweller in Brahmā, Śiva, etc. All beings —

---

28. *Bhagavad-Gītā,* X.42.

from Brahmā down to inanimate objects — are subject to *karma*, bound to material bodies and are incapable of giving liberation to aspirants. Nārāyaṇa is the only worthy object of meditation and worship for those who want to be liberated from the bondage of *karma*, as He is not only unbound by *karma*, but He is the controller too.

In Viśiṣṭādvaita tradition, the form of Nārāyaṇa is made of *śuddha sattva*, which has been described as a spiritual substance not included in *prakṛti*. Just as God has a special name, He has a special Divine form, which is not a manifestation of a formless consciousness, but an ultimate part. It is one with His unique and inherent nature (*svarūpa*). There is nothing anthropomorphic about it, though its description may suggest that idea. In his commentary on *Bhagavad-Gītā*, Rāmānuja describes that form of Nārāyaṇa as:

> His one celestial permanent form is a treasure store of infinite qualities such as radiance, beauty, fragrance, tenderness, charm and youthfulness, which are inconceivable, celestial, wondrous, eternal, flawless, supremely excellent and appropriate to Him.

He dwells in the highest abode (*Vaikuṇṭha* or *Parama Pada*), which is not included in *prakṛti*. The natural senses and intelligence of the human beings — because of their impurity — cannot experience this form in His abode. But to a pure mind of an intensely devoted aspirant, He will reveal it.

The Universality of Rāmānuja's Teaching

Man functions at different levels; he relates to others intellectually and emotionally, but his essential nature is spiritual. There are opposite features in human personality, like love and hatred. Though seemingly there is need to cultivate love, in reality, this is not true. The opposite qualities are the inhibiting factions that have to be neutralised. One's true nature is to love; there is only mental restraint in discovering it.

Despite one's exposure to the teaching that the "Self is love", it is difficult to understand and to realise this Self-brimming with love. To realise this, the emotional traits should relax in the awareness of the Self. There is auto-criticism and self-disgust in all, a nagging doubt whether one is normal or not. These swinging moods and their experience show that man does not have total control over himself.

Moods determine man's emotional profile; and one has reason to doubt whether one is normal, because this vague feeling seems to get confirmed, when one is unable to control one's emotions in day-to-day life. Hindu traditional scriptures have recognised this aspect of human personality. Further, one looks forward to the prospect of a better moral life.

Rāmānuja says that man's emotional aspect has its roots in *Īśvara*, who resides in the heart of every being as the Inner Ruler (*antaryāmin*). The dualities of love and hate, right and wrong, good and bad that are gradually perceived are judgements of the mind. They do not touch Reality. So man's spiritual nature remains ever free from the judgements of the mind.

According to Hindu philosophy, an embodied human soul (*jīvātman*) is a partial expression of the Supreme Soul (*Paramātman*), which is the source of the manifested universe. Although in essence the two are the same and are indivisible, still the soul has become subjectively separated from the Supreme Soul and is destined to become united with Him again in consciousness, after going through an evolutionary cycle in the manifested universe. The mental process through which this unification of the soul and the Supreme Soul is attained in called *bhakti*. It is through intense love and devotion to the Supreme that the soul can attain Him.

Devotion need not have a religious support. But man is a religious being by instinct. There is a natural yearning in him for something beyond, for something that does not belong to his sensual and intellectual pleasures. Religion is a means for ennobling one's heart for the realisation of God. Man offers prayers daily to reach this end. Religion is mostly a personal concern and consists in the practice of certain principles. It is any system of faith and belief. A religious man is like an ardent patriot. The word "religion" usually denotes a way of life that helps one to reach an ideal or the highest goal of life.

Religion is not for many. Only some people can be religious. *Bhakti* proceeds from a real need. When man feels that he needs something beyond this world, something above all material forces, then he becomes a devotee. Constant meditation on the object, that is above all material forces, is also devotion.

Truth as well as Reality, like God, is the perfection of purity, constant and permanent light; and by taking refuge in Him, man leaves his sinful deeds behind. Only the eye of spirit can acquire the gaze of this Light.

Hindu traditions have formulated the steps, which an individual can decide on for success in his life journey. They lead him to the goal of enjoying permanent bliss in God's kingdom and consist in performing the scriptural duties as a service to God without any attachment to the results. Certain duties are to be performed for securing material prosperity, which should help him in carrying out the tasks mentioned in the stated injunctions. When observed in accordance under divine directions, all these will take man on the road to liberation.

Desire by itself is not to be condemned but should be turned towards enjoying the presence of God. The goal of one's action should be to serve God, whether one is religious or not. All actions performed by a person, who has oriented his life towards the spiritual goal, are acts of worship. Even if a person is non-religious, his simple act of providing food to the family members becomes a sort of worship of the Almighty, who resides in all. For a householder, all his actions right from his profession to his duties become transformed into worship, if he has devotion and dedicates his actions to the Supreme. The householder has to lead an active life to discharge his duties towards his family and society; and hence the spiritual quest at this stage involves developing devotion and orienting all actions towards the spiritual goal. This active stage in life will automatically lead to the stage of contemplation, after all the worldly duties have been discharged. When a spiritual aspirant reaches this level of spiritual evolution, worldly attachment will drop away on its own accord. Even while leading an active life in this world, it is possible to evolve spiritually, if one has the right approach.

When one's thoughts are always centred on the Supreme, the mind will develop concentration. Once the mind gets a taste of the peace resulting from the concentration on God, it will seek this peace instinctively. Initially, this requires efforts by allotting a specific time everyday to prayer and contemplation, but with practice the mind will be attuned to God effortlessly. This is similar to the comfort one feels in one's own home and the instinct to return, when one is away from home.

When the mind is sanctified with intense devotion, the Supreme accepts and enjoys immensely whatever the devotee offers. The value in worship is the inward yearning of the heart. *Īśvara* is to be worshipped in heart and soul.

Even if man's daily life is not considered as religious, it may be consecrated and transformed into worship. What a man does, what he eats and what he offers may be consecrated by the thought that the Supreme is the ultimate agent and the enjoyer of fruits. All the activities of life change over to worship, if He is looked upon as the doer, the enjoyer, the being propitiated and the deed itself. Adoration is placing the Supreme, be it God, the Reality or the Ultimate Truth, at the centre of life with love. This life is converted into a continuous sacrifice to the Highest. If one worships Him with love and lives in Him, God in His turn lives in him.

RĀMĀNUJA'S INFLUENCE ON BHAKTI IN INDIA

Everything in this universe is under the direct control of the Supreme Vāsudeva, and nothing can be gained without His grace. Devotion is a gift of God. The devotees have to choose God alone for aiding and completing the course of *sādhanā*.[29] The *Bhagavad-Gītā* declares, "Seek refuge in Him alone with the whole of your being. By His grace, you shall find supreme peace and eternal abode."[30] The *Kaṭha Upaniṣad* also says, "He reaches the end of the journey, the highest abode of Viṣṇu".[31]

One should worship God and follow Him alone to attain the Highest. Without surrendering oneself to God, one cannot get over the obstacles of *bhakti-yoga*. God alone is to be chosen for leading one to *bhakti-yoga* and for helping one to complete it successfully. Rāmānuja explains the significance of self-surrender (*prapatti*) as related to *bhakti-yoga*: Self-surrender to God is a necessity for the commencement of *bhakti-yoga*.

The universality of Viśiṣṭādvaita as a philosophy of religion lies in its synthetic insight into the truth and the spiritual transformation of insight into universal love. "*Sat* (Truth) is one, though the seers describe it in different ways."[32] Just as the water of all the rivers flows into the sea, the worship offered to all deities finally reaches the one God.

Rāmānuja's synthesis consists in his conclusion that all ideas and names ultimately connote *Brahman* or Nārāyaṇa and that the worship of deities like Indra is really the worship of Nārāyaṇa, the inner ruler of all beings.

---

29. Method or means adopted to achieve a goal.
30. *Bhagavad-Gītā*, XVIII.62.
31. *Kaṭha Upaniṣad*, III.9.
32. *R̥gveda*, I.164.46.

The silent power of love conquers everything in a mystical way. The vitality of the Vaiṣṇava movement is largely traceable to the influence of Rāmānuja, who himself represents the ancient tradition of Vedānta hospitality and love.

Devotion consists in converting self-centredness into God-centredness and turning the mind away from sensuality to the spiritual love of God. Equipped with the sevenfold *sādhanā* (*sādhanā saptaka*) and disciplined by the eightfold Yoga (*aṣṭāṅga yoga*), the devotee chooses any of the 32 meditations (*upāsanā*) and meditates on God.[33] Meditation consists not only in the intellectual knowledge of God, the feeling of his loving presence, but also the uninterrupted practice of devotion until the moment of death. Reflection clarifies the nature of devotion as the loving recollection of a prenatal contact with God. The feeling changes the recollection into a loving experience and will make the mood a devotional habit. In the course of time, love of God becomes a thirst for communion. The most inspiring truth of Viśiṣṭādvaita is its definition of God as love. Love mediates between thought and will by inspiring the former and illumining the latter. Śrī Kṛṣṇa brings out the inspiring message: "Whoever with true devotion worships any deity, in him I deepen that devotion and he ultimately reaches Me"[34] and "Even those, who worship other divinities, worship Me."[35] Even the lowest of the low and the worst sinner can attain God, if they trust the Supreme.

The Viśiṣṭādvaita tradition, worked out by Rāmānuja, invites humanity to dive into divinity and be merged in its immortal bliss.

THE BHAKTI MOVEMENT IN NORTH INDIA

The *bhakti* movement in north India is traceable to Rāmānanda (CE 1300–1411), who was deeply influenced by the teachings of

---

33. See Chapter on "Practical Approach to Devotion".

34. *Bhagavad-Gītā*, VII.21.

35. *Bhagavad-Gītā*, IX.23.

Rāmānuja. He was initiated into the truth of Viśiṣṭādvaita. Being a radical reformer, he refused caste distinctions in religion. He vitalised religion by freeing it from religious excesses and spread the message of universal nature of devotion. He is regarded as the source of the *bhakti* movement in north India; to him Rāma is *Brahman*, and there is no other God apart from Rāma.

Religion is the spiritual realisation of God by every person irrespective of social distinctions. The twelve disciples of Rāmānanda, who, like the twelve apostles of Jesus, ardently spread the faith all their life and by teachings in their mother tongue, came from all classes of society, but especially from the unprivileged backgrounds.

Raidas, a cobbler by birth, is said to have initiated Mīrā Bāī into the meaning of devotion. He insisted on the need for democratising devotion by service to all. Sena, a barber, made the king of Band Hogar (north India) a disciple of Vaiṣṇavism. Dhannā was a farmer, and Pīpā was a Rājpūt prince. Shukānanda, Asānanda, Paramānanda, Mehānanda and Ānanda belonged to the order of Rāmānuja too. The poet Kabīr is regarded as the greatest of Rāmānanda's disciples. He is said to be the son of a brāhmaṇa widow, who was brought up by a Muslim weaver. The story is told that Kabīr resorted to a device to obtain the grace of Rāmānanda. In the darkness of an early morning, he lay himself down on the *guru*'s path on the bank of the river Gaṅgā. Rāmānanda, touching the head of Kabīr, cried "Rāma, Rāma", and Kabīr felt that it was the *mantra* given to him by the *guru* for meditation. He did his best to unite Islam and Hinduism by synthesising the spiritual aspects of Vedānta and Sufism. A cotton cleaner at Ahmedabad (north India), named Dādū, believed more in God-realisation than in blind faith in the scriptures. He had interviews with King Akbar who was having in mind to bring divergent faiths together in a common bond of love. Sūradās, blind from birth, dedicated his poetic talents to the service of Śrī Kṛṣṇa. Tulasīdās was a brāhmaṇa, who had a genius for devotion to Rāma and composed his immortal *Rāmacaritamānasa* in Hindi language, which is highly valued for its moving power.

Philosophers, namely Nimbārka, Mādhava, Vallabha, Kṛṣṇa Caitanya, Jayadeva, the writer of the immortal lyric poem *Gīta-Govinda*, the mystics, Nāmadeva, Ekanātha, Tukārām, Rāmdās all affirm the necessity of devotion and self-surrender. True spirituality lies in the performance of one's duty with the heart set on God. All people are spiritually one in devotion though socially different.

In short, a seeker after God prefers devotion to liberation. Viśiṣṭādvaita prescribes a course of Vedānta culture or *sādhanā* — moral, spiritual and religious practices — to free oneself from the confusions of *avidyā* and the fetters of *karma* so that one attains God. *Sādhanā* consists in the build-up of devotion by *karma-yoga*, *jñāna-yoga* and *bhakti-yoga*.

7

Practical Approach to Devotion

The task of those who seek to cross the ocean of *saṁsāra*, rendered dangerous by the crocodiles constituted of the six passions (ardent desire, anger, greed, delusion, haughtiness and hatred), is very difficult indeed, if it is undertaken without the help of *Īśvara* as the boat. Therefore, resort to the boat of the worship of Śrī Hari (another name of Viṣṇu, the Supreme Being), the Supreme Lord, and cross this ocean of misery which is difficult to cross.

— *Śrīmad Bhāgavata,* IV.22.40

What great difficulty is there in communing with the Śrī Hari, who, like the sky, is pervading the hearts of all including yourselves, who is the soul of one's soul and who is the most genuine well-wisher and friend of all beings? And what special virtue is there in pursuing the vulgar enjoyments of the senses which can be had even in animal bodies? — *Śrīmad Bhāgavata,* VII.7.38

Neither philosophers nor contemplatives can attain the Lord with as much ease as those who are endowed with loving devotion.

— *Śrīmad Bhāgavata,* X.9.21

If a man, having by some good fortune got the rare embodiment in a healthy and perfect human body, fails to take shelter at the lotus feet of the Lord, he will fall into the pit of worldly life drawn by the attractions of the fleeting sense-objects and domestic affections, just as an animal falls into a well (covered or camouflaged with attractive grass). — *Śrīmad Bhāgavata,* X.51.47

Even though a person might have gained control over his senses and the *prāṇa,* if he has not surrendered himself at the feet of the Lord, all his efforts to discipline the extremely fickle mind, which is like an uncontrolled horse, will result only in the pain and trouble of striving, and he will be overwhelmed with deep sorrow because of failure. His condition will be like that of a party of merchants in the mid-ocean without a helmsman to direct the boat.

— *Srīmad Bhāgavata*, X.87.33

Consciousness of Devotion

"Having obtained *rasa* he becomes full of bliss."[1] *Rasa,* used in the sense of affection, *rāga-bhakti,* is the association of the soul in the Divine with love. It is a personal feeling. Moreover, the sense of awareness that "I am a devotee" may increase the ego in man, which becomes the cause of his downfall.

What is essential in the beginning is the desire to love and this love should provide happiness to man. Then this love is to be diverted to God or an object of merit, which a person naturally likes. Of course, in the beginning there will be vicissitudes in the content of devotion because of the imbalance in human nature arising from the three *guṇa*s. After a progressive practice, the mind learns to hold the object of love. The speed of success varies from one person to another, depending on the environment he finds himself in.

It is a utter necessity that makes man love God. At times it can just be the desire to live. When the time comes that man cannot live without God, who is above all material forces and beyond this world, then he automatically becomes a devotee of God. At this stage, there will be a development of his spiritual quest, and he feels the need to know God and to yearn for Him as his protector. Just as a hungry man goes in search of food, the sheer need makes man go in search of God. He, who desires God, will get devotion. Need makes man embrace devotion as his highest ideal and makes his senses aim at it. He will slowly work through his abilities to reach God.

1. *Taittirīya Upaniṣad*, 27.

Just as a mischievous but intelligent child who can be tamed, so too a person with tender feelings and love can be made to subjugate his heart to God. Rāmānuja provides a captivating example: A warrior adored his wife so much that he could not bear her suffering a trace of sunshine and hence held an umbrella over her head. Rāmānuja found him fit to be transformed and took this lover to the *sanctum sanctorum* of Śrī Raṅganātha's temple in Śrīraṅgam (south India). After witnessing the charm of the idol Raṅganātha, he got transformed totally and became a guardian of the Lord. Therefore, if the heart is filled with love, devotion flows on its own.

Usually, progress is gradual, and it is difficult to gauge one's progress. It is like the slow movement of the hand of a huge clock; it is like the study of language by infants. It is not easy to see the progress, although it is taking place all the time. The progress of a spiritual devotee can be compared to a man asleep, who is carried on a stretcher. He is not aware of the movement, although it is happening all the while. He will realise his progress not before he finds himself at the destination, that is, when he wakes up.

Man's outlook on spiritual life must be entirely different from that which concerns his worldly enterprises. In worldly matters, man's view is quantitative, and measurement is the technique to evaluate the progress or failure. However, he will not enter the realm of the spiritual world, until he gives up this method of calculation.

The spiritual devotee is like a hereditary cultivator. He will not take up agriculture as a business, but for the love of it. As soon as there is a drought or fall in the price of grains, the businessman gives up the work and takes to some other occupation, while the hereditary cultivator will not do the same. A genuine spiritual devotee considers spiritual practice as the only thing worth doing and carries on without looking for loss again. He firmly establishes in the hope that his faith and aspirations are getting stronger which is a sign of progress. There will be periods of ups and downs, when the thin flame of aspiration seems to disappear. But these are the phases that the genuine devotee will have to wait patiently for the mood to move away like a passing cloud. If man's longing for God is becoming increasingly captivating, he is on the safe track and is going forward. Moreover, peace, purity and strength will manifest in him.

Developing Devotion

"Let a man lift himself by himself. Let him not degrade himself, for the self alone is the friend of the Self and the Self alone is the enemy of the Self."[2] Man must work for God-realisation through the apt regulations of his mind, which alone is man's friend and foe. Those, whose minds are fixed on God as their end, who seek abiding union with Him and who possess supreme and eager faith, belong to the best class among men.

Many scriptures explain God, His powers, etc. in detail. But the proper understanding of the knowledge of God does not come before acquiring the personal experience in life. Those who have failed to get His experience, will become non-believers in God. But there are many, who believe in God, even without His experience.

Normally, each person undergoes only three states in his daily life, namely sleep (*nidrā avasthā*), dream (*svapna avasthā*) and waking (*jāgrat avasthā*). One does not care to seek or search for a further state. But the experience of God will take place in the fourth state, called *turīya avasthā* (also *samādhi*). Therefore, man can have the experience of God, who runs the universe, only after crossing over the three ordinary states of sleep, dream and waking.

God, the ultimate Truth, has to be experienced and realised in the depths of the fourth state (*turīya avasthā*). Certain practices are essential to reach this state. "Practising the method of

2. *Bhagavad-Gītā*, VI.5.

meditation, the sages realised that Being, who is the God of religion, the Soul of philosophy and the Energy of science, who exists as the self-luminous power in everyone, who is the source of intellect, emotions and will, who is one without a second."[3]

He, this Supreme Being, is called God, *Brahman*, *Paramātman*, etc. The joy of experience induced man to call God with different names, giving different meanings and forms. The whole universe is pervaded with His great power, *Brahman* of the Vedas and the Upaniṣads. So, the entire universe was named *brahmāṇḍa*, and the part of His power in man was called *piṇḍāṇḍa*.

In almost all the scriptures, God is called omniscient, omnipotent, omnipresent, etc. The Supreme Entity (*parātattva*) is named *Brahman* in Vedas, Viṣṇu in Purāṇa and Śiva in Tantra literatures. When man is able to cross over his ordinary state of consciousness by his own efforts and is able to expand it further, then only he is capable to have the experience of God, the Supreme Entity.

At first, one should strive to understand oneself completely. This means that he should realise his own soul (*ātmā*). Unless he realises his own *ātman*, he cannot at all have the realisation of God. When man is in the waking state, he is conscious of his body. So, *ātmā* will have the bodily experience of pain, misery, etc. During sleep, his mind will consciously experience many mental impressions in dream. But when man is in deep sleep, he will not have any emotions or memory; that is to say: man is neither the body nor the mind, but the real consciousness, that has left the body and mind behind. This real consciousness is *ātmā*. When this *ātmā* is in a body, it is called *jīvātmā*; the Supreme Entity is *Paramātmā*. Without the realisation of *jīvātmā*, realisation of *Paramātmā* will not take place. So, when self-realisation is attained through certain spiritual practices (*sādhanā*), the same practices will also lead man to God-realisation.

3. *Śvetāśvatara Upaniṣad*, I.3.

If the Self is referred to as mind, then the subdued mind is the friend of man, and the mind which is not controlled, is his real enemy. By the self, that is, by the mind, which is not attached to the sense objects, one should strive to transcend the Self. One should not, meanwhile allow the Self to be on the decline through an uncontrolled mind.

Life is like an ocean, in which the soul with a body (*jīvātmā*) is like an object, which might sink. The lingering attachments of the mind to objects are the causes of drowning. A mind with such attachments is a foe. Through certain disciplines, the mind may be kept aloof from such objects of attachment; then the mind is a real friend. "For him, who has conquered his (lower) Self by the (higher) Self, his Self is a friend, but for him, who has not possessed of his (higher) Self, the very Self will act like an enemy."[4]

The mind is the friend of him, by whom the mind has been conquered. But for him, whose mind is not conquered, the mind — like an enemy — remains hostile. "The mind of the man is the cause of his bondage and his release. Its addiction to sense objects is the cause of his bondage. Its separation from sense objects is the means of his release."[5]

Hinduism speaks of six mental enemies. They are ardent desire (*kāma*), anger (*krodha*), greed (*lobha*), delusion (*moha*), haughtiness (*mada*) and hatred (*mātsarya*).

Suppose a man wishes to buy a costly car, but cannot do so because of certain reasons, his desire to buy the car is his *kāma*. If his wife taunts him, saying that he is still not able to buy the car, her mockery makes him angry with himself and with his wife. This is *krodha*. Then he does everything to buy the car.

---

4. *Bhagavad-Gītā*, VI.6. Lower self is referred to the mind, when it is addicted to sense objects; higher self is referred to the mind, when it is not addicted to sense objects.

5. *Viṣṇu Purāṇa*, 6.7.26.

This is *lobha*. At this stage, he becomes self-centred. He thinks that he is in a high status and always moves around in his car; this is *moha*. Supposing an old woman tries to cross the road, while he is driving along, he becomes arrogant and assaults her. This is *mada*. When some day, he realises that his neighbour has a better car and is happy with it, it makes him develop hatred towards his neighbour. This is *mātsarya*. So, from desire arise anger, greed, delusion, haughtiness and hatred. If one cannot subdue one's desire, the same desire will envelop all its family members, namely *krodha*, *lobha*, *moha*, *mada* and *mātsarya*. Since the mind is the root cause of all these evils, it should be brought under one's control.

Lord Yama, the God of death, while instructing Naciketā on *brahma-vidyā* says

> Know the individual self as the master of the chariot and the body as the chariot. Know the intellect as the charioteer and the mind as verily the bridle. They call the organs (*indriya*) the horses, the organs having been imagined as horses (know) the objects as the roads. The discriminating people call that self, the enjoyer, when it is associated with body, organs and mind.[6]

Speaking of the Self *Bṛhadāraṇyaka Upaniṣad* says, "It thinks as it were and shakes as it were."[7] Though the Self is absolutely inactive, it appears to think and act, because the intellect does so. The proximity of the intellect to the Self creates this feeling of identification. So, "Man, however, who has, as his charioteer, a discriminating intellect and who has under control the reins of the mind, attains the end of the road, that is the highest place of Viṣṇu."[8]

Somehow, man's mind is to be taken to this highest level. This is the goal. By controlling the mind with all the sense

---

6. *Kaṭha Upaniṣad*, I.iii.3, 4.
7. *Bṛhadāraṇyaka Upaniṣad*, IV.3.7.
8. *Kaṭha Upaniṣad*, I.3.9.

organs, *jīva* should be led towards *paramātman* and then get fixed on him.

Generally, one assumes that happiness is attained by money. To earn more money, one gives more work to one's mind. This attitude causes mental strain resulting in mental tensions, which in turn leads to physical as well as mental diseases. It can be observed that poor people — unless greedy — are not generally affected by these chronic diseases, because their body works more than their mind does. But rich people, on the other hand, suffer from such diseases, because their mental thinking goes to the extremes. Part of the money thus earned, will be spent on curing the diseases. Their entire life will be caught in these poisonous surroundings, which bring endless sufferings. Therefore, it is wrongly assumed that money will give permanent happiness. Money can only give certain external comforts not happiness. Happiness should come from within the mind. Man thus spoils not only his external but also his internal surroundings with such wrong assumptions.

Desire in life is essential, but one should never cross the limits of one's desires. Man must work hard and earn the money that is essential. Just as consuming excess of food spoils the physiological system, so too, excess of mental work to amass material wealth, spoils the mind itself. Instead of remaining a slave to money, man should become a master of it. He must routinely invest some part of his day in earning the knowledge that is essential to move towards God, who alone can give him total happiness. Once man tastes this joy, the joy of remaining closer to God, he will never feel like withdrawing from that happiness. This experience of joy is to be the goal in life for everyone.

Lord Kṛṣṇa says

He who works having given up attachment, resigning his actions

> to God, is not touched by sin even as a lotus leaf (is untouched) by water.[9]

He did neither ask to keep away from worldly life nor to renounce work, but to work offering it to God, in whom alone lays real happiness. When one renounces his attachment to the finite ego and its likes and dislikes and places all his actions in the eternal God, he will for ever remain happy. So, the only way to achieve everlasting happiness is devotion. The aim is to lead the soul (*jīva*) nearer to the Supreme Soul (*Paramātman*), which should be the supreme goal in life.

The aim of devotion is to establish a definite relationship between man and God. Devotion is the love to be cultivated towards the One, who is to be propitiated. This love is a form of affection towards an object inseparably connected with joy. It is impossible to long for joy from an object without feeling affection towards it. Affection is most important in devotion.

"Affection is what dwells in pleasure."[10] Where there is no love, affection cannot reside. By nature, human beings are attracted to any person or object due to the pleasure it provides, however meagre it may be. People may be fascinated by a person, because they desire some kind of pleasure from him, be it physical, mental or emotional. When a particular object gives man the pleasure of emotional satisfaction, he becomes devoted to it. The soul in bondage — having lost the direct source of joy — starts searching for it in the external world, and anything that provides a small fraction of joy becomes dear to him. When a specific pursuit gives intellectual satisfaction, man will be devoted to it too. When he is frequently dissatisfied, he further searches for the subtle and constant joy and realises that it is within himself. At this stage, he understands that this inner joy is independent of external circumstances. Man feels contentment after the experience of this inner joy, bliss essence.

---

9. *Bhagavad-Gītā*, V.10.

10. *Pātañjala Yoga Sūtra*, II.7.

Devotion is the kind of affection accompanied with love, respect, high esteem, delight, etc. The element of sincere devotion on the part of an individual is the main reason in promoting a close relationship between God and the longing soul. Devotion must be nurtured and made to grow by personal efforts.

Desires arise from a sense of imperfection, which is characteristic of a man, who identifies himself with the ego. Once this ego is transcended, mental perfection is attained, since man will not feel the sense of imperfection. Such a feeling stays on in the mind when man finds something material outside himself, but a perfect man is not aware of anything other than God.

Śrī Kr̥ṣṇa speaks of the mental states of devotees:

> When a man completely casts off all the desires of the mind, his Self finding satisfaction in itself alone, then he is called a man of steady wisdom.
>
> He who is not perturbed by adversity, who does not long for worldly happiness, who is free from worldly attachments, fear and wrath, is called a man of steady wisdom.
>
> He who is not attached to anything, who neither rejoices nor is vexed when one obtains good or evil, his wisdom is firmly fixed.
>
> When he completely withdraws the senses from their objects, as a tortoise draws in its limbs, then his wisdom is firmly fixed.[11]
>
> He is said to be a steadfast *yogī*, whose heart, through knowledge and realisation is filled with satisfaction, who having conquered his senses never vacillates and to whom a clod, stone or gold are the same.
>
> He who has equal regard for well-wishers, friends and foes, for those who are related or indifferent to him, for the impartial and malicious and even the righteous and the sinful, he stands supreme.[12]
>
> He who never hates any being and is friendly and compassionate to all, who is free from the feeling of "I" and "mine" and even-minded in pain and pleasure, who is forbearing, ever content and

11. *Bhagavad-Gītā*, II.55-58.

12. *Bhagavad-Gītā*, VI.8-9.

> steady in contemplation, who is self-controlled and possessed of firm conviction and who has consecrated his mind and understanding to Me. Dear to Me is the one who is thus devoted to Me. Whom the world cannot afflict, he who is free from (worldly) joy and anger, fear and anxiety, he is dear to Me.[13]

Lord Kr̥ṣṇa gives instructions for developing devotion:

> With their mind wholly in Me, mentally enlightening and always speaking of Me, they are satisfied and delighted. To them, ever steadfast and serving Me with affection, I give that intellect by which they come to Me.[14]

Devotion makes the mind flow towards God. By purifying the emotions, it directs the intellect towards Him. The human mind is always restless. It is not only unsteady and turbulent, in which thought waves of various kinds furiously rage, but also powerful like a mad elephant. It is difficult for man to bring the mind under control. Therefore, he has to apply the means repeatedly, striving through various devices to fix the mind on God with a view to realising Him. Man can conceive the Divine in his own way as the perfect being and love and worship Him in his heart. This practice fixes man's mind on God, bringing in him the definite conclusion that God alone is the supreme object of love. Nothing in this world brings the least charm for him. In this state, he entertains no attraction, not even for the rarest enjoyment of the world. He devotes himself with exclusive love and supreme reverence to the constant remembrance of God alone.

Means of Developing Devotion

- Charitable gifts, vows, austerity, worship through divine symbols like fire, repetition of divine names (*japa*) scriptural study, concentration and several such spiritually uplifting disciplines generate loving devotion to Lord (Śrī Kr̥ṣṇa).

---

13. *Bhagavad-Gītā*, XII.13-15.

14. *Bhagavad-Gītā*, X.9-10.

- Learning, austerities, regulation of breath, kindliness, pilgrimages, gifts, repetition of *mantra* — none of these practices can purify the soul efficiently as the constant remembrance of the Lord (that is, evoking Him in the heart).
- Hearing (*śravaṇa*), recapitulating (*manana*) and meditating (*nididhyāsana*) are the necessary means to develop devotion. These exercises are like the shelling of grains. This shelling is to be continued until the grains are husked.
- The cultivation of tranquillity (*śama*), control of senses (*dama*), withdrawal of the senses from their objects and preventing them from going after the sense objects (*uparati*), forbearance (*titikṣā*), ardent faith (*śraddhā*) and concentration of mind (*samādhāna*) are essential in developing devotion.
- "Therefore he who knows thus, having become tranquil and self-controlled, withdrawing himself from desires, forbearing all pains of opposites, gaining concentration of mind, sees the soul (*ātman*) in himself."[15]
- Developing the concept of devotion, Śrī Kṛṣṇa says,

> Being endowed with the true knowledge of the soul (*ātman*), the devotee should check his mind from all outwards tendencies, discarding attachment (*rāga*) and hatred (*dveṣa*) that originate from the contact of the objects of senses. He must withdraw himself to a secluded place convenient for meditation.
>
> The activities of the mind, body and speech should be made conducive to meditation by control over the body and the mind.
>
> He must engage himself in meditation (*dhyāna yoga*), day in, and day out, developing an attitude of disinterestedness in everything other than the object of his meditation.

15. *Bṛhadāraṇyaka Upaniṣad*, IV.4.23.

> He must check the force of the latent impressions (*vāsanā*) and give up passion, anger, greed, delusion, arrogance, hatred, etc.
>
> He must liberate himself from the clutches of mineness and must rejoice the "Self-experience". Such a devotee realises the state of *Brahman* (*brahma-bhūta*). He desires nothing other than the attainment of the Lord. Such a devotee is blessed with the supreme devotion towards God.[16]
>
> Focus your mind on Me, be My devotee, be My worshipper, bow down to Me. Engaging your mind in this manner and regarding Me as your Supreme Goal, you will come to Me.[17]

Devotion is not a sterile remembrance of God's qualities, His form, His beauty, etc. but is the fixing of the mind on God without interruptions. This meditation is love of God because of which every act, performed by the devotee, is dedicated to God. By doing so, he gets submerged in the huge flood of his love towards God, considers Him alone as dearest to him, thinks of Him alone and engages himself in activities that please Him. He dedicates his heart and soul to the eternal service of his Lord. He serves God alone in all his actions.

The *Bhagavad-Gītā* expounds that only those devotees who perform all their duties — secular and religious — in a spirit of devout service to God, with firm conviction of attaining Him alone as their goal, and worship Him with meditation, salutations, praise and prayers with immeasurable joy, would very soon be saved from sorrows.[18] They alone would be blessed with divine communion. Śrī Kṛṣṇa says that every devotee should

---

16. *Bhagavad-Gītā*, XVIII.51-54.
17. *Bhagavad-Gītā*, IX.34.
18. *Bhagavad-Gītā*, XII.6-7.

strive to know and think of Him alone. He asks Arjuna to set his heart firmly upon Him and decide that He alone is the object of attainment, because only devotion can lead the devotee directly and quickly to reach the highest goal.

> For those who dedicate all actions to Me, hold Me as their Supreme God, intent on Me and worship Me, meditating on Me with exclusive devotion. Of those whose minds are thus focused on me, I become soon their saviour from the ocean of mortal life.[19]

Bhakti is the means to reach God. This intense love for God seeks after nothing but to attain divine communion. But it is not easy to achieve steadfastness in God, who was never before seen by the devotee, whose mind is drawn towards the objects of senses by his residual impressions (*vāsanā*).

The *Bhagavad-Gītā* teaches the ways of attaining steadfastness in God:

- Fixing one's mind on God by means of practice,
- Thinking lovingly, without any break, of the many auspicious qualities of the Lord and attaining firmness of meditation. One can gain this firmness by constant practice,
- Fixing the mind repeatedly on God, who is auspicious and far from imperfections. Practice (*abhyāsa*) and renunciation (*vairāgya*) are the two powerful means to check the outward tendencies of the fleeting mind,
- Curbing the mind from running to undesirable objects through renunciation, and
- Through practice, it must be bound to live in the object of attainment.

By this double process, the residual impressions (*vāsanā*) will be subdued, and the mind will be brought under control. By

19. *Bhagavad-Gītā*, XII.6-7.

constant practice, the mind remains firmly in the Lord, and with the help of such firm meditation, the devotee attains his goal.

SUBSIDIARY MEANS

But the mind is ever-changing and difficult to conquer. It may engage itself in such pleasures that are soon realised in this world. So, it might not be possible for the mind to practise and dwell in God. The mind may be impelled to engage itself only in worldly activities and never in practice. To such minds, the *Bhagavad-Gītā* shows another way of attaining firm meditation on God. Śrī Kr̥ṣṇa advises such devotees to associate themselves with some activity or the other that is related to God, according to their psychological background. By doing so, they will gradually attain, through practice (*abhyāsa-yoga*), a steady memory and steadiness of mind in God. So, people of such temperaments and abilities are required to engage themselves in activities, which are really devout services to God, such as building of shrines, raising flower gardens for the worship of God, lighting lamps for God, cleaning temple precincts, bringing flowers for worship, making garlands to decorate of holy images, reciting the holy names of God, praising the Lord with hymns, prayers and salutations, and so on. These activities enrich the devotee's devotion towards God; they are to be done with immense love for God and for the sole purpose of His pleasure. By following these different activities, the devotee will, in fact, be reflecting upon the glory of God, because all these activities are sacred, they are dedicated and related to God, and they comprise the reflections upon the Supreme Being. By doing so, the devotee becomes capable of meditating upon the auspicious qualities of God and ultimately attains Him through steadfastness. The *Bhagavad-Gītā* further says,

> If you are incapable of even this practice of repetition, then devote yourself to My deeds (service). For even by working for My sake,

> you will attain perfection. If you are unable to do even this, then, taking refuge in any disciplined activity, renounce the fruit of all actions with the self-subdued.[20]

Lord Kṛṣṇa suggests that if a devotee is not capable of doing even these divine duties that immediately precede the stage of *bhakti-yoga*, he should practice *karma-yoga* or the performance of disinterested actions, which leads him to Self-realisation, which in turn awakes in him intense love for God. The knowledge of the real nature of God will increase his love for God alone.

The example of a prince illustrates this. As a child, a prince wandered out of the palace to play and was taken away by hunters. He was brought up in the hunters' village and followed their activities. Soon after, he learnt from some honest and sincere well-wishers about his parentage and future destiny; he developed intense love for his father, the king, and went in search of him. Just like the prince, man will also develop deep love for God, after he realises his own soul. His love for God becomes spontaneous and intense.

The teachings of the *Bhagavad-Gītā* are adapted to the capabilities of several devotees and their practical needs. It prescribes different ways, which are practicable even for an ordinary devotee, keeping in mind the drawbacks and limits of the devotees in general. To encourage them to follow some practice (*sādhanā*) and to remove their depression of being unable to follow the direct way of attaining intense devotion, *Bhagavad-Gītā* suggests, as a first step, the path of *karma-yoga* (action) to them, which would eventually, perfect the practice of devotion.

The path of *karma-yoga* can only be efficient, when the mind is purified of all impurities in the form of attachment (*rāga*) and hatred (*dveṣa*) through disinterested actions. When the devotee has renounced his desire for the fruits of all his actions, he will

20. *Bhagavad-Gītā*, XII.10-11.

attain inner tranquillity (*śānti*), which gradually leads him to higher and higher stages of devotion. The mind only becomes calm, when its impurity is washed away by the means of detached action (*niṣkāma karma*, desireless action). Meditation upon the true nature of the soul becomes possible, only when the mind has attained tranquillity; one achieves Self-realisation only after meditation on the Self. Intense love to God will only be born of Self-realisation. To a devotee, who is incapable of following the path of *bhakti-yoga* instantaneously, meditation on *ātman* is more helpful than any other means. In the path of *bhakti-yoga*, a devotee is required to practice the various virtues that are conducive to the path of *sādhanā saptaka*.[21] These virtues are also enumerated in the *Bhagavad-Gītā*:

> He who has no ill-will to any being, who is friendly and compassionate, free from egoism, the I-ness, even-minded in pain and pleasure, and patient, the *yogī* who is ever content, self-controlled, unshakable in determination, with his mind and understanding given up to Me — he is My devotee and dear to Me.[22]

Being endowed with these noble dispositions, renouncing the fruits of all his actions (*karmaphala-tyāga*) he would attain higher stages of devotion through realisation of his Soul.

Renunciation of the fruits of actions destroys the sources of unrest and brings about inner calm and peace, which are the very foundation of a spiritual life. In such a life, knowledge and meditation become subordinate to devotional mind.

---

21 Purification of the body by consumption of *sāttvika* food, which leads to the purity of mind (*viveka*), getting rid of sensual attachment or anger for securing mental tranquillity (*vimoka*), repeated reflection of God, who is immanent in the human souls (*abhyāsa*), performance of the religious duty, which will provide inner mental strength (*kriyā*), development of ethical virtues such as honesty, integrity, compassion, benevolence, non-violence, etc. which will give inner purity (*kalyāṇa*), freedom from despair due to disappointments and unexpected calamities (*anavasāda*), and lastly not to be overpowered by excessive joy, so that tranquillity of mind is not disturbed (*anuddharṣa*).

22. *Bhagavad-Gītā*, XII.13-14.

The devotees of the *bhakti* path are classified into two categories, namely those who are capable of following the path of devotion directly and those who are incapable of doing so.

For the cultivation and development of devotion, certain points are to be noted:

- The knowledge of the individual soul and the Supreme Being through preceptors and holy books.
- Purification of the mind and activation of the proper disposition to maintain the purified mind through continuous and conscious effort.
- Implicit faith in the saving grace of God, through which alone the cultivation, development and fulfilment of a devotional life is possible.

The school of Viśiṣṭādvaita expounds the process of development of devotion as:

- Love of God, which is caused by the close association with people of *sattva* temperament and the study of scriptures.
- Performance of disinterested actions, lovingly dedicating the fruits thereof to the Lord.
- Reflection upon the true nature of the individual Self by the grace of God.
- Realisation of the Self as subservient to God.
- Realisation of the truth that the highest object of attainment in life is communion with God.
- Ardent desire and determination to obtain the vision of God, who is to be served.

The Concept of Purity in Devotion

The true aim of all religious treatises is devotion to God. The wise man, who takes to it, is the best of all. When God is pleased, devotion culminates. There is no greater delusion than devoting oneself to sacred treatises and not to God; such devotees are always under bondage.

Devotion consists in firm and overwhelming affection for God with a sense of His greatness. Liberation can only occur through this. Those, who get into the bliss of God, will have the experience of that bliss in themselves. But those who do not enter this state, enjoy God with their senses and mind, even if they are ordinary householders.

He who thinks of God as all and of himself as emanating from Him, and who serves Him with love, is a devotee. Without love, devotion is simply of an inferior type. But by reading and reflecting on the scriptural sayings, one would not only remove the mental taints but also increase one's devotion. When the mind is removed of impurities, love occupies its place.

The great devotee, Prahlāda expresses the wish that he may have the same attachment to God as one has for the sense objects.[23] One must find supreme pleasure in God. It is this natural and spontaneous attachment to God that is called *bhakti*. *Bhagavad-Gītā* says,

> Devotees live with their mind focused on God, their life centred on Him. They inspire one another by speaking of Him always. They live in contentment and bliss at all times.[24]

Devotion is a state of mind, which slowly merges in God and brings the mind and the soul along with it.

The principle means, by which devotion is attained through the grace of God, is the purity of heart. For the heart to be pure, one should purify the intellect, the emotions and the ego, which in turn strengthens the mind. The sole condition of knowing God is to aim at the purity of the three functions of the mind, namely intellect,

---

23. *Viṣṇu Purāṇa*, 1, 20, 19.

24. *Bhagavad-Gītā*, X.9.

emotions and ego. Jesus Christ puts this great truth in his oft-quoted words "Blessed are the pure in heart, for they shall see God."

It has been already said that *jñāna-yoga* purifies the intellect, *bhakti-yoga* the emotions and *karma-yoga* the ego. Man is free to adopt any of these paths. But to achieve the end quickly, it would be better to attempt a synthesis of these paths. However, as the mind is potentially homogeneous, any single path — strenuously pursued — would necessarily result in the purity of the entire mind; just as physical exercises, though confined to particular limbs or organs, necessarily result in the health of the whole organism. The path of devotion recommends a way for purifying the emotions in order to provide a proper basis and motive for the service of God. This path is considered the easiest of all.

There are certain means for attaining the purity of heart — some are external and some internal. They may seem to be difficult in the beginning, but the pleasure that results from the application of devotional principles is indescribable and incomparable. It springs from the cheerfulness arising from the knowledge of the Self. It is the non-sentient, transcendental bliss from the vision of the Self or the being with God. It is the highest pleasure, which arises from the gratification of the desire to be with God. It is supreme delight in the Self — due to the complete transformation of desires. "That experience, which is like a nectar, is *sāttvika*", says the *Bhagavad-Gītā*.[25] *Sāttvika* pleasure springs from complete self-control, control of the sense organs, the mind and the intellect. When it is attained, all sufferings are destroyed and the mind becomes peaceful (*śānta*). This peaceful state is required for the development of devotion.[26]

The mind becomes quiet, when it is free from all taints. *Śānta* is the calm state of mind, characterised by the complete cessation

25. *Bhagavad-Gītā*, XVIII.37.

26. Emotion of devotion (*bhakti rasa*) springs from peace and serenity (*śānta rasa*).

of its determinations and agitations. Rāmānuja regards *śānta* as the cultivation of the habit of restraining the sense organs from their natural tendency to enjoy their objects that cause mental impurity, which in turn causes mental restlessness. A restless mind, hankering after objects of enjoyment, cannot enjoy the supreme eternal Bliss. A restless mind cannot be the bliss of the Self. A person who does not meditate on *ātman* and whose mind cannot rest in it, cannot enjoy the bliss of beatitude. A tainted mind is not free from activities. So, it cannot enjoy the bliss of tranquillity. The mind should be purified of its impurities first. Listening to the scriptures, reflection on sayings, sense-restraint, mind control, endurance of pleasure and pain, withdrawal of the sense organs from their objects, dispassion for happiness and desire for liberation, should be practised earnestly and diligently until devotion becomes firm, strong and pure. Devotion is a royal science, a royal mystery, the supreme purifier and is realised by direct experience, pleasant to practise and is abiding.[27] Rāmānuja explains the purity of mind as freedom from anger and other emotions. The mind is free from uneasiness owing to anxiety for worldly objects. The transparency of the mind renders it fit for acquiring the immediate experience of the Supreme Self. Śaṅkara considers the purity of mind as self-abiding in its true nature.

Freedom from anger, anxiety, afflictions, actions, realisation of hopes and potencies is regarded as purity of mind. When the mind is freed from the impurities of doubt, desire, anger, envy, greed, attachment, pride, hatred, deceit, hypocrisy and falsehood, it becomes pure. When it is purged of the modes of *rajas* and *tamas*, it is regarded as pure. Mental purity is a saintly quality.

The purity of motivation is also very important to keep the purity of heart. Rāmānuja regards the purity of motivation as mental freedom from anxiety for other objects, which are different from the Self. Purity in motivation is the inner purity

---

27. *Bhagavad-Gītā*, IX.2.

of the mind accompanied by the purity of actions performed. In one's social conduct, the mind should be free from hypocrisy in one's behaviour with others, free from falsehood and fraudulence. The absence of hypocrisy is present in the mind by showing one's affection towards others. Hypocrisy is absent in straightforwardness, which is composed of sincerity or harmony of thoughts, words and actions. It is an essential factor of the purity of mind. It also implies the treatment of one's son, friend, wife, enemy and oneself, without any distinction.

In ordinary love, pleasure culminates in pain. It is the desire for enjoyment of tangible pleasures. An individual turns his mind away from God, directs it to the external objects of pleasure (owing to ignorance) and so suffers from pain of the embodied life. Sensual pleasure is always attended by tangible pain. Real pleasure, namely Bliss and peace (*śānti*) emerge from the absence of sensual pleasure and pain. "The *śānta* state of mind brings steadfast devotion to God."[28] When the mind is turned away from sensual pleasure and pain and is constantly fixed on God, who is the infinite Bliss, a devotee feels bliss.

To acquire and maintain the purity of heart, certain virtues like the cultivation of mental qualities, such as patience, good character, *śama*, *dama*, moral observances and so forth, are to be practised which will be dealt with later.

Śama is the steadfast attachment to God by the control of the external sense organs. *Dama* is the control of mind. Contentment is the conquest of sexual desire and greed. Charity is the non-punishment of the offender. Austerity is the renunciation of desires. Heroism is the conquest of the inner nature, while subordination to the sentient nature (of oneself) is pitiable. Wealth is the excess of good qualities. Happiness is the defeat of pleasure and pain. Hell is the predominance of *tamas*; heaven is the abundance of *sattva*. Compassion is intolerance of other's

28. *Śrīmad Bhāgavata*, XI.19, 36.

suffering. Knowledge is the true knowledge of the Self and Reality. Mastery is the power of controlling and guiding others. Tenderness is the melting of the heart by love. Śrī Kṛṣṇa recalls the duties such as austerity, purity, forbearance, uprightness, knowledge, special knowledge and faith as a means to control the senses and the mind.[29]

The *Śrīmad Bhāgavata* declares that the devotional practices destroy the taints of the mind produced by sins; they purify the mind. The seeds of sins cannot be completely burnt by penances, control of the sense organs and the mind, charity, truthfulness, purity of the body and mind, restraints and moral observances, though they can subdue them temporarily. The potencies of sins remain intact and generate other sins; penances without faith and devotion cannot purify a devotee of all his sins and their seeds. But supreme devotion to God can destroy all sins and burn up nescience (*avidyā*), which is their seed. Devotion destroys sins, just as fire burns a peace of wood to ashes. It destroys *avidyā* and purifies the mind of all.

Devotional practices such as the sight and the company of saints, listening to the excellence of God, chanting His name and glory, constant recollection of the Supreme, salutations to Him, worship, etc. destroy all sins, remove all misery and mental agony and dispel the darkness of ignorance. They purify the mind and produce higher knowledge and dispassion.[30] These acts involve frequent thoughts of God, the Pure and the Holy, which destroy the contrary thoughts of impurities and sins. Withdrawal of the mind from impure thoughts and its concentration on God weaken them, because they are no longer nurtured. Śāṇḍilya, who evolved the philosophy of devotion, confirms the teaching of the *Śrīmad Bhāgavata*. The acts of *bhakti sādhanā*, such as muttering and chanting the name of God,

29. *Bhagavad-Gītā*, XVIII.42.

30. *Śrīmad Bhāgavata*, XII.13, 23.

salutations, worship, prayer, meditation and the like, destroy all sins and impurities of the mind and purify it.[31] Listening to and chanting God's name and constant recollection of Him are atonements for sins. When a sinner repents his sins, the best form of compensation for his sins is the constant recollection of God. The act of devotion, however slight, can destroy great sins. Thus, devotion itself is the powerful expiation of all sins.

As said earlier, according to Rāmānuja constant and firm recollection of God is achieved by taking pure food, the absence of attachment to any object of pleasure, the frequent practice of concentrating the mind on a divine object, the study of scriptures, the performance of sacrifices, charity, austerity and dispassion, the practice of virtues like truthfulness, simplicity, compassion, benevolence, non-injury and successful thoughts, the absence of depression owing to grief and the absence of excessive joy. The purity of food generates the purity of mind, which improves the capacity of recollection. *Brahman*, the Absolute, ought to be sought through penance, celibacy, faith and knowledge. Self-control, mind control, listening to the scriptures and reflection on them are the duties relating to all stages of life. Listening and reflection are the means to the acquisition of knowledge. Frequent meditation on God, the object of prayer, is like a continuous stream of thought. God can be known through devotion, which increases purity.

The practice of virtues (*sādhanā*) is meant to bring in the natural perfection of the human soul by purifying the various faculties of the mind, especially the purification of emotions. The best way to succeed in it is to seek the constant loving association with God in one's own heart. One should always remember God; never should He slip away from memory. All

---

31. *Śāṇḍilya Bhakti Sūtra*, II.32.

rules are nothing but ancillary to these two. "By any method, whatsoever, one should focus the mind on God."[32]

THE CONCEPT OF PURITY IN BHAGAVAD-GĪTĀ

"Even a hard-baked sinner, if he comes to have an unswerving love to God, he soon becomes righteous and obtains lasting peace. My devotee never perishes."[33] During *sādhanā,* the devotee should hold the firm and right belief that God is always present by his side and that he is protected in His presence. All evil inclinations for attraction and repulsion, joy and grief, lust and anger and all worldly thoughts and doubts should be driven out of the mind. In this way, the mind should be purged of all impurities and made serene with the help of dispassion. The devotee should guard against sleep, lethargy, carelessness and other obstacles. He should bring the mind thoroughly under control and merge it in God with personal efforts, withdrawing the mind from external objects. Withdrawing his love from the outer world, the devotee should fix it on God and obtain an insight into the virtues, the glory, the truth and the mystery of God. The sight of God's form, exchange of words with Him, the touch of His person, thinking of Him and chanting His name, the obeisance offered to Him confers the highest sanctity even on the vilest sinner. The least remembrance, hearing and chanting God's glory and virtues possess purifying properties.

Bhagavad-Gītā stresses on the qualities of food to be taken by a devotee. His food should be conducive to influence devotion. The constitution of man's mind is determined by the kind of food he takes, and a man's faith corresponds to his mental constitution.[34] If a man's diet is pure, his mind too will be pure as a matter-of-course; the purity of thought, the feeling of faith

32. *Śrīmad Bhāgavata*, XI.13 14; VII.1.31.

33. *Bhagavad-Gītā*, IX.30-31.

34. *Bhagavad-Gītā*, XVII.7.

and other qualities and actions too depend on the purity of mind. When the mind is pure, the sacrifice, charity, penance, etc. will also be pure in nature.

The *Bhagavad-Gītā* advises the practice of worship of gods, devotees, one's elders and wise men, and the cultivation of purity, straightforwardness, continence and harmlessness as bodily penance.[35]

Austerity of speech consists in uttering only such words that are inoffensive, truthful, agreeable and free from all impurities of speech.[36] These virtues and practices remove all impurities of speech and purify it along with the mind. Mental austerity is the cheerfulness of mind, placidity, contemplation on God, control of the mind and the perfect purity of inner feelings.[37]

The mind should be freed from dejection and fear, anxiety and grief, agony and perturbation, restlessness, lust, anger and greed. It should be cultivated with the permanent blooming of virtues, like forbearance, love, politeness, etc. which will remove all mental impurities. Desire, anger and greed are the triple gates of hell bringing the soul to ruin. Therefore, these three states should be avoided.[38]

Man commits sins of various kinds under the impulse of desire. Infatuated by anger, man resorts to violence, retaliation and other sinful acts. Greed, the insatiable desire to take all that one can get with no thought of others' needs, involves man in the major sins. When he falls prey to desire, anger and greed, the quality of his thoughts, feelings and conduct begin to decline. Desire, anger and greed drive him to actions, which ruin his body, fill his mind with evil thoughts, impair his reasoning and

35. *Bhagavad-Gītā*, XVII.14.

36. *Bhagavad-Gītā*, XVII.15.

37. *Bhagavad-Gītā*, XVII.16.

38. *Bhagavad-Gītā*, XVI.21.

vitiate all his activities; as a result his life on the earth is robbed of its joy, peace and purity. When man understands that these evils are solely responsible for his degradation in every form, then only will he refrain from them. Having given up desire, anger and greed, and focusing on cultivating moral virtues, a devotee can aspire to attain the Supreme Goal.

Scriptures on devotion inculcate among devotees the attitude that holy company is necessary for the growth of one's spiritual life. Holy men are persons endowed with equanimity in all up-and-downs of life. They are full of mercy and friendliness to all. They are serene in temperament; goodness is their ornament. Holy company is one of the most important factors to strengthen faith and devotion. "Understand the true nature of knowledge by approaching illumined souls, prostrate before them with reverence, serve them and question them repeatedly. They will impart to you the saving Truth."[39] The company of holy men is highly conducive to obtain the purity of mind. Their good qualities bring great change in the mind of all.

The conception of a *guru* plays an important role in the purification of mind. Though God alone can bring spiritual enlightenment to a devotee, the spiritual master, under whom the devotee received the guidelines, forms the human medium. There is an intimate relationship between the conceptions of the *guru* and the personal god. The practice is to meditate on the *guru* first and then merge him mentally in the personal god.

Purity is an important factor. It sustains faith and longing for the Supreme. It is also useful to combine prayer with austerities like fasting, observance of vows, worship, etc. All these would add seriousness and concentration to the prayer. But, it has to be understood that God is not like a father in granting prayers. He is the judge of all, presiding over the *karma*s of all beings. If a man's *karma* is too adverse, the prayer may not be

---

39. *Bhagavad-Gītā*, IV. 34.

granted, as it may go against all moral laws. So, while it is legitimate for a devotee, who has intense faith in God, to pray to Him, he should not lose faith, if his prayer is not fulfilled. However, the assurance is always there: "Even if you be the most sinful of all sinners, you will cross over all sins by the boat of knowledge (concerning God) alone."[40]

For Sri Kṛṣṇa assures:

> For, I am inexpressibly dear to the man of knowledge and dear is he to Me.[41]
>
> He in whom there is surpassing love for Me, I hold him also as surpassingly dear to Me. You shall come to Me alone.[42]

Bhakti-yoga is possible only for those people, to whom God is very dear and who are free from all evils. Evils are so huge for some that the expiatory rites, which would wash them off, cannot be performed in the limited time of one's lifespan. In the *Bhagavad-Gītā,* Arjuna thought that he was unfit to follow *bhakti-yoga*, considering his so many evils. To remove Arjuna's grief Kṛṣṇa advises him,

> Completely relinquishing all *dharma,* seek Me alone for refuge. I will release you from all sins. Grieve not.[43]

To succeed in *bhakti-yoga,* one should seek God as refuge. God is supremely compassionate, the refuge of all without considering the differences of character among them. He is an ocean of tenderness for those dependent on Him; He will release the devotee from evil and sins, He will purify the heart and will take His abode in the devotee's heart. Supreme devotion to God is itself the best purifier of man's heart.

---

40. *Bhagavad-Gītā*, IV.36.
41. *Bhagavad-Gītā*, VII.17.
42. *Bhagavad-Gītā*, XVIII.65.
43. *Bhagavad-Gītā*, XVIII.66.

CONCEPT OF PURITY IN YOGA-SŪTRA

The *Pātañjala Yoga-Sūtra* also speaks of developing external purity (purity of the physical body) and internal purity (purity of the mind). It is well known that beneath the skin (that gives physical beauty) there is nothing but a mass of flesh, bones, all kinds of secretions and waste products, which arise disgust in the mind, when they come out of the body. Yet, man completely identifies with his body, so, despite his knowledge of its contents, he does not feel disgust for it, but regards it as his most loved possession. Many think that they have a physical body, which has a soul and not that the soul has a body.

With the purification of the physical body, man becomes increasingly sensitive and begins to see things in the true light. The purity of the physical body is to be brought about by ordinary external processes. It is essential as it enables the devotee to use his body for the devotional practices without any hindrance from it. Purity is attained from penance, which destroys the dirty veil of impurities. When physical purity is attained, the sense organs become purified too. "Purity contentment, austerity, self-study and self-surrender constitute observances."[44] In Yoga, the word "purity" is used in relation to man's vehicles, *kośa*.[45] Man can cognise the body not only with his physical senses, but also with super-physical vehicles, which serve as the instruments of emotion, thought and other spiritual faculties. Purification implies the elimination of those bodily and mental conditions that prevent man from exercising their proper functions, namely attaining the goal in view. A pure mind easily and naturally thinks pure thoughts and feels pure emotions; it becomes difficult for the pure mind to entertain undesirable thoughts and emotions in the same way as it is difficult for an impure mind to entertain high and noble thoughts and emotions. Purification is a positive practice in Patañjali's Yoga system.

---

44. *Pātañjala Yoga-Sūtra*, II.32.

45. The five *kośa*s are : *annamaya*, *prāṇamaya*, *manomaya*, *vijñānamaya* and *ānandamaya*.

Patañjali says that faith, courage, retentive power and keen intelligence are essential for *samādhi*.[46] *Samādhi* in the Yoga of Patañjali equals the highest stage of devotion in *bhakti-yoga*. Faith means the strong aspiration of the mind. It sustains the devotee like a benevolent mother. While faith is a mental tendency, devotion is a mental action. Through purification, the mental tendency should be brought to a state where all mental actions are directed towards God. Faith is the firm conviction that the Supreme (or God) exists. Faith is the state of inner certainty that is present, where a purified mind is irradiated by the light of the intellect. It is impossible to reach the goal without this kind of faith. In such a faithful devotee, courage is born. Retentive power comes to the courageous. When memory is freed from disturbance, the keen intellect shines to the maximum limits.

To reach the desired goal *Yoga-Sūtra* recommends the constant practice of one truth or one principle.[47]

The mental distractions or impediments are disease, debility, doubt, inadvertence, sloth, sensuality, wrong understanding, non-attainment of the stages of progress, and inconsistency in maintaining the reached stages. "Pain, dejection, unsteadiness of limbs, spasmodic inspiration and expirations are the companions of distractions."[48] All these above-mentioned obstacles keep the mind impure. They cause mental distractions, which hinder the devotee's practice of concentration and meditation. For the removal of these obstacles, there should be constant practice on one truth or one principle. When the mind is dependent on one truth, all distractions are stopped; and thereby the mind is purified. Similarly, the mind is clarified by cultivating the attitudes of friendliness, compassion, gladness

46. *Pātañjala Yoga-Sūtra*, I.20.

47. *Pātañjala Yoga-Sūtra*, I.32.

48. *Pātañjala Yoga-Sūtra*, I.31.

and indifference towards happiness, misery, virtue and vice respectively.[49] The devotee should cultivate the feeling of friendship towards all living beings engaged in the enjoyment of pleasure and the feeling of compassion towards the vicious. Then the mind becomes transparent, one-pointed, steady and fit for meditation.

While Patañjali prescribes the *aṣṭāṅga yoga* principles of *yama* (restraint), *niyama* (observance), *āsana* (posture), *prāṇāyāma* (breath regulation), *pratyāhāra* (abstraction), *dhāraṇā* (concentration), *dhyāna* (meditation) and *samādhi* (spiritual absorption),[50] Rāmānuja advises the principles of *sādhanā saptaka*[51] to remove the impurities of the mind. The practice of the first five external components of *yoga* removes the gross impurities. The subtle impurities are to be destroyed by the practice of the three internal components (*dhāraṇā, dhyāna* and *samādhi*) of Yoga. Patañjali also gives importance to food habits, which counts as an external purification. Internal purification implies to wash away the mental impurities.

Dedication of all actions to the highest preceptor, *Īśvara*, is one of the most important actions in the realisation of *Īśvara*. While study of scriptures, the repetition of *praṇava* (*OṀ*) purifies the mind, cultivation of the attitudes of harmlessness, truthfulness, abstinence from theft, continence and non-

---

49. *Pātañjala Yoga-Sūtra*, I.30-33.

50. *Pātañjala Yoga-Sūtra*, II.29.

51. Purification of the body by intake of *sāttvika* food, which leads to the purity of mind (*viveka*), getting rid of sensual attachment or anger for securing mental tranquillity (*vimoka*), repeated reflection of God, who is immanent in the human souls (*abhyāsa*), performance of the religious duty, which will provide inner mental strength (*kriyā*), development of ethical virtues such as honesty, integrity, compassion, benevolence, non-violence, etc. which will give inner purity (*kalyāṇa*), freedom from despair due to disappointments and unexpected calamities (*anavasāda*), and lastly not to be overpowered by excessive joy, so that tranquillity of mind is not disturbed (*anuddharṣa*).

acceptance of gifts and contentment are secondary means in the purification of the mind. When the mind is pure, naturally the heart becomes pure.

Full aspiration for *Īśvara* is deep meditation on *Īśvara*. This is the fastest and easiest way for purification. The devotee simply surrenders himself to the will of *Īśvara* and merges all his desires with the Divine Will. His emotions will be gradually purified by submitting himself to *Īśvara*'s will and doing *niṣkāma karma* (desireless actions); then emerges the dissolution of the "I". Love is the driving force in devotion, which brings about the weakening of the ego. With this destruction, the spontaneous and uninterrupted flow of love towards *Īśvara* arises and through His grace, *Īśvara*'s knowledge manifests.

Concentration, Contemplation and Meditation in Devotion

Devotion is a mental action and as such, the mind plays a very important role in it. The mind's tendency is always to seek peace, which is its real nature. But it is influenced by the force of the senses. The senses, in conjunction with the mind, are noted for their waywardness, running after any object they like, any time they like and at will. The mind whose nature is also unsteadiness, is the medium through which man grasps the object. In fact, mind is possessed of three energies having the qualities of illumination (*sattva*), activity (*rajas*) and inertia (*tamas*). Mind undergoes modifications, since its objects are sometimes known and at other times unknown. It assumes the form of all objects and thus apprehends them. Just as a magnet attracts a piece of iron by its own power, so too the senses attract the mind by their own influence, relate it to themselves and transform it into their forms. The forms that the mind thus projects are not always true, because the mind is capable of injecting other forms. It is absolutely necessary to wash out these impurities of the mind to make it free from its subjugation to the senses. Likewise, the subtle impurities in the form of habitual potencies should be washed out too. Once these impurities are weeded out, mind becomes capable of concentration.

CONCENTRATION

Concentration (*dhāraṇā*) is to focus one's thought and effort on one object. *Dhāraṇā* means to hold the object firmly, to retain it in the mind. Retention of a definite and determinate perception is concentration. The mind remains focused on one point, it does not oscillate between two ends. Patañjali[52] defines concentration as the confining of the mind to a limited space (object of concentration). Concentration is the first step for the achievement of God-realisation; in *bhakti*, it is the first step for achieving communion with God. Just as the same earth, on which a child falls, becomes the very support for its rise too, so also with the help of the support of concentration, a devotee, even if he falls down, rises once again to reach his goal. Concentration is the increasing, intense degree of alertness and the power of attention.

In *dhāraṇā*, the mind is confined to a limited sphere or territory, which allows a limited freedom of movement. The mind is turned in, as it were, within a limited mental territory and has to be brought back immediately, if it turns out. The reason is that every object has innumerable aspects, and the mind can consider these aspects only one by one. While it takes up one aspect after another, it is moving and yet really fixed on the object of concentration. Or, the object may involve a process of reasoning, consisting of many logically related steps and forming an integrated whole. Here too, it will be found that there can be no movement, which really leaves the object of concentration. It is only when the mind gets out of touch with the object and an unconnected and irrelevant object enters the mind that *dhāraṇā* is considered as interrupted.

52. Author of *Yoga-Sūtra.*

Paradoxically, the mind agitates violently, when one tries to fix it in one place and it flies stubbornly away elsewhere. If the mind leaves the sphere, while it should be held concentrated, the concentration is said to be broken.

Concentration consists in keeping the mind continuously engaged in the object of consideration and bringing it back immediately each time when there is an interruption. One should try to reduce progressively, the frequency of such interruptions and ultimately eliminate them. Then complete focusing of the mind on the object should be aimed. Vague and blurred impressions should be replaced by sharply defined mental images, accompanied by an increasing degree of alertness and the power of attention. As long as the mental images are blurred and confused, it is not easy to concentrate on them. If the mind does not get a good hold on clear mental images, they tend to slip away easily. The capacity to form vivid and sharp images and to be able to see them clearly is necessary for an efficient practice of *dhāraṇā*. The conditions of the mind during the period, when it is engaged with the object, and the frequency of the interruptions, which break the connection, are both important in concentration. As the grip on the mind becomes stronger, the frequency with which the distractions appear becomes lesser. In the practice of concentration, the mind should be moulded into the desired object. It has to be weaned away from other objects and fixed on one centre. Arjuna tells Śrī Kṛṣṇa:

> O! Kṛṣṇa! My mind is very fickle, impetuous, and stubborn. I think restraint of it is as difficult as that of the wind.[53]

Apart from being unsteady, turbulent and powerful, the mind is also unyielding. It clutches with all its force at whatever it takes a fancy for, and more or less, identifies itself with that object. Arjuna is an ardent devotee of Lord Kṛṣṇa. At this stage,

---

53. *Bhagavad-Gītā*, VI.34.

the Lord draws and attracts the devotee's heart towards Him. When one's personal efforts fail and when one submits oneself to God, He himself shows the ways to reach the aim. Śrī Kṛṣṇa comforts Arjuna:

> The mind is restless, no doubt, and difficult to curb, Arjuna. But it can be brought under control by repeated practice and by the exercise of dispassion.[54]

Practice (*abhyāsa*) is the repetitive attempt to direct the flow of thoughts towards the object. In devotional practices, the flow of thoughts is to be directed towards God to establish the link between God and the practitioner (*sādhaka*). Practice should be carried on with firm conviction that God is the highest and the only truth. The supreme goal in life is to realise Him, to be united with Him.

Certain practices for concentration are prescribed, following which the mind will be able to withdraw from all abstractions. With the help of faith, reverence and steadfast reason, mind should be repeatedly concentrated on God. "Drawing back the restless and fidgety mind from all objects after which it runs, he should repeatedly fix it on God."[55] The mind is very restless and shaky. It will not stick to a particular object for any length of time. When the practitioner fixes the mind on God with great effort and imagines that he has succeeded in his efforts, the very next moment he finds that it has given him the slip and has run far away. Therefore, the devotee should be alert and should not allow the mind to think of anything else than God. But despite alertness, the mind will slip away. The mind recoils from God because of ignorance and delusion. The moment the devotee notices that his mind is running away in pursuit of other objects, he should drag it back at once with great caution and firmness, without the least hesitation, and concentrate it on God.

54. *Bhagavad-Gītā*, VI.35.

55. *Bhagavad-Gītā*, VI.26.

If the devotee becomes feeble at this situation, he will not succeed in meditation. Whatever objects the mind may run after, the deity of one's choice should be thought about in that very object.

One should offer mental worship to God, like repeating the names of the deity of one's own choice considering such a name to be God's own name. A concentrated, fully conscious, sincere utterance of the name of God is equal to hundreds of absent-minded repetitions. Out of 1,000 repetitions, only one may have been done properly. That is why the name of God is to be repeated many times. Concentration can also be developed by imagining the luminous form of a deity seated in the centre of consciousness or imagining the Divine in the form of light, but not in terms of material light. Then it is possible to realise the centre of consciousness as luminous too.

One may take up symbols for concentration. Symbolic representations take the devotee to a higher mental stage and nearer to God. Offering prayers, reading and studying the Holy Scriptures that reveal the truth about God and His creation and joining an assembly of holy persons (*satsaṅga*) also help in the practice of concentration.

Repeated prayers should be offered to God with a sincere, humble mind and heart, imploring that the mind's restlessness may disappear and that the mind may get concentrated on Him. The love of God should not be negative but positive and creative; God should not only be served in the Divine form, but also in all forms that the Divine manifests.

There are many people who dislike (or even hate) the worship of images, which are the representations of God, thinking it to be idolatry. But if reasoned properly, it will be understood that this kind of worship is the only way to have a direct communion with God. The worshippers of trees and stones do not worship all of these kind but only distinctive trees and stones in the name of God. These worshippers are the true idealists. They can feel the omnipresence of God and become capable of reaching the highest stage of devotion. These worships are helpful in concentration.

Practice will meet with success, only when it is carried out with faith and reverence and continued for a sufficient length of time without a break. Irregular, inconstant and desultory practice can never lead to success.

Practice is like a beautiful channel for the flow of thought currents in the direction of God. Practice promotes dispassion, which is like an embankment to restrain the flow of current towards the worldly objects of enjoyment. Practice and dispassion help each other and are means of subduing the mind. When the mind is restrained, the process of concentration becomes easier. Concentration of the mind means focusing the mind on the desired object. God is the focusing centre for the devotee on *bhakti mārga*.[56] The mind is ever unsteady and stubborn to give up its habits, and the intellect does not firmly adhere to one supreme conviction. A devotee should try his best to convert the mind and the intellect to orderliness and submission and turn them towards God by regular training with the help of reason and dispassion. Only then, the senses will not indulge in their respective objects, but will meekly follow the devotee's will and remain tied down to where it directs them to be. The mind will then be in concentration according to the devotee's will, and the intellect will firmly adhere to the conclusion of his choice.

The *Chāndogya Upaniṣad* indicates the healthy condition of both, the body and mind. "When food is pure, the mind is pure. When mind is pure, memory becomes firm."[57] Concentration is difficult without the power of memory. The word "food" should be understood in a wider sense. Every sense has its own food in

---

56. The Path of Devotion.

57. *Chāndogya Upaniṣad*, VII.26.2.

the shape of an object of enjoyment. Memory depends upon the health of the mind (*sattva*), which in turn depends upon the health of the body. The health of the body depends on the food. Eating too much induces sleep and lethargy and creates various disorders in the physiological system through accumulation of undigested matter. Relinquishing food altogether and observing total fasts sometimes bring a severe strain on one's energy of mind, senses and vital organs. With a lack of energy, the devotee can neither sit steadily nor can he fix his mind on God. The food taken should therefore not be more than one's digestive capacity can cope with, and it should be of *sāttvika* type that keeps the mind alert. A regulated and reasonable diet and recreation tend to promote the quality of *sattva* in one's body, senses and mind and enhance their purity and liveliness, increasing the power of concentration.

On the control of mind, Patañjali says,

> The mind can be controlled by persistent practice and non-attachment.[58]

Practice and detachment are apparently simple words, but they require tremendous efforts of human will, and they stand for various practices. Patañjali states that *abhyāsa* is the effort for being firmly established in a particular state that is concentration of the mind on God. Practice is the course of proceeding with the means to reach at the aim. This practice is not at all an easy-going path. The restraint of mental operations requires many qualifications for its achievements and cannot be easily attained.

> That practice becomes firmly grounded on being continued for a long time, without interruptions and reverent devotion.[59]

These practices must be continued uninterruptedly for a long time. The path must be trodden with devotion and in a spirit of

58. *Pātañjala Yoga-Sūtra*, I.12.

59. *Pātañjala Yoga-Sūtra*, I.14.

reverence. Complete change in the nature of the devotee is so fundamental in practice that he must be prepared to continue the work, until he gains firm concentration.

The devotee has to remove all impure thoughts and emotions from his mind and should only respond to pure thoughts and emotions corresponding to the object of concentration. One should develop the capacity to devote oneself wholeheartedly and persistently in pursuing one's aim: concentrating the mind on God. The duration of success depends on the evolutionary stage of the devotee, the time already given to this practice in previous lives, and the effort that he makes in this life. If the practice is intense, the result will be obtained faster. If he continually worries when the success will be his, it shows his lack of real interest.

Withdrawing the senses from their objects is *pratyāhāra,* the fifth limb of *aṣṭāṅga yoga* (Yoga of eight limbs). When *pratyāhāra* is achieved, concentration (*dhāraṇā*) becomes easy. Once the intellectual activities are controlled, then meditation (*dhyāna*) becomes smooth.

Without wholly renouncing the thoughts of the world, the mind cannot be united with the object of concentration. It is indispensable for all practitioners. Perfection in concentration is only attained, when freed from all attachments for action and worldly objects.

CONTEMPLATION

> O! All-virtuous Lord! Without thee I seek neither abode in the uppermost heaven nor the positions of *Brahman,* the Creator, neither sovereignty over the entire globe, nor dominion over the netherworld, neither the achievements of Yoga nor the everlasting freedom from rebirth.[60]

---

60. *Śrīmad Bhāgavata Purāṇa,* VI.11.25.

This should be the mind of a true devotee, who does not wish to be separated from God, not even for a moment. God is the only thought for him. When a love-intoxicated devotee, who remembers God with exclusive devotion, can no longer bear his separation from Him, God too begins to feel this separation unbearable. For, His vow is: "However men approach me, even so do I seek them."[61] Because of their exclusive love for God, the devotees want to see Him only and always. Contemplation and meditation in devotion are like the both sides of the coin — knowing and loving God.

After gaining perfection in concentration, the process of contemplation takes over. Contemplation is the careful study of the object of concentration. The wisdom revealed by it impresses on the mind. Fixing the mind on the object and reflecting on it is contemplation. It is the intense concentration of thought in the mind with the aim of realising some definite understanding of the object of concentration. Contemplation gives the knowledge of the object and makes the mind believe in it. This is faith, without which devotion is impossible. Contemplation is a form of intense learning. But God cannot be realised by profound learning. Yet, one should remember that

> This Self cannot be known through much learning or through the intellect, or through much hearing. It can be known through the Self alone that the devotee prays to, this Self of that seeker reveals Its true nature.[62]

In *bhakti-yoga*, concentration, contemplation and meditation are on God alone. Giving full attention on God is concentration. Contemplation is to know the nature and glory of the Soul. Knowledge of the nature of the Soul and God (or absolute *Brahman*) is a precondition for cultivating intense devotion in

---

61. *Bhagavad-Gītā*, IX.29.
62. *Kaṭha Upaniṣad*, 1.2.23 .

bhakti-yoga. Contemplation is a quite and deep concentration, while meditation is a quite and sustained contemplation.

If concentration (*dhāraṇā*) is keeping the mind collected, that is, steady abstraction of the mind, *dhyāna* is abstract contemplation. *Dhyāna* is especially religious meditation. It is constant contemplation in the mind. Contemplation means complete elimination of all personal preconceptions, the I-ness and the sense of attachment. Concentration is possible, if the determination to reach the very end persists in mind. Contemplation consists in the control of the senses and the concentration of thought. It gives rise to firm memory due to clear understanding. Firm memory is the base for *dhyāna*.

Contemplation helps in overcoming mental impressions gathered in the present life (*saṁskāra*). These impressions are like pet animals that have become attached to a person by fondling and feeding them for a long time. Even though the practice of meditation might not remove entirely these past impressions, yet one can obtain union with the Supreme through prayer and meditation, if one has firm faith in God.

MEDITATION

Bhakti-yoga is the same as worship (*upāsanā*), knowledge (*vedanā*) and *dhyāna*. It implies a series of unceasing meditation upon God, culminating in the direct perception of God.

Dhyāna is a succession of memories (or remembrances), which is unbroken, like a stream of oil. "When firm memory is attained, there is the loosening of all knots."[63] Such memory is of the same form as direct perception. Steady meditation has the same character as direct perception, that is to say, the devotee has the experience of God.

It is to be noted that *dhyāna* does not mean mere gazing at an object. In the initial stages, the mind has to be focused on the

63. *Chāndogya Upaniṣad*, VII.26.2.

object of contemplation. It means a constant and continuous reflection on the Divine form with all its glory. According to Rāmānuja, it means reflection on the essential nature (*svarūpa*) of the Divine Personality (*rūpa*) with His auspicious qualities or the attributes (*guṇa*) of God. It amounts to a conscious effort to think continuously and repeatedly of all the glories of God to obtain the vision of the Supreme. The flow of thought towards God should be like an unbroken stream of oil poured from a vessel. This firm meditation on God is called *bhakti* or *upāsanā*.[64] It is considered well established.

> When reflection or higher understanding is strong, memory becomes strong, when memory becomes strong; there is release from all knots (doubts) of the heart.[65]

The *Vedānta-Sūtra* also states that meditation is to be done with deep devotion towards God.[66] Anything devoid of love to God is not pleasing to Him and will not lead to the desired goal. The goal in devotion is to keep constant contact with God. And meditation has to be practised until the end. "Living, indeed, thus throughout his life, he reaches the world of *Brahman*."[67] Contemplation is a thoughtful study. During the development of steady contemplation, the mind takes to meditation on it and absorbs completely in the object forgetting its surroundings. That is to say, the mind is in constant company with the object of meditation and nothing else disrupts it. The feeling of a constant desire to serve God is the result of devotional meditation.

---

64. *Chāndogya Upaniṣad*, uses the word *dhruva smṛti* for *dhyāna* or *upāsanā*. (VII.26.2). The word *upāsanā* is generally used for meditation on *mantra*, called *mantropāsanā*. When the form of God is meditated with the help of a *mantra*, it is called *upāsanā* on a particular deity, because different deities have different mantras for *upāsanā*.

65. *Chāndogya Upaniṣad*, VII.26.2.

66. *Vedānta-Sūtra*, IV.1.4.

67. *Chāndogya Upaniṣad*, VIII.15.1.

God chooses him, who loves Him. So, one should love God intensely. Lord Kṛṣṇa himself revealed this secret that the man of knowledge (*jñānin*) is His dearest.[68] God chooses the one who has the knowledge of Him, for whom His constant remembrance becomes dear, because of his intense love for Him, who is the object of his meditation. The intensity of love for God leads the devotee to yearn for the divine vision. Meditating love essentially implies clear knowledge of the Divine. Firm meditation is the knowledge of the object of meditation; it is to be repeated without any intermediary interruptions. This remembrance, the clear perception of God, is the means of *mokṣa*. Meditation is the concentration of mind on one object, namely the god of one's choice[69] in *bhakti*, uninterrupted by the ideas of different other objects.

The main text that enjoins meditation on God says,

> The Self is to be seen, to be heard, to be reflected upon, to be meditated upon.[70]

This statement contains the fundamental instructions on meditation; it forms the crowning precept of the Sage Yājñavalkya to his wife Maitreyī. The universal cause is to be the goal of all meditations. "The Self is to be contemplated upon" is a confirmation of what is already established by hearing. Reflection on what is heard should be undertaken more than once. Then the knowledge of the object of meditation is clearly perceived. When the knowledge of the object of meditation is acquired, meditation on it becomes firm.

Bhakti as meditation is manifold, because of the form of meditation. The Upaniṣads embody 32 kinds of meditation on *Brahman* (*brahma-vidyā*), which enjoin that the only object of

68. *Bhagavad-Gītā*, VII.17; X.10.
69. God of one's choice refers to a personal God.
70. *Bṛhadāraṇyaka Upaniṣad*, IV.5.6.

meditation is *Brahman* and neither the matter nor the *jīva*.[71] For those desirous of release, they also prescribe the method of intuiting *Brahman*. Besides certain attributes, which are common to all, each meditation, *vidyā* embodies one or more special attributes of *Brahman*, which distinguishes it from others. While some *vidyās*, like *udgīta-vidyā*, are the means to spiritual realisation, others are for the attainment of empirical fruits. Meditations aiming at an object of desire other than the contact with God provide only limited results.[72]

In *dahara-vidyā*, it is stated:

> In the city of *Brahman* (human body), there is the place in the heart of the form of a small lotus, and within it, the small *ākāśa*. What is within it is to be sought after. That is to be known.[73]

This practice of meditation is common to all even today: meditation on the heart[74] (*hṛdaya*), considered as the abode of God. This technique of meditation defines *ākāśa* within the lotus of the heart as neither matter nor *jīva* but *Brahman* and praises the Infinite who, owing to his boundless love towards the devotees, becomes the finite in the hearts of all beings as the object of meditation.

Nyāsa-vidyā is self-surrender: to conceive what is in conformity with the will of God, to reject what is disagreeable to God, to have firm faith, as "He will save me", to seek Him alone as the protector, and to surrender one's Self to Him in modesty.

A devotee should select a good and worthy object for *dhāraṇā*. The form of God alone, who is highest among all objects, is fit for concentration. Meditation is a type of thinking or

71. See end of sub-chapter.

72. *Brahma-vidyā*, such as *antarakṣi-vidyā*, *dahara-vidyā*, *bhūma-vidyā*, *śad vidyā*, *madhu-vidyā*, *upakosala-vidyā*, *śāṇḍilya-vidyā*, *puruṣa-vidyā*, *vaiśvānara-vidyā*, *pañca-agni-vidyā* and so on are means for attainment of *mokṣa*.

73. *Chāndogya Upaniṣad*, VIII.1.1.

74. Not to be confused with the physiological organ.

concentration of the mind on God's image. Single-minded attention is the chief means of meditation. Thinking of God's form, qualities, actions and serving Him deeply are all different types of meditation. For those who are used to meditation, there is no restriction of place, time and conditions.

> Those persons, who meditate on and pray to God with single-minded devotion are delivered by Him from the cycle of birth and death.[75]

Meditation produces endurance of pleasure and pain, of heat and cold and of hunger and thirst, washes off all impurities and vices and produces devotion, Liberation and God-realisation. When the devotee reaches perfection in the practice of meditation, having firm belief in the omnipresence of God, he always contemplates on Him, in active life just like in the hours of meditation. Both, the *Bhagavad-Gītā* and the *Kaṭha Upaniṣad*, say, "It is said that the senses are great. But greater than the senses is the mind, and greater than the mind is understanding. But what is even greater than understanding is He."[76]

To find success in the aim, withdrawing the senses from their corresponding outward objects or retraction is the first step. This serves to shut the mind against all unessential impressions coming from the outside world. Because of that, the mind ceases to be affected by external influences. By this practice, the devotee learns to confine his mind to a limited area and can concentrate on the knowledge that is essential for achieving his goal. When he brings his senses thoroughly under control, he qualifies himself for concentration. With the devotee's mind in *dhāraṇā*, he is fit to enter into contemplation, which implies the study of the object of concentration carefully, giving serious thoughts to it and reflecting on it. The concentrated and contemplated mind passes on to *dhyāna*.

---

75. *Bhagavad-Gītā*, XII.6-7.

76. *Kaṭha Upaniṣad*, I.3.10; *Bhagavad-Gītā*, III.42.

> The man of faith, zeal and self-control attains knowledge. Having attained knowledge, he immediately attains supreme peace in the form of God-realisation.[77]

The purpose of meditation is to help man obtain a direct and immediate experience of his basic nature as bliss. In the ordinary waking state, the mind is going outward through the passages of the senses, and so it gets the knowledge of the external nature.

Consciousness is like a line between two points, say, "X" and "Y"; "X" and "Y" standing for the subjective side and line between "X" and "Y" the objective side. Just as the line makes the two points disappear in our perception, so too the objective existence of this world takes over the subjective aspect of the creation. Consequently, just as man loses the awareness of the nature of the subjective aspects of the line, he loses the awareness of the subjective aspect that is behind the creation. He is entirely identified with the body-mind-complex and the experiences that are brought through it. It is like the line identifying itself with the two individual points. Meditation is a process whereby this tendency of identification is removed, enabling a clear perception of the subjective and the true nature of the universe. It is just like realising the reality of the two points "X" and "Y" by simply extracting all the attributes (past, present and future) that were transferred to the line.

> In respect of each of the senses, attachment and aversion to objects are fixed. One should not come under their sway, for they are impediments in one's way (of reaching the goal).[78]

> Shutting out the external sense-objects, fixing the gaze between the eye-brows, controlling the outgoing and incoming breaths that move through the nostrils, with the senses, mind and intellect restrained and free from desire, fear and anger, the sage, who has liberation as his highest goal is indeed ever free.[79]

---

77. *Bhagavad-Gītā*, IV.39.

78. *Bhagavad-Gītā*, III.34.

79. *Bhagavad-Gītā*, V.27-28.

In meditation, detachment of the body-consciousness is to be achieved through absorption in the object of meditation. If the concentration is firm and real, then, this detachment occurs immediately and automatically, just like a reader who forgets himself while reading a book of personal interest, his mind intensely absorbed in it. His consciousness is fused with the reading that occupies the field of his attention. Likewise, while practicing meditation on the Deity with a personal form (as in *bhakti*), the body-consciousness is to be overcome. Usually, the practitioner reflects more on himself than concentrating on the Deity, which in turn gives rise to dispersion and the loss of the meditative state of mind.

The process of concentration should begin by sitting in a steady posture, practising *prāṇāyāma*, excluding all other thoughts and fixing the mind on any object of high virtue. At first, it is difficult to fix the mind on an object and so the thought has to be repeated constantly in the mind. Then concentration will change over to contemplation and meditation.

A distinction should be made between the general technique of *prāṇāyāma* and the technique of *prāṇāyāma* applied in Hindu religious or meditative rituals:

The general technique of *prāṇāyāma* is:

> Facing east, sit cross-legged with an erect back. Fold the index and the middle finger of the right hand. Bend the right arm to bring the right hand in front of the nose. Then close the right nostril with the thumb and inhale through the left nostril. At the end of the inhalation, hold the breath for 5 or 10 seconds according to your capacity. Close the left nostril with the ring and the little finger. Open the right nostril and exhale through the right nostril. Keeping the left nostril closed inhale through the right nostril. Again, hold the breath for 5 or 10 seconds according to your capacity. Then close the right nostril, open the left nostril and exhale through the left nostril. This forms one cycle.

In all meditative or religious practices, only inhalation through the left nostril followed by a holding of breath and exhalation through the right nostril is applied. This forms one *prāṇāyāma*. In all Hindu rituals, a *prāṇāyāma* is accompanied by *Gāyatrī Mantra.*

The *Gāyatrī-mantra* for *prāṇāyāma* is:

oṁ bhuḥ, oṁ bhuvaḥ, oṁ suvaḥ (to pronounce *ogum suvaha*),
oṁ mahaḥ, oṁ janaḥ, oṁ tapaha, oṁ satyam (to pronounce *ogum satyam*),
oṁ tat saviturvareṇyam bhargo devasya dhimahi. dhiyo yo naḥ pracodayāt,
Oṁ āpo jyotiraso-amṛtam brahma bhurbhuvassuvar-oṁ.

There are two ways of doing this type of *prāṇāyāma:*

During inhalation (*pūraka*), the first part of *Gāyatrī-mantra* is mentally recited. During the holding of breath (*kumbhaka*), the second part of *Gāyatrī-mantra* is mentally recited and during the exhalation (*recaka*), the third part of *Gāyatrī-mantra* is mentally recited. This type of *prāṇāyāma* is also practised in the standing position.

During *pūraka*, one *Gāyatrī-mantra* is mentally recited. During the holding of *kumbhaka*, according to the capacity, one, two or three *Gāyatrī-mantras* are mentally recited. During *recaka*, according to the capacity, one or two *Gāyatrī-mantras* are mentally repeated. This type of *prāṇāyāma* is practised in the standing position too.

Meditation is not easy; there is no doubt about it. But for one, who has reverence and love for God, and who firmly believes that meditation would be easy by constantly remembering God all the time, meditation becomes easy. It is certainly difficult for one, who lacks faith and love.[80]

Meditation in devotion is a state of mind, in which the thought of God, exclusive of everything else, abides spontaneously without

---

80. *Bhagavad-Gītā*, IX.12.

any effort. This state is attainable after mastering the knowledge of the Self as derived from the teacher and the scriptures, because meditation is based on the strength of the knowledge of the Self.

Meditation, which is a form of intense concentration of the mind, is the uninterrupted stream of similar cognitions of an object. Meditation can also be described as a reflection on an object with a focused mind. A person with a fixed mind does not deviate from the state of absorption, in which he has fixed the object. For example, a person who is aiming an arrow with a focused mind, fails to perceive a group of children walking on a nearby road. One-pointedness of mind should be cultivated with care, before taking up the process of meditation. By adopting the method of making use of the lower steps as temporary substitutes for the highest and meditating on it, the practice of meditation becomes easier.

While teaching Sage Nārada on *bhūma-vidyā* (also called *brahma-vidyā*) Sage Sanatkumāra tells him to worship the texts consisting just of "names" as if they were the Ultimate Reality or *Brahman*, just as one would worship God in an image.[81] Sanatkumāra teaches Nārada the process of worshipping by explaining gradually the higher steps: name, speech (that is, conceiving, expressing thoughts and ideas), the mind (including speech and name), the ego (through which one directs the mind) and the intellect (that comprehends an object and examines it).

When Nārada was not satisfied with these worships, he obtained instructions for the next higher stage, namely contemplation, that is greater than all the previous ones. Contemplation is the process of firmly establishing one's thought on the object intended. It results in a clear understanding of the object of concentration through observation and reflection on this object. A proper understanding of scriptures is necessary for contemplation, as without reflection one cannot understand

---

81. *Chāndogya Upaniṣad*, 7.1.4; 7.2.1, 7.3.1, 7.4.1, 7.5.1, etc.

the scriptures. When there is no understanding, recollection is not possible. Without recollection, the mind cannot hold the unbroken memory of the object of concentration. That is why the study of scriptures[82] is considered as a support for contemplation and meditation.

Apart from reflection and clear understanding, purity of mind is an essential condition that is needed to hold the continuous memory of God. Purity of mind depends upon the capacity to receive only proper impressions. As said earlier, meditation is the concentration on one object, uninterrupted by the ideas of different things incompatible with the object of meditation. It is a continued representation of the object of meditation in one's mind, so that the knowledge of the object becomes increasingly vivid.

Hearing (*śravaṇa*), reflection (*manana*) and steady meditation (*nididhyāsana*) are prescribed in the process of practice of devotion.[83] Hearing consists in receiving ideas from preceptors, sacred texts, etc. about the knowledge of God. Reflection is rationally establishing in one's mind that the instructions of the teacher and the holy texts are true. It serves the purpose of fixing in the mind what has already been heard. Steady meditation is the incessant contemplation of this very idea, that is, setting one's mind completely on God. Grasping the virtues and glories of God, as well as the truth relating to Him, by the intellect, and making a firm resolve with supreme faith, and dwelling constantly on the idea of God alone in the mind are necessary conditions to develop faith and reverence. Lord Kṛṣṇa says

> Fix your mind on Me, be devoted to Me, worship Me, and make obeisance to Me, thus linking yourself with Me and entirely depending on Me, you shall come to Me.[84]

---

82. *Svādhyāya*.

83. *Bṛhadāraṇyaka Upaniṣad*, II.4-5.

84. *Bhagavad-Gītā*, IX.34.

Bhakti-yoga is based on the following three points and their proper understanding helps to progress in devotion:

1. Fixing the mind on God with deep devotion,
2. Following the different modes of worship of God, and
3. Offering salutations, bowing down to Him, and dedicating oneself to God.

Dhyāna is mainly a mental act in the form of an unceasing, loving meditation on God, but is also a multiform ethical, religious and spiritual discipline to be undertaken and continued over a long time for the purpose of attaining God. According to the Vedānta, God cannot be seen by the visual organs, but He can be comprehended by the mind that has been cleansed of its impurities through the practice of constant meditation with loving devotion to Him. *Muṇḍaka Upaniṣad* says,

> "One can realise Him while engaged in meditation."[85]

Śrī Kṛṣṇa confirms this:

> I will bestow on you a divine eye. Behold My lordly Yoga.

He further says,

> Single-minded devotion is the only means of attaining God's vision.[86]

God is not bound to appear in an embodied form before one, who treads the path of knowledge.

> Sacrifice is a means by which knowledge is brought about. This knowledge is something absolutely different from the knowledge of the textual means.[87]

---

85. *Muṇḍaka Upaniṣad*, III.1.8.

86. *Bhagavad-Gītā*, XI.8 and 54.

87. *Bṛhadāraṇyaka Upaniṣad*, IV.4.22.

This knowledge is denoted by words such as *dhyāna, upāsanā,* etc. It is of the nature of remembrance, which has attained the form of direct and clearest perception, by practising daily, it attains excellence and when continued, it becomes the means of attaining *mokṣa*. Such a meditation arises from the grace of the Supreme Being, who is pleased by the performance of the daily and occasional acts. In householders, knowledge stands in need of all daily and occasional works. Just as the horse, which is a means of locomotion, stands in need of harness, so too, the knowledge of the Divine or meditation on Him stands for a means to liberation.

The *Bhagavad-Gītā* also says,

> The acts of sacrifice, charity and penance performed by them serve to purify their heart,

and adds,

> They should be performed without attachment and hope of reward.[88]

Although a person is engaged in the performance of works, he should possess calmness, self-control, etc. because they are of the nature of concentration.

According to Rāmānuja, *dhyāna*[89] is an important stage in *bhakti-yoga* and needs loving devotion to God. *Śrīmad Bhāgavata Purāṇa* mentions nine modes of devotional worship, including contemplation on the glory of God, which helps to cleanse the mind from its impurities and to secure stability to perform *dhyāna-yoga* leading to the vision of God.

> There are nine forms of devotion to the Lord: to hear the names, episodes of God, to sing of His name and glories, to remember

---

88. *Bhagavad-Gītā,* XVIII.5-6.

89. The different terms used in the Upaniṣad, such as *upāsanā, dhyāna, smṛti santati,* Vedānta, *darśana,* are to be taken to mean *bhakti.*

> Him (His name), to render service unto Him, to worship Him, to pay obeisance to Him, to dedicate all actions to Him, to confide to Him as a friend, and to offer one's body and belongings to His service and care.[90]

Nammāḷvār, the south Indian Saint of great fame, says that the devotee resorts to the contemplation on God's deeds, when separation from God causes anguish in him.[91] When it is practised continuously, it takes the form of uninterrupted remembrance of the object of contemplation. This is called *smṛti santati* or *upāsanā*, an unbroken series of recollection of the object of meditation, comparable to the uninterrupted flow of oil. It is a continuous and steadfast concentration. When *upāsanā* gains intensity by repeated and continuous observance, it assumes the form of vividness similar to that of a direct vision of the object of contemplation. Thus, *dhyāna* leads to *dhruva smṛti* (steadfast concentration), which assumes the form of *upāsanā*, and *upāsanā* results in the direct vision of God. Only such a meditation — perfected to the extent of being similar to the vision of the Supreme Being — is considered as the means for liberation.

Rāmānuja acknowledges the need for *aṣṭāṅga yoga* disciplines, based on *Viṣṇu Purāṇa*,[92] which clearly states that contemplation on the Supreme is to be accomplished with the aid of the first six limbs of *yoga* (*yogāṅga*). Before embarking on *dhyāna*, concentration on the object of contemplation is to be practised. Concentration of the mind presupposes invariably the mental purity through cultivation of ethical virtues (*yama*), observance of duties (*niyama*), a steady posture (*āsana*), control of breath (*prāṇāyāma*) and withdrawal of the sense activities from the mundane world (*pratyāhāra*). Then follow *dhāraṇā* and *dhyāna*. The

---

90. *Śrīmad Bhāgavata Purāṇa*, VII.5.23.

91. *Thiruvaimoli*, V.10.5.

92. *Viṣṇu Purāṇa*, VI.7.91. *Aṣṭāṅga yoga* or the eight limbs of Yoga: *yama, niyama, āsana, prāṇāyāma, pratyāhāra, dhāraṇā, dhyāna* and *samādhi*.

same, when practiced for a long period, culminates in actual realisation or the vision of the Supreme. This final stage of Yoga leads to the state of Isolation (*kaivalya*). In Viśiṣṭādvaita Vedānta, this final stage culminates in the vision of the Supreme Soul[93] leading to *mokṣa*.

Though *bhakti-yoga* covers *aṣṭāṅga yoga* of Patañjali, its scope is far wider and covers much more than the latter. *Vedānta-Sūtra* refers to the need of a steady posture, the concentration of mind and a proper congenial atmosphere for contemplation.[94] In the *Vedānta-Sūtra,* there is no specific mention of *yama* and *niyama* of Yoga. But it emphasises the need of developing calmness (*śama*), control of the senses (*dama*), etc. as an aid to *upāsanā*.[95]

Rāmānuja is of the opinion that the purity of food is essential for the knower of *Brahman*. "When the food is pure, mind becomes pure. When the mind is pure, the remembrance is firm."[96]

Further, the sevenfold ethical disciplines known as *sādhanā saptaka*,[97] which Rāmānuja proposes, is an essential requirement for *bhakti-yoga*; it covers some of the features of *yama* and *niyama*. They are:

1. Purification of the body by consumption of *sāttvika* food, which leads to the purity of mind (*viveka*),
2. Getting rid of sensual attachment or anger for securing mental tranquillity (*vimoka*),

---

93. *Paramātmā sākṣātkāra* (direct perception of the form of the Supreme Soul or God).
94. *Vedānt-Sūtra*, IV.1.7 and 11.
95. *Vedānta-Sūtra*, III.4.27.
96. *Chāndogya Upaniṣad*, VII.26.2; Also refer to Chapter on: "Means according to Rāmānuja"; However, according to *Manu-Smṛti*, X.10.4, there is one exception: when there is danger to his life, he can take food from anywhere. He is not stained by sin like a lotus leaf is not stained by water.
97. Sevenfold discipline propounded by Rāmānuja.

3. Repeated reflection of God, who is immanent in the human souls (*abhyāsa*),
4. Performance of the religious duties, which will provide inner mental strength (*kriyā*),
5. Development of ethical virtues such as honesty, integrity, compassion, benevolence, non-violence, etc. which will give inner purity (*kalyāṇa*),
6. Freedom from despair due to disappointments and unexpected calamities (*anavasāda*), and lastly
7. Not to be overpowered by excessive joy, so that tranquillity of mind is not disturbed (*anuddharṣa*).

These disciplines help the devotee to accomplish progress in meditation on God. Moreover, they bring freedom from the web of desires, leading to calmness of the mind. The process of concentration, contemplation and meditation would be very difficult without mental tranquillity, if not impossible. "Let him meditate with calmness of mind."[98] Steady remembrance of God results from mental tranquillity.

> He, who with his mind disciplined through Yoga in the form of practice of meditation and thinking of nothing else, is constantly engaged in contemplation of God, attains the supreme effulgent divine *Puruṣa* (God).[99]

Dhyāna or *upāsanā* is the constant remembrance of God, like the uninterrupted flow of oil. It is the process of focusing the mind on God in a proper environment. For this, the devotee is recommended to choose a proper place and time and to adopt a sitting posture, which is most conducive to *dhyāna*. When the recollections, acquired by practice, bring the clearness and distinctness of a direct perception of the form of God, then meditation gives rise to

98. *Chāndogya Upaniṣad*, III.14.1.

99. *Bhagavad-Gītā*, VIII.8.

devotion. Mental concentration is possible only in the above-described way. Physical immobility is a necessary condition for meditation in a sitting posture. Śrī Kṛṣṇa says,

> Having established in a clean spot, a firm seat, neither too high nor too low, having covered with sacred grass, then with a deer skin[100] and then with a cloth. There sitting on that seat with a mind concentrated upon a single object and holding the mind and senses in check, he should practice *yoga* for the purification of his own Self.[101]
>
> Meditation has to be practised in a level and clean place, which is pleasing to the mind.[102]

According to Sāṁkhya philosophy, meditation consists in the suppression of *rajas*, which produces restlessness, and *tamas*, which hinders the real perception of objects. Therefore, it is necessary that *sattva* predominates over *rajas* and *tamas* to enable the mind to be free from attachment, mobility and inertia. This freedom is necessary for a steady and meditative mind. Success in suppressing mental functions can be achieved by dispassion and practice. It can be attained by the clarity of discriminative knowledge, which constitutes supreme dispassion.

Patañjali defines meditation as "uninterrupted flow of mind towards the object (chosen)".[103] In other words, the uniform flow untouched by any other cognition is *dhyāna*. Concentration is the confinement of the mind to a place. This is the first step of meditation and is the sixth part of *aṣṭāṅga yoga*. When the devotee succeeds in removing the distractions completely and continues the concentration on the object for a long time without any interruption, then he reaches the stage of *dhyāna*. The difference between *dhāraṇā* and *dhyāna* is that in the former, there is the

---

100. The deer should have a natural death.
101. *Bhagavad-Gītā*, VI.11.12.
102. *Śvetāśvatara Upaniṣad*, II.10.
103. *Pātañjala Yoga Sūtra*, III.2.

occasional appearance of distraction in the mind, while in the latter the flow of mind towards the object of meditation is uninterrupted. Meditation is thus a constant succession of cognition within the space of the intended object of meditation. The content of consciousness, with which the mind remains in continuous contact, is fixed and yet variable. It is fixed in the sense that the area, within which the mind moves, is defined and remains the same. It is variable, because within that limited area, there is movement. It is like the microscopic vision of a tissue, where the field of vision is defined and limited within a circle, and nothing can be seen outside of it. But within that circle of light, there are constant movements of all kinds. This is the dual nature of the content of consciousness in meditation. As said earlier, the continuity of the content of consciousness is the only thing that distinguishes concentration from meditation. The continuity may be compared to the flow of a river or that of oil poured from one vessel to another. Every break in the continuity means distraction. Distraction in continuity means a lack of adequate concentration and a lack of mastery over the activities of the mind. If the mind is diverted from the chosen object, some other object has taken its place, as there is always continuity in the movement of mind. It is only in the restrained or suppressed state (*nirodha*) that the continuity of the movement of mind cannot be broken by any other object occupying the mind.

The Sanskrit word *nirodha* means suppression or restraint. *Nirodha* is involved even in the preliminary practice of *dhāraṇā*, if studied carefully. In trying to practice *dhāraṇā*, the will is trying to suppress distractions all the time and substituting in their place the one object, on which meditation is to be performed. To replace a distraction by the chosen object, in each of these efforts there must be a momentary state, in which neither the distraction nor the chosen object is present, and the mind is really without any content of consciousness. It is like the moment when the direction of a moving object is suddenly reversed, there is a moment, when the object does not move, but stays at rest. Because, the state of *nirodha* is momentary. *Nirodha* in the practice of *dhāraṇā* and *dhyāna* is that momentary unmodified state of mind, which intervenes, when one impression, which holds the field of consciousness, is replaced by another impression.

If distraction breaks the continuity, there is not much harm done, because the mind can take up the thread immediately and continue the process going deep into the study. The appearance of distraction is the result of insufficient mastery over the mind and a corresponding lack in the depth of concentration. According to Yoga, the mind is getting ready for the real practice, when this state of meditation is attained. In *bhakti-yoga*, the mind is getting ready for the real practice of devotion, when it flows continuously towards God.

When the state of *dhyāna* is well established and the mind can hold the object of meditation without any distractions, it is possible to know the object more intimately than in normal perception. But this does not bring the direct knowledge of its very essence. This state merely is a primary condition, which qualifies the devotee to enter upon the task of investigation, just as a Master's degree of a university qualifies a student to enter a course of independent research. Only when the mind is completely isolated from external influences and has reached the intense state of meditation, can it successfully contact the Divine. Those, who concentrate their minds and meditate on God, and who pray Him with sincere faith and with their minds absorbed in Him, are constantly united with Him.

A stable knowledge of an object is acquired by fixing the mind on it. This knowledge is definite, distinct and unwavering like the non-flickering flame of a lamp. It is the effect of focusing the mind on the object of meditation. Yoga believes in the existence of a Supreme Person. It regards meditation on this Supreme Person and dedication of all duties to Him as the means of total restraint of the mental modes. It also considers the discriminative knowledge of the Self as different from God. Success in the control of mental modes can be achieved by repeated meditation.

Concentration, contemplation and meditation form the most important aspects of devotion. It is not important, whether one sees the form of the object or not. It is the mental state, which is important and which should have a continuous attitude of prayer. Perfect concentration is only possible, when the devotee eliminates all desires from his mind except that for contact with God. To have the desire to be in contact with God really is no desire at all, as it puts an end to all other desires.

While practising concentration, a devotee can have God's picture in front of him, and looking steadily at it, he can say prayers or do *japa*[104] prescribed for that Deity; and at the end he can try to visualise the form of the Deity. Love is the foundation for concentration. So the devotee can choose any Deity he loves the most, while sitting for meditation. With eyes opened, he can offer prayers mentally. The power of the chosen Deity is in the prayers. The prayers are the Deity set to sound. That is to say, the devotee is in communion with the Deity through sound. To develop concentration he has to withdraw his mind from all external things and think that he is clinging to God's feet as his only support in life. If he has attachment for many things and persons in life, it will be difficult to be attracted towards God. After offering prayers, he may let his mind be absorbed in God or try to mentally visualise His whole Being. The real problem is that the mind does not acquire concentration, because it is interested in many other things and enjoyments of the world. These have to be counteracted by contrary thoughts. The devotee has to develop the spirit of non-attachment through the process of discrimination. Of course, this will be a slow process passing through enjoyments and sufferings.

---

104. Repetition of *mantra* or God's name.

Usually, meditation is done in the heart,[105] the centre from which consciousness radiates. The lotus, on which the Deity is meditated upon, is only a symbol of that centre. Meditation should be done with the feeling in mind that the form meditated upon is the Supreme Being. It is important to keep the body and mind relaxed during meditation.

In intense meditation, the devotee tries to cross the barrier that separates consciousness from the subconscious mind. Certain impressions lingering in the subconscious mind, which the devotee is unaware of, come up to produce many sensations that will be felt in meditation. This may give rise to fear too. At that time, the devotee should stop meditation and take to prayer. Offering prayers to God with intensity, will bring God near to the devotee and remove his fear. When the love for God dominates in the heart, the prayer, *japa* of a *mantra* and meditation become one and the same. Perfect meditation can be achieved, only when one has singleness of purpose. Śrī Kṛṣṇa says,

> I am easy of access, O Arjuna, to that *yogin* who is ever integrated with Me, whose mind is not in anything else but Me and who ceaselessly recollects Me at all times.[106]

But control of mind is very difficult — just as the control of air. Only through practice and the spirit of non-attachment, one would be able to achieve it; and there is the time factor too. Describing the nature of devotion, Śrī Kṛṣṇa says,

> Focus your mind on Me, be My devotee, be My worshipper. Bow down to Me. Engaging your mind in this manner and regarding Me as the Supreme Goal, you will come to Me.[107]

---

105. Heart is not to be confounded with the physiological heart. Here, heart is the place, which is the place of the soul, usually situated to the right of the lower part of the heart, but left of the sternum.

106. *Bhagavad-Gītā*, VIII.14.

107. *Bhagavad-Gītā*, IX.34.

Through concentrated *japa* and prayer, one gradually attains the state of meditation. The devotee patiently has to steer through them all through practical means like saying prayers, repeating *japa*, offering flowers, fruits and lighting lamps to God, etc. "God is the greatest of all purifiers and most auspicious among all auspicious objects."[108] There is nothing on earth as purifying as the knowledge of the truth about God.

In the beginning, one can meditate only for a short time. Concentration without any alteration in one's feelings, desires and will should not be done. The mind should be disciplined through *japa*, prayers and contemplation or through all of them. The real yearning makes the practitioner struggle hard to reach the goal.

After mediation, one might feel a rush of energy. This should be diverted towards a higher channel, which makes the mind calm, that is, free from restlessness. The calm mind helps in rising to a higher plane of consciousness, the divine plane. It should be kept in mind that one has to adjust oneself between one's inner and one's outer life on a higher plane of spiritual practice. In devotional life, the main thing is to have a sense of proportion and adjustment. One should adapt oneself depending on the situation and avoid creating frictions. A nice atmosphere should be created around, which should be felt by all. The devotee should apply grace and dignity in all his actions.

In the spiritual path, there are more psychical than physical difficulties. Repetition of the divine name, along with the thinking of the meaning or the ideal it stands for, gradually removes the obstacles from the mind and makes it fit for meditation. Meditation culminates in absorption in the Divine and finally in illumination and actual contact of one's soul with the Divine.

Meditation should be preferably learnt from a *guru*. A spiritual master is capable of kindling the mind in the right way, so that

108. *Mahābhārata*, Anuśāsana Parva, 189.9.

the perfection in the process of meditation results soon. Still the devotee should put in his efforts to the best of his abilities.

Means to Different Stages of Devotion

Nārada defines devotion as the nature of supreme love for God. It is single-minded love directed towards God, which is devoid of any desire for wealth, happiness, virtue and liberation. The nature of supreme love for God is indescribable. It can only be experienced by a devotee, but cannot be described by him.

> It is like the experience of the joy, which a dumb man has, when he tastes something sweet.[109]
>
> Supreme love for God is devoid of *sattva*, *rajas* and *tamas*, that is, devoid of attributes. It is of the nature of a homogeneous and integral subjective experience, subtler than the subtlest, manifesting itself automatically in the wake of the fulfilment of certain conditions, and expanding every moment.[110]

Devotion is independent of causes; and its content is a perennial fountain of eternal bliss, it becomes increasingly enjoyable as it deepens and strengthens in the course of time. One can never become satiated with devotion; and so it is something that can be enjoyed all the time. Devotion springs from God, who is immanent in the *jīva* as its inner guide. It is directed towards Him, transcendental, continuous, incessant and ever-expanding. While it is veiled by *avidyā*, it can be revived by destroying nescience. It is experienced in subtler and subtler forms; and its sweetness can never be experienced in its entirety.

Everyone has the experience of love towards something or somebody now and then. In devotion, this natural love of the world is directed towards God after purifying and strengthening the emotion of love. This emotion of love does not require some

109. *Nārada Bhakti-Sūtra*, 52.

110. *Nārada Bhakti-Sūtra*, 54.

other proof to recognise it, for it is self-evident. "Supreme love for God is in the nature of tranquillity and supreme bliss."[111]

A devotee is one who has dedicated himself to God, who has acquired undivided devotion to God, thinks of Him only, recollects Him only, meditates on Him only, loves only Him and performs all actions for Him only. All his thoughts and emotions are directed towards God.

But the dawn of devotion or love for God grows out of a divine discontent in man. This discontent results in an aspiration for God, a longing to know more of Him, to move closer to Him and a feeling that life is purposeless, if it is not used to reach Him. Devotion develops knowledge, discrimination, dispassion, etc. As man increasingly begins to feel the joy of divine communion, worldly enjoyment will become insipid to him. Spiritual life is a need to develop devotion to God.

The basis of spiritual life is to have a great yearning in the mind for having a greater understanding of God and one's relationship with Him. The object of all spiritual practice is to intensify the spiritual yearning. The practice should be persisted with one's full capacity, until one reaches the stage of absolute resignation to the Divine. The practice should be deemed as a natural function, like taking food, etc. in spite of being busy in many other ways. Spiritual maturity can only come through the development of a firm moral nature, by becoming less and less self-centred in one's look, by cultivating deep and steady aspirations for the Divine and by systematic practice of devotion. Success in the practice is gained through certain means prescribed for a devotional life. The natural perfection of the human soul manifests only when the various faculties of the mind are purified and coordinated harmoniously. The spiritual practices are meant to effect this through the cultivation of various faculties of the mind. Devotion is mainly concerned with the culture and the

---

111. *Nārada Bhakti-Sūtra*, 60.

purification of emotions. The intellectual culture has got a place only in so far as it is necessary and helpful for the proper development of emotions, which is effected through an ardent love of God. Devotion is only a means. Various disciplines help one to achieve devotion. They aid the devotee to avail himself of the Divine grace, which always seeks to bless the devotee with devotion to God. Unless the lower stages are given up, the higher ones cannot be attained in spiritual life. It can be compared to the seed that decays and disappears, before it develops into a tree. Unless man ceases to be what he is, he cannot be, what he ought to be. When man becomes dispassionate to the material world, he will acquire knowledge and faith in higher divine bliss. Then the spiritual endeavour becomes firm and is productive of the best results.

"Renunciation and service, detachment from worldly objects and practice — these disciplines form the cornerstone of all spiritual disciplines."[112] Renunciation of the ego is the essence of spiritual practice. The renunciation is not complete, until the ego is destroyed. The prime characteristic of devotion is the complete self-surrender to God; every action done with this attitude has a due place in devotional life. Self-surrender is only another name for the effacement of the ego; any work that is selfless has a place in spiritual life.

Those who have had the experience of the upward struggle and the consequent realisation, and who, being deeply moved by the miseries of the world, stretch out a helping hand to those who begin their spiritual path. *Bhagavad-Gītā* considers undivided devotion as a means to the realisation of God, the Supreme person.[113] Lord Kṛṣṇa says

> He, who constantly worships Me through the Yoga of exclusive devotion — transcending the three *guṇa*s (*sattva, rajas* and *tamas*), becomes eligible for attaining *Brahman*.[114]

---

112. *Śrīmad Bhāgavata*, IV.22, 21.

113. *Bhagavad-Gītā*, VIII.22.

114. *Bhagavad-Gītā*, XIV.26.

> Unswerving and undivided devotion to God is true knowledge, because it is a means to the knowledge of Him.[115]

Bhagavad-Gītā emphasises devotion as the best means to God-realisation.

He who is constantly engaged in hearing, singing and dwelling on God's virtues, glories and pastimes, reciting and muttering His names, contemplating on His being and other such practices, who looks upon the mind, the intellect, the body, other organs and everything else as belongings of God and who continues to perform all actions in a disinterested way, for His sake and as an act of service to Him, regarding himself as a mere tool in His hands, is said to worship Him through the Yoga of exclusive devotion.

A devotee who serves, prays and worships God with single-minded devotion, completely transcends his psychical nature, composed of *sattva*, *rajas* and *tamas* attains union with Him. Such a devotee is tranquil, devoid of attachment, love and hatred, compassionate to all creatures, free from enmity and equal to all. He fixes his thought on God alone. Undivided devotion to God and constant meditation on Him generate his release from the embodied life. The *Śrīmad Bhāgavata* says,

> Supreme devotion is unswerving devotion or the most intense devotion to God.[116]

To reach this stage, certain means (*sādhanā*) of devotion are to be followed. God is Truth and can be attained by unswerving truthfulness. Faith in God is the first step to cultivate devotion. *Śrīmad Bhāgavata* prescribes *śraddhā* in hearing God's name, attributes and actions as one of the means to acquire devotion. Belief is the precondition of faith, and faith is a precondition of devotion.[117]

---

115. *Bhagavad-Gītā*, XIII.11.

116. *Śrīmad Bhāgavata*, I.15.33; II.3.10 and 11.

117. Faith (*śraddhā*) is the capacity of the mind to accept on trust, the ultimate →

Faith is belief in God, which is deeply tinged with an emotion producing transparency and tranquillity of the mind that are essential means to realise the supreme end. Faith is the pre-acceptance of God with sincerity and the resolution to live in such a way that it leads to this intuitive experience. The power of intuition is developed only from faith. One should also have faith in the scriptural sayings that inculcate spiritual doctrines based on the intuitions of the great seers and the disciplines laid down by them.

Acceptance of certain practices and of devotional observance that have come to one through family traditions, are the preliminary stages of devotional exercises. When it is made dynamic by faith, this acceptance of scriptural values becomes genuine devotion.

Faith in God and a devotional ideal are necessary for man's happiness in life and they increasingly gain necessity today compared to the earlier periods in human history, for without these virtues man will become more and more corrupt and unhappy. In fact, in the disciplinary stages, the devotee keeps a sense of real distinction between himself and God, which is essential for his practice. In the advanced stages, he will understand that true devotion alone can generate true love. They are complementary in their maturity though they may look different in the beginning.

Generally, man thinks of God as the Supreme Creator. Divine Majesty always lies in the forefront of his thought. To win the favour of such a being, prayer and adoration are considered necessary. The more one thinks of the basic relation between him and the Supreme Being, the more one earns emotional

---

→ and otherwise understandable facts of life with a power very near to that of conviction. Trust is always the basis of a reliable authority, namely a scripture or a teacher. Scriptures are revealed literature. The great teachers are men of illumination and power. Belief in God deepens into faith and faith deepens into devotion.

sustenance from Him and one is assured of His capacity and readiness to save him from the bondage of the world of experience. It ends in self-surrender through philosophic reflections and adorations. This type of devotion is mixed with knowledge. This element of knowledge is essential, as man cannot love anything without some preceding knowledge of the object or the person. But the need for knowledge ceases, when a strong link of affection is established.

When man has adoration for something outside himself, it becomes external devotion. It is based on the unenlightened feeling that God is external to man, that He dwells in a particular place or action — a temple, a shrine, a holy mountain, on the bank of certain rivers, in pilgrimages, in the worship of images, symbols and sacred books and so on. Higher than this, is the passionate worship of a chosen Deity or a personal God in the heart (*iṣṭa devatā*). It clears the worshipper's mind of many filaments of superstition and gives a healthy direction to the spirit of devotion.

The purest (*sāttvika*) devotion is that where the worshipper loves God for His own sake and not for obtaining any rewards. In the other two types of devotion, God is worshipped for the sake of benefits which are not necessarily material gifts that come from His grace.

When devotion is pure, there is peace in the devotee, for God graces him with the awareness in his heart. This peace is so great that he gradually learns to search for Him only and always. When He comes to dwell in man, man becomes indifferent to external prosperity, and His absence is his greatest adversity. When He is present in man, man can tide over every difficulty.

Some of the devotional means, the devotional teachers prescribe, are:

- Keeping the company of saints,

- Talking about God,
- Chanting His excellence,
- Explaining His message,
- Serving the spiritual guide with sincerity as His medium,
- Practising restraints, observances,
- Worshipping God daily with constancy,
- Muttering a mystic sound or formula (*mantra*) symbolising Him,
- Showing respect to His devotees,
- Detachment for objects of pleasure,
- Sense control and mind control,
- Reflection on the nature of the Ultimate Reality.

Nārada, the great devotee, says that the renunciation of the objects of enjoyment and the company of the people who are engrossed in worldly pleasure, serves as a means to devotion.[118] Just as, one who has attachment to worldly objects is absorbed in them, so too, one who is attached to God is absorbed in Him. The hindrance to the emergence of devotion is due to the company of worldly attached persons. The mind has the natural inclination to turn towards the objects of pleasure. As the mind is the basis of all sense operations, the senses will follow, when the mind turns away. On the other hand, evil company will strengthen the natural inclination of mind. So, the company of vicious persons should be shunned by all means.

Nārada also says that listening to God's attributes, as given to Him by His devotees, and chanting His name and glory in their company, are the means for the attainment of devotion. Scriptures, inculcating devotion, should be studied and reflected upon, and the actions, which are enjoined by them as conducive to devotion, should be performed. Thoughts favourable to

118. *Nārada Bhakti-Sūtra*, 35.

devotion should be entertained, and actions favourable to it should be performed.

The devotee should meditate on God without thinking of pleasure and pain or gain and loss. Non-injury, truthfulness, purity of the body and mind, compassion, faith in God and other virtues conducive to devotion should be cultivated.

Dedication of all actions to God is an essential element of devotion. Rāmānuja says that constant recollection of God is achieved by taking pure food, by the absence of attachment to any object of pleasure, concentrating the mind on divine objects, the study of Vedas, performance of sacrifices, charity, austerities and dispassion, the practice of virtues (truthfulness, simplicity, compassion, benevolence, non-injury and successful thought), absence of depression due to grief and avoiding excess of joy. Muttering the name of God (*japa*), fasting, charity and prayer to God are aids to the knowledge of the Supreme. Sense control, mind control, listening to the scriptures and reflection on them should be part of the daily life at all stages of life. All great teachers mention these as means of devotion.

Preparatory devotion is the sentiment of devotion generated in the mind by external stimulation from disciplines, environment and contact with other devotees. It manifests under proper conditions, but often disappears, when the external environment changes. Keeping the mind at a high spiritual level, without any external aid, is possible only at an advanced stage of spiritual life. In the development of devotion, two stages are spoken of. The first is called disciplinary devotion. In this stage, man takes the help of external aids to keep up a devotional mood. Constant hearing of the divine excellences, singing devotional songs individually or collectively, hearing devotional discourses and practising ritualistic worship are some of them. But it is only when loving attachment to God is established in the mind, that one will approach Him spontaneously without any external aid. This is a higher stage of spiritual development, which comes only by long and continuous practise of disciplinary devotion. To arrive at this stage, one must practice devotional disciplines continuously for a long period, until the subconscious mind is filled with these ideas. The Divine is an ocean of peace, strength and joy. He is within every being. When one feels that level of his being, then one will steadily establish in the higher states of joy. A true devotee will try to keep up the remembrance of God by repeatedly uttering His name, offering all his actions to the Supreme, whether it is personal or professional.

Studying of scriptural texts is part of one's spiritual practice. But it should not be studied for scholarly interests. These texts are meant to keep the devotee's mind in touch with Divinity. It is not a waste of time, but a necessity to keep up the ideals of the devotee. Even the professional and domestic work should become spiritual practices by dedicating them to the Divine, from whom the universe has come and by whom it is imprisoned. Devoting some time daily in the morning and evening for spiritual practices, the devotee can maintain an equilibrium between his worldly duty and his spiritual life. If the devotee considers and applies the attitude that all his energies are from the Supreme and thinks sincerely that he is offering all his energies and works to God in carrying out his duties, then all his actions, thoughts and motivations would become of an equal value as meditation.

PRECONDITION TO DEVOTION

Diet, recreation, activity, sleep and wakefulness of the devotee should not offend or go against the instructions of the scriptures and should be kept within the bounds considering the temperament, health and taste of the practitioner. A complete code of moral virtues and many duties are counted as preliminary conditions for a person following the path of devotion. A devotee, who is in the primary stage, should meditate upon the beauty of God and all his qualities and glories and learn to regard himself as His servant. One of the conditions of meditation upon God as the master, is to train oneself in dedicating all actions to Him. Reciting His name, listening to His glories and talking of His glories with joy are the stages in devotional practices, and they will gradually grow into a truly natural irresistible emotion. This emotion deepens into love. It is associated with a sense of possession by God and absolute detachment from other things.

Adoration and worship of a personal God is essentially needed in devotional practices. A devotee always follows *saguṇa bhakti* (devotion attributing qualities to God or the divine object), in which the personal God stands before him for all time, because he communicates his emotions with Him alone. *Saguṇa bhakti* includes all disciplinary stages of devotion. Meditation on the form of the personal God is the best form of devotional exercise.

Repetition of God's name or a prescribed phrase (*japa*) is accepted in all forms of spiritual disciplines. Lord Kr̥ṣṇa says, "Among offerings, I am the offering of *japa*."[119] To bring out its superiority to every other offering, Śrī Kr̥ṣṇa calls it His very Self. The Code of Manu (the Hindu Constitution) speaks very highly of *japa*:

> *Japa yajña*[120] is ten times more valuable than a ritual, the same, when practised in a low whisper, is hundred times more valuable, while mental *japa* is a thousand times more valuable than the same.

The *Pātañjala Yoga-Sūtra* says, *OṀ* is His (the Supreme Person's) designator and recommends its repetition as one of the ways of steadying the mind.[121] *OṀ* also known as *praṇava* is termed as a one-syllable *mantra* fit for repetition. "Of all significant words

119. *Bhagavad-Gītā*, X.25.

120. *Japa yajña* is the ritual of repeating God's name or any prescribed *mantra* with ardour.

121. *Pātañjala Yoga-Sūtra*, I.27-28.

praṇava stands the foremost, for it is an appellation of God."[122] Śrī Kṛṣṇa speaks of *praṇava* as His own Self. "I am the secured syllable *OṀ*."[123] The repetition of the word *OṀ* brings God-realisation; there is identity between the word and its meaning.

Performance of *japa* or silent repetition of the divine name is an important part of the devotional discipline. It comes under remembrance (*smaraṇa*) and is an aspect of devotional practice. Continuous repetition of divine names helps the remembrance of Him and develops love for Him. The superiority of *japa* is based on its freedom from dependence on any other particular object, time, place or other requirements. Moreover, while other sacrifices are not permitted for all, *japa* can be practised by all, irrespective of age, sex, caste and stage of life, at all times, in all places, in one form or another. There is another advantage in repeating divine names. It does not need any special instruction or guidance from anybody. There are no regulations for any ceremonial purity in repeating God's names mentally. "A spiritual man attains his goal through *japa* alone, whatever else he may perform or not."[124]

Buddhism, Christianity and Islam pay the same tribute to the Divine names.

In devotional language, the word *mantra* is used for the names or the invocation of an aspect of the Deity with some seed-letters (*bījākṣara*). It is transmitted for generations from a master to the disciple for devoted and concentrated repetition. A *mantra* is more than a prayer and is in itself a word of power. It is a sound-manifestation of the Deity; and through its repetition, the devotee is enabled to grasp the reality of the Deity. The repetition and the consequent rhythmical vibrations of the subtle sound regulate

---

122. *Bhagavad-Gītā*, XVII.23.

123. *Bhagavad-Gītā*, X.25.

124. *Manu-Smṛti*, II.87.

the unsteady mind of the devotee providing him harmony, which enables to seize the reality of the Deity.

Mere repetition is not sufficient; the power of the *mantra* can be evoked only by the concentration of the devotee. Just like it is not sufficient to have an axe to cut down a tree, one also needs the appropriate knowledge and the technique for its usage. So too, the devotee should have the correct understanding of the *mantra*'s significance and should be motivated by unconditional faith and aspiration. The essential point in understanding the significance of a *mantra* is that it is the Deity, who is in the sound form and by repeating the *mantra,* the devotee communicates with the Deity. The power of the *mantra* is roused through faith and aspiration. Faith consists in the uninhibited acceptance of the spiritual tradition, the teacher and the efficiency of the discipline (*sādhanā*) by the mind; failing this, the mind cannot exert the *mantra* with force. The devotee's strength and steadiness of spiritual aspiration are equally important. The devotee should have the thirst of heart, the longing and his soul should reach out for the Supreme Being — the most essential requirement in spiritual practice. When the power of the devotee is roused through understanding, faith and aspirations and unites with the power of the *mantra* through devoted and concentrated repetition, accompanied with contemplation, then enlighten-ment comes to him. He becomes established in harmony, fit to communicate with God.

It is by the subsidiary forms of devotion — called *sādhanā bhakti* — that perfect concentration is attained. The ascending stages in devotion depend upon the intensity of practice. Supreme devotion (*parā-bhakti*) is actually the devotion that arises after the realisation of God. Subsidiary devotion is a means thereof. This is in the form of chanting God's name, singing his glories, etc. The devoted service is the highest. Śrī Kṛṣṇa says,

> The *yogin* is superior to the performers of austere penances, and is considered to be superior even to those who possess (much)

knowledge. The *yogin* is superior to the performers of religious rites too. Therefore, O Arjuna, do you become a *yogin*. He who, with his inner self directed to Me, has ardour and worships Me — he is deemed by Me the most accomplished, as compared with the *yogin*s and also with all (others).[125]

DEVOTION AS A MEANS

Devotion as a means (*sādhanā bhakti*) is generated by devoted spiritual practices, which help in developing devotion. All forms of *sādhanā bhakti* produce affection towards God, because they aid to develop and acquire the affection needed to approach the Supreme.[126] From *sādhanā bhakti* arises mental purity (the destruction of sins, which cause impurity of mind, intellect, etc.). Various kinds of devotional means are elaborated in the scriptures, some of them are: worshipping God with all accessories, singing His glories, repeating His names and so forth are the best. All these purify the heart and help to aim at supreme devotion. There is no rule that they should be practised all together, or only some of them, or in any particular order. Any of them, when practised sincerely and intensely, can please God and thus give rise to supreme devotion.

Devotion as an end is produced by the grace of God. Some adopt devotion with its subsidiaries as a means to liberation. Some practise devotion for its own sake. Devotion is an end to them, who practise devotion to please God, because their devotion is a means to communicate with God. When devotion is practised for its own sake, it destroys the limitations (*upādhi*) of the embodied soul and consequently, destroys bondage. This brings forth

---

125. *Bhagavad-Gītā*, VI.46, 47.

126. Suppose one makes some extra effort to earn more money, with the help of which he would like to perform a special worship or go on a pilgrimage. In such cases, even though the effort is apparently worldly, it is to be considered as a subsidiary to devotion, since the end aimed at is devotion.

liberation, which is of the nature of immortality and is obtained through devotion to God. All devotional means lead to liberation only through the generation of supreme devotion.

> Through that supreme devotion he comes to know Me in reality, what and how great I am, and thereby knowing Me in essence, he forthwith enters into My being.[127]

The result of supreme devotion is God-realisation. The form of God-realisation varies according to the sentiment and the faith of the worshipper during the period of his spiritual discipline.

Cultivating devotion by *karma-yoga* (*yoga* of action) and *jñāna-yoga* (*yoga* of knowledge) develops into definitely determined love to God. When this type of love is established in the devotee, he feels God is both, the means and the end. Then he realises his inseparability from God, just like the radiance is inseparable from the sun and lives only in the love of God. He feels that God is absolute bliss; he renounces the pleasures of wealth, the happiness of *kaivalya*[128] and other types of satisfaction, realising that he exists for serving God. Devotion increases with the intensity of self-renunciation. Service to God is entirely different from all other services. The will of God as a ruler is the will to love and be ruled by love. The will of the devotee is his response to the Divine call and His attainment with the redeeming purpose, by developing the attitude of service to God.

Śrī Kṛṣṇa answers the specific question regarding the means to cultivate devotion with, "Concentrate and fix the mind on Me". This looks simple but in practice, one experiences how tough it is to tame the mind. For instance, when a person sits in his prayer room for worship, his mind will not be steady. To keep it subdued is as difficult as controlling the wayward wind. Kṛṣṇa spells out the method in four graded steps.

---

127. *Bhagavad-Gītā*, XVIII.55.

128. Isolation from the influence of the three *guṇas*.

Concentration requires discipline and constant practice:

- When the mind is intensely concentrated on Him, the devotee will abide in Him. But this too is difficult in the beginning, as the mind will refuse to entreat God,
- So, the next stage prescribed is to realise Him by practice (*abhyāsa*), which consists in constant retraction of the mind from worldly matters. If even this is hard to practice,
- Then one should dedicate all actions to God. If this practice is arduous too,
- Then one should take refuge in God.

The different types of prescribed devotional practices are:

- Single-minded devotion to God,
- Constant practice and discipline,
- Listening and chanting his names, and
- Giving up the fruits of one's actions.

A devotee should feel that all he does is under the direction of God.

OBSTACLES TO DEVOTION

Vanity, extravagance and loss of faith are the obstacles to devotion. Vanity tempts a person to make a parade of his devotion. He is pleased with the reputation he gets for spirituality and is displeased, when others do not recognise his merits. This is no true devotion. God's grace will not come to the devotee through vanity and pride, but through boundless humility and perfect charity. A true devotee should practise his devotion in secret. He should be gentle, kind and forgiving towards others. He should always endeavour to make himself pure and others happy. All this should be done with perfect naturalness and ease and with no idea that all should know this. Spiritual pride

— in whatever form — is deadlier than earthly pride. It ruins the soul faster than worldly vanity.

A true devotee should also be free from extravagance in all its forms. His devotion should be neither excessively emotional nor unnecessarily self-torturing. Śrī Kṛṣṇa says,

> Yoga (*bhakti-yoga*) is not for him, who eats too much, nor for him, who eats too little. It is not for him, who is given to too much sleep, nor for him, who keeps vigil too long. But in the case of a man, who is temperate in his food and recreation, restrained in all his actions and regulated in his sleeps and vigils, *yoga* (*yoga* of devotion) will put an end to all his sorrows.[129]

Regulated actions are duties performed with due regard to society. The stage of life, the conditions, the circumstances, study of scriptures, sleep and wakefulness should be regulated according to the devotee's nature and requirements.

Rāmānuja's Indications for Devotional Exercises

The system of Viśiṣṭādvaita Vedānta has a rich tradition. Rāmānuja is the chief expositor of Viśiṣṭādvaita. He led a saintly and simple life and was a genius of synthesis. One of his main contributions to Viśiṣṭādvaita is the justification of the supreme values of devotion (*bhakti*) and self-surrender (*prapatti*). He explained how devotion and *prapatti* are interrelated in all the ways.

Every philosophical system gives great importance to *sādhanā*. A thorough understanding of the true knowledge of Reality leads one to *sādhanā*. Viśiṣṭādvaita also considers that *sādhanā* is very important and dedicated itself to it. Like other great preceptors of the past, Rāmānuja also emphasised that one should follow the prescribed *sādhanā* for one's transcendental evolution. His concept of *sādhanā* is the twofold aspect of *bhakti* and *prapatti*.

---

129. *Bhagavad-Gītā*, VI.16-17.

Sādhanā is a means to an end. Etymologically *sādhanā* is that (goal), which is to be accomplished through practice. It is the process that unites the devotee with the goal of his aspiration. The word *sādhanā* has a wide connotation and implies all kinds of means for attainment of all types of aspirations, both worldly and spiritual. Rāmānuja restricts its connotation to the meaning "for achieving spiritual perfection". Different schools of Vedānta have expounded the philosophy of *sādhanā* in their own characteristic ways and prescribed action, knowledge, devotion or self-surrender as the aids for perfection.

Anyone can apply the principles of *sādhanā*. The theory of evolution, both ancient and modern, acclaims the human being as the finest product of creation, endowed richly with an enormous power of thought and deed that could be directed towards the attainment of perfection. Man has been the subject of study from the very early times. The sages have arrived with wisdom at the fundamental truth that the Supreme is an eternal principle — different and distinct from matter. This revelation of the eternity of the Self is the pivot, on which the entire structure of *sādhanā* is based.

Any devotee would certainly aspire to obtain answers to some questions: Is the *jīva* self-explanatory? Is he himself the creator of the universe? Is there an all-powerful, all-knowing, blissful Creator other than the *jīva*? If so, how is the soul related to that Creator? Is he one with Him or different from Him? What is the nature of matter? Why is the soul related with matter? When can it sever its relation from matter and how? The answers to these questions will only be understood, when man realises his situation in the physical and metaphysical universe as well as the goal he has to attain.

Naciketā, the son of Sage Uddālaka, was only worried about three problems, namely that of the Universal Being, that of the devotee and that of the means. Yama, the God of Death himself, instructed him in this triple philosophy of the end, the way and the Reality. The philosophy of *sādhanā* centres round the devotee (the disciple) or the finite Self related to the Universal Self.

The philosophy of Rāmānuja is based on the central thought that *Brahman* is the foundation of all existence, which only exists to glorify Him. Rāmānuja insists on the validity of all Upaniṣads and strikes out a unique path of interpretation based on the authority of tradition. It is a path of synthesis, by which all scriptural statements become equally significant.

Rāmānuja formulates an important interpretation of the apparently divergent texts without harming any of them. Creation is nothing but the manifestation of *Brahman* in the *cit* and the *acit* of the gross state. The world of matter and selves was existing with *Brahman* even before the creation of this world of names and forms. At that time, it existed in a subtle form, and it was impossible to analyse it, as there was no differentiation of names and forms. After creation had taken place, this world of matter and selves became distinguishable both, in name and form. *Cit* and *acit* existed as a part of Reality in the state of effect. Only matter and the Self undergo any change in creation but never the cosmic principle, the Absolute Reality. These two entities, namely *cit* and *acit*, are adjectival in nature and characterise *Brahman* in both, the primordial and the consequent stages. That is why, Reality is the One Absolute characterised by *cit* and *acit*.

The finite Self has lost its native state of consciousness due to its beginningless *karma*, by means of which it has bound itself down to the empirical life. The state of bondage is a state of reality and involves happiness, misery and rebirth. By following certain disciplines of *sādhanā*, the finite Self can get rid of this miserable plight and attain the state of liberation to enjoy the unlimited joy of Divine experience. The goal, one has to attain, is a positive Reality, which can only be achieved by personal efforts.

According to Rāmānuja, the finite selves are innumerable; they are not only different from matter but also are different from the Supreme Being. These individual selves are eternal, self-luminous, very minute and blissful in nature; they are substantive consciousness and qualified by attributive consciousness. Being different and distinct from the body, the sense organs, the vital airs (*prāṇa*) and the attributive consciousness, they are entirely supported, controlled and used by the Supreme, only for His satisfaction.

Based on the scriptures, Rāmānuja holds the Self to be atomic and declares that it resides inside the heart. *Śrīmad Bhāgavata* says,

> The Supreme Being along with the finite Self has entered into the internal cave of the heart.[130]

So, knowing the Supreme Being and the means to it, are most valuable to a devotee. The *jīva* cannot take delight without God. Therefore, the achievement of the unlimited bliss of the Divine communion and eternal service to Him are man's highest aspirations. The soul should become conscious of God. A devotee must yearn for a complete and comprehensive vision of the Supreme.

Rāmānuja was convinced that the Absolute *Brahman* of the Upaniṣad is itself *Īśvara* of religion, who is the supreme Vāsudeva, the inner Self of all. *Brahman* of the Upaniṣad is Sarveśvara or the Supreme God of religion. He is the first and the foremost, the God of compassion. His abundant mercy is for one and all without any distinction.

The Absolute of the Upaniṣads, *Para-Brahman*, who is the all-self and ultimate goal of humanity, is the ever-existent means of salvation and the universal Redeemer. The natural flow of His

130. *Śrīmad Bhāgavata*, I.2.11.

grace is checked by the *karma* of human beings at certain times. God is Himself the endeavour as well as the goal of all. Divine communion alone is the end of all beings; the primary means that has to be chosen is Himself. Spiritual perfection, devotion and self-surrender are the ways of clearing away the obstacles that withhold the spontaneous flow of Divine grace.

Rāmānuja holds that the specific name of the Supreme Being is Nārāyaṇa. He declares that God is the highest goal that everyone should attain. All other aims are delusions, because achieving any other thing is certain to involve the *jīva* in misery, sorrow and dissatisfaction. God alone is of the nature of supreme joy. Man finds joy in Him only; therefore God is the highest good that is to be attained.

The terms Viṣṇu, Nārāyaṇa,[131] Vāsudeva,[132] *Bhagavān* and *Brahman* denote the same Ultimate Reality referred to in the Upaniṣads. On this basis, Rāmānuja states that the term *Brahman* denotes the Supreme Being, who is identified with the name Nārāyaṇa on the authority of the Upaniṣad.

Affirming that *Brahman* is Nārāyaṇa, Rāmānuja intimates that the Reality of the Upaniṣad is a personal God associated with the Goddess Śrī. The doctrine of the Goddess Śrī forms a distinguishing feature of Śrī Vaiṣṇavism. Śrī is the beloved consort of Nārāyaṇa; and the Divine Couple constitutes the Ultimate Reality together.

One of the qualities attributed to Śrī is that she listens to the pathetic pleadings of the devotees. Everyone seeks Her. Śrī also

---

131. *Nara* stands for sentient and non-sentient entities in the universe. *Nara* meaning "Supreme Being", *Āyana* means "abode". *Nārāyaṇa* means "one who is the foundation of all sentient and non-sentient entities in the universe".

132. *Vāsudeva*: The root verb *vas* means "to reside", the suffix *deva* denotes that He shines (*divyati*).

means "to remove". So, Śrī is interpreted as the one who removes the sins of the devotees who seek Her refuge. She is also the one, who promotes good in the universe.

In the words of Rāmānuja, Śrī is the Divine Queen of the Ruler of all celestial beings. There is perfect similarity between God and Goddess in all respects. She has all characteristics of the Lord, appropriate to His status. He is inseparably related to Śrī; Nārāyaṇa is adored with Śrī. She holds the position of the Mother of the Universe, who extends the accessibility of the Divine to one and all — even to those who do not believe in devotion. It is the nature of the Mother to have the greater concern for the weak. In the system of Śrī Vaiṣṇavism, adoration and prayers to Śrī are offered to seek her grace. Rāmānuja insists on this point and he practically took refuge in Śrī before the commencement of his writings, rituals, etc.

Self-realisation is a part of God-realisation. In this approach, the devotee realises the adjectival nature of the finite Self, which attracts him towards the Supreme or God in full measure; and he proceeds steadily on the path of devotion to reach Him. Devotion to God is an unbroken meditation upon God, which is to be practised continuously by the devotee in the state of embodiment.

Rāmānuja's concept of *sādhanā* is remarkable for its spirit of synthesis. He has given right importance to *karma*, *jñāna* and *bhakti* and has assigned the proper place to each one of these. He does not discard one for the other. According to him, *karma-yoga* leads to Self-knowledge, which in turn leads to the knowledge of God. Action and knowledge are significant and necessary limbs of devotion.

Rāmānuja expounds a synthesis between Divine grace and human effort. Divine grace is indispensable for Liberation, but the human effort also has a role in winning it. Though God is omniscient and omnipotent, He does not bind one being to the state of embodiment and sets another being free according to His will and pleasure. He serves man according to his desires and aspirations. As a benevolent redeemer, He waits for man's eagerness to be saved. Therefore, a minimum of human effort is necessary to obtain Divine grace.

Upāsanā or *bhakti* is a form of knowledge to Rāmānuja; and there is no difference between devotion and knowledge. So, devotion is described as a kind of knowledge, having the nature of incessant, unlimited love towards God. Devotion does not contribute to the attainment of any other kind of aim, but only to the attainment of God. Knowledge in devotion is of the nature of meditation, which transforms itself into the love of God.

A long process of spiritual culture is essential for the attainment of the knowledge in devotion. It does not mean action in a general sense, but the action in the form of a special kind of experience. Rāmānuja identifies devotion with *dhruva smṛti* or *upāsanā* (the uninterrupted flow of intellectual love), since devotion is a kind of expansion of knowledge.

According to Rāmānuja, *bhakti-yoga* presupposes certain vigorous disciplines, which he calls *sādhanā saptaka*. They are meant for the sublimation of the feelings and the training of the intellect. They are (1) discrimination, (2) control of passions, (3) practice, (4) sacrificial work, (5) purity, (6) strength and (7) suppression of excessive joy.

Discrimination is the purification of the body, which is essential for the purity of the mind. The food one takes must be pure. Rāmānuja states that food should be free from the three kinds of impurities:

1. It must not be impure by its very nature, such as too exciting, too hot, too cold, unripe and such other impurities,
2. It must not be taken from wicked and accursed people, and
3. It should be free from impurities like dirt, insects, bacteria, etc.

The food taken goes a long way in determining the devotee's mental constitution, and so the devotee is advised to take pure food.

Controlling passion means freeing oneself from the cycle of desire and anger. This is indispensable for Divine realisation. Conquest over one's senses is the most essential aspect for successfully meditating upon *Brahman*. The devotee attains mental tranquillity, when he totally detaches himself from the grip of desire and anger.

Practice is an unceasing effort in fixing the mind on the auspicious form of the Supreme Being, who is immanent in everyone. Practice here is the uninterrupted meditation on God. This is termed as *dhyāna-yoga* and is to be practised at the prescribed time and space (for better results). This practice is only preparatory to obtain the steadfastness at the time of meditation. One should meditate forever on that Divine presence to attain steadfastness in the Divine.

The performance of the prescribed duties according to the stages of life and one's ability strengthens the power of one's meditation. But the scriptures do not ordain what is impossible of being achieved. "One, who is engrossed (devoted) in spiritual effort, is the chief among the knowers of *Brahman*."[133]

The practice of virtues implies the application of the eight qualities that are conducive to virtue:

1. Truthfulness (that which is conducive to the good of all living beings),
2. Integrity (the sincerity in thought, word and deed),
3. Compassion (the quality of being unable to bear the suffering of others and the spontaneous action of doing good to others),

---

133. *Muṇḍaka Upaniṣad*, III.1.4. According to Indian traditional scriptures Vedic recitation, sacrifices, penance, etc. are to be followed, as they are means of purification.

4. Benevolence (the absence of greed),
5. Non-injury to others (human or animal),
6. Non-coveting of others property,
7. Freedom from despair and melancholy, and
8. Freedom from excessive merriment.

In the scheme of *sādhanā saptaka,* the devotees have to gain the true knowledge of the nature of the soul and of *Brahman* (or God) from the scriptures and holy preceptors. The disciple must have absolute faith in the saving grace of the preceptor. When one is thus instructed into Divine wisdom, one develops into *brahma upāsanā* (meditation on God, the Supreme Being). From then on, he embarks on his pilgrimage to reach the ever-auspicious Lord, striving all the time to overcome the insurmountable obstacles on his way. Human mind is formed of the three *guṇa*s, (*sattva, rajas* and *tamas*). He has to put his individual effort to subdue the *tāmasika* and *rājasika* forces for a successful spiritual life. So, *karma-yoga* has been prescribed to divest the mind of all *rājasika* and *tāmasika* tendencies and to conquer the temptation of the senses. The scriptures therefore ordain that all *karma*s prescribed for the stages of life are to be observed throughout one's life for developing and completing the means of spiritual perfection.[134]

When *karma-yoga* is perfected, it culminates in the experience of the Self (*ātma avalokana*) — either directly or through *jñāna-yoga. Jñāna-yoga* is the stage, when the devotee contemplates on the native state of the Soul, which will lead to devotion towards the Supreme Soul.

DEVOTION AND SELF-SURRENDER

In Rāmānuja's system, devotion is a steady and ever-increasing remembrance of God, which is practised with intense love for God. The knowledge of God is identified with the love of God.

134. Rāmānuja's commentary on *Vedānta-Sūtra,* 1.1.1.

The devotee develops such intense love towards God that he arrives at a stage, where he cannot bear himself without realising Him. The devotee sees God through his heart, when this meditation becomes intense and perfect; it results in a vivid perception of the Supreme Being. The devotee has to surrender himself totally to God to conquer the obstacles in his devotional approach.

Viśiṣṭādvaita emphasises the fact that self-surrender is necessary for a successful course of *bhakti-yoga*. Self-surrender is a direct and valid means to *mukti*. Even if *bhakti* and *prapatti* are both valid means to liberation, each is meant for different classes of devotees. Those who are incapable of adopting the principles of *bhakti-yoga*, may observe self-surrender and attain their highest goal of life.

Rāmānuja maintains the distinctive nature of devotion and self-surrender. He upholds that both are valid means to liberation and expounds the twofold aspects of *prapatti*. Self-surrender completes *bhakti-yoga*; and so it functions as a limb to it. It also operates as a means to liberation; and in this aspect, it is a substitute for *bhakti-yoga*.

Bhakti-yoga is superior to *karma-yoga* and *jñāna-yoga* as it leads the devotee directly to the realm of his realisation. Its sole purpose is the attainment of God and being united with Him. This union is natural, sweet and gentle. The devotee feels the joy of keeping company with God even from the very beginning. Lord Kṛṣṇa says,

> This (devotion) is the royal science, the royal mystery, the supreme purifier. It is realised by direct experience. It is in accord with *dharma*,[135] it is pleasant to practice and is abiding.[136]

Even at the time of *sādhanā*, the devotee feels the delight of Divine experience. It is lovely (*priya*) by its very nature, and so it is by itself of the form of beatitude, as it causes Divine experience.

135. *Dharma* is that, which constitutes the means for the highest good.

136. *Bhagavad-Gītā*, IX.2.

Yet, it happens to be the ultimate means of attaining the Godhead, which alone is of the type of unlimited delight.

As devotion is extremely delightful, it is also easy to practise. It is ever-growing and never vanishes, not even after getting the Divine experience. On the other hand, it remains ever eternal with all. *Bhakti* is the means to *mukti*, and this state of liberation is qualified by devotion.

It should be noted that though Rāmānuja propounds the doctrine of devotion as a means to attain Liberation, he also admits the efficacy of *prapatti* as a direct means to God-realisation. In his *Vedārtha Saṁgraha*, which describes the means to *mokṣa*, Rāmānuja declares that the Supreme is attained through devotion, which is an uninterrupted, loving flow of memory of Him, and which has taken on the character of the most vivid and immediate vision of God. But this depends entirely on *prapatti*. Only by offering one's all and one's very Self at the feet of God does one develop *bhakti-yoga*.[137]

Prapatti is not an invention of Rāmānuja. It is enjoined in all sacred Hindu scriptures. It was observed by the savants of the past, such as the great Nātha Muni and Yāmunācārya, the great predecessors of Rāmānuja. Goṣṭipūrṇa, Rāmānuja's preceptor, initiated him to *prapatti*. Rāmānuja taught the doctrine of *prapatti* to his innumerable disciples and opened the gates of liberation to the majority of human beings, who were depressed, owing to their inability to follow the hard disciplines of *bhakti-yoga*. Rāmānuja holds self-surrender as a direct means to *mukti*. He also describes that self-surrender is not meant for perfecting other means, but to attain the eternal service of God. Rāmānuja was convinced that *mokṣa* was impossible without one's complete surrender at the feet of God. In his *Vedārtha Saṁgraha,* he states that there is no way of liberation without surrendering absolutely to God.[138]

---

137. *Vedārtha Saṁgraha* of Rāmānuja.

138. *Vedārtha Saṁgraha*.

The philosophy of *sādhanā* in Viśiṣṭādvaita is based on the fundamental truth of Divine grace and human endeavour. Human effort, which is adopted for the awaking of the Divine grace, is of two categories, namely devotion and Self-surrender. According to this school of thought, these are the only two ways of gaining spiritual perfection.

Because of its universal character, Rāmānuja's concept of *sādhanā* is of supreme importance to all. *Bhagavad-Gītā* sums up the essential features of *bhakti-yoga* in one significant verse, which refers to three points. "On Me fix thy mind, be devoted to Me; sacrifice to Me; prostrate thyself before Me; harmonised thus in thy Self, thou shalt come unto Me, having Me as thy Supreme Goal."[139] First, the devotee should fix his mind on the Supreme Being. This act is *dhyāna*. Secondly, he should engage himself in the different modes of worship of the Supreme Being. Thirdly, he should do other acts such as offering salutations to Him. This denotes one's dedication to God.

Non-meditative forms of Bhakti

Rāmānuja mentions of several modes of devotion, other than the meditative mode, and considers them as legitimate. They are praise (*stuti*), bowing down with obeisance (*namaskṛti*), striving or making an effort (*yatna*), reciting the Name of the Lord (*kīrtana*), worshipping an image (*arcanā*) and complete prostration (*praṇāma*).[140] He says that they are not the substitutes of yogic meditation.

> "If, resorting to *bhakti-yoga* which has the form of exclusive love for Me due to reflection on My qualities, you are unable even to do that *karma* to Me from which *bhakti-yoga* arises, then perform the *akṣara-yoga* or *dhyāna-yoga* which has the form of reflection on the essential character of the *ātmā*.[141]

139. *Bhagavad-Gītā*, IX.34.

140. Rāmānuja's commentary on *Bhagavad-Gītā*, IX.14 and 34; XI.55; XII.10; *Vedārtha Saṁgraha* of Rāmānuja.

141. Rāmānuja's commentary on *Bhagavad-Gītā*, XII.11.

While commenting on the 34th poem of 9th Chapter, he says,

> Therefore, in this way, you will engage yourself, for the sake of pleasing Me, in secular activities like those needed as the means for bodily sustenance, and religious activities like the obligatory and occasional rites, considering them to have been prompted by Me and find sole delight in complete subservience to and absolute dependence on Me. You will always be lovingly engrossed in uttering My names, making efforts to serve Me, prostrating to Me and similar activities. You will meditate on the whole universe as being under My governance and having subservience to Me as its sole delight. Meditating on the multitudes of My qualities which are exceedingly dear (to you), and offering (Me) everyday this worship as defined, you will attain Me alone.[142]

The Supreme is to be meditated upon by the devotee as his inner Self. *Prapatti* at the feet of God is essential for the commencement as well as the perfection of *bhakti-yoga. Prapatti* becomes possible and effective only under the following conditions:

- One should attune oneself to the will of God, by keeping away from transgressing divine laws.
- One should be convinced that there is no other means of redemption than the Supreme Lord.
- One should have that firmness of mind which is needed for placing unshakable faith in the Lord.
- One should be convinced of the redemptive will of God.
- One should actually entrust the Lord with the burden of one's protection with a feeling of thorough subservience to Him.

RĀMĀNUJA'S GUIDELINES

- Holy men are to be worshipped by paying them the same respect as one pays to one's spiritual teacher.

---

142. *Bhagavad-Gītā*, IX.34.

- The devotee should cultivate sincere faith in the teachings of great preceptors in days of yore.
- He should not be satisfied just with the acquisition of worldly knowledge, but should study repeatedly the works dealing with the greatness of God and the wonders of His creation. If the devotee is favoured with the sparking wisdom by the *guru*'s grace, then the attraction of the senses will cease for him.
- The devotee should learn to treat all his feelings with indifference.
- He should enjoy listening to the names and glories of God's devotees with as much relish as uttering God's names and glories himself.
- He should bear in mind that one who renders service to God's devotees, attains God faster.
- Dedicating himself to the service of God and his devotees will save the devotee from impediments that come in the path of his practice.
- The devotee should never consider his life for acquiring any selfish advantage, but must endeavour to realise the ideal.
- Everyday, some time should be devoted to the contemplation on the greatness of the devotee's spiritual preceptor and some time of the day to the reading of the Holy Scriptures.
- The company of those who pursue the path of self-surrender to God, ought to be always sought and one should spend some time in the company of other devotees.
- He who has truly surrendered himself to God's mercy, should not have any thought on his future, which is

entirely at His disposal. One's present life is entirely determined by one's past *karma*. So, it is not necessary to brood over it.

- Performance of all duties should be considered as a service rendered to the Supreme Being.

All traditional scriptures should be studied with respect, conviction and devotion and should be taught to others too. This is a service most pleasing to God. One can also spend his life in the service of God in the sacred places. One can stay, where one is immersed in contemplation on God, praying, repeating holy *mantra*s (*japa*), or seeking a holy man, who is full of wisdom, devotion and without desire, moving with him in such a way that he may be kind towards the devotees, which is itself a means for salvation.

Care should be taken in selecting friends. Those who like God are friends, and those who hate Him are enemies. The worldly minded are the indifferent ones. The sight of friends brings joy to the heart and that of enemies make the heart tremble. The sight of the indifferent is like coming across stocks and stones. Association with friends and holy men will confer spiritual illumination on the devotee.

One should shun the company of enemies and should be silent towards the indifferent. Hankering after worldly benefits will surely make one move away from God. Remembering that the all-merciful Being is ready to provide all that man prays for, he should ward off the enemies.

Glossary

Abhyāsa	Continuous and uninterrupted practice with conviction.
Abhyāsa-yoga	The practice of repetition.
Ācāra liṅga	One of the two aspects of *iṣṭa liṅga* (*ācāra liṅga* and *guru liṅga*).
Acit	Non-sentient matter; primordial cosmic matter (*prakṛti*).
Acyuta	One of the names of Viṣṇu.
Adbhuta	Wonder.
Ādhāra	The quality of being a support.
Adharma	Unrighteousness, wickedness, sinful actions.
Ādi ātmika	Miseries or sufferings related to the body and the mind.
Ādibhautika	Miseries or sufferings caused by living beings, relating to animate objects.
Ādidaivika	Miseries brought by Nature.
Āditya	The Sun.
Ādiyajña	Divine person, or Supreme person, unmanifest aspect of God.
Āgama	Revealed Scripture, the treatises dealing with the modes of worship of God and matters relating to temples. To join, to reach, to come to (the goal).

Agni	Fire, consecrated fire.
Agnihotra	Offering oblations to the sacred fire.
Aikya sthala	The highest devotional state when the individual soul unites with Lord Śiva, the Supreme Soul.
Aiśvarya	Lordship, one of the six principal attributes of God.
Aitareya	A Vedic sage; name of a Brāhmaṇa and an Upaniṣad.
Ākiñcanyam	Destitution.
Akka Mahādevī	One of the female personalities of Vīraśaivism.
Akṣara	Imperishable, immutable, a syllable letter.
Akṣara-yoga	Another name of *dhyāna-yoga.*
Āḷvār	One who is deeply immersed in God's experience. A Vaiṣṇava saint of south India.
Ānanda	Bliss, blissful, an essential attribute of *Brahman.*
Ānanda śakti	Power of joy.
Ānandopāya	Blissful means.
Ananta	Infinite, that which is not conditioned by space, time or another entity, a distinguishing attribute of *Brahman.* Name of the Primordial Serpent. Timeless and eternal.
Ananyagatitvam	Seeking the Lord as the sole refuge with complete aversion to all fruits other than liberation.
Āṇava upāya	Personal effort, one of the means in Śaivism.
Anavasāda	A mental state unaffected by afflictions. Cheerfulness.
Āṇḍāl	A women saint in Śrī Vaiṣṇavism.

Aṅga	A component.
Aṅga sthala	Part of the classification scheme in Vīra Śaivism.
Āñjaneya	A very important character in the epic *Rāmāyaṇa*.
Antaḥkaraṇa	The internal organ comprising *buddhi, ahaṁkāra* and *manas*.
Antaryāmin	The inner controller, the immanent Supreme Self.
Anuddharṣa	Tranquillity of mind, non-exultation.
Anukulasya saṁkalpam	Determination to perform whatever is pleasing to the Lord.
Anupāya	No-means. Another name for *ānandopāya*.
Anurāga	Affection, attachment, passion.
Anurakti	The highest love for God.
Apahata pāpman	One who is sinless. One of the epithets of God.
Apāna	Breathing out, one of the five vital airs.
Aparā	Lower, a dependent reality.
Aparā bhakti	Preparatory stage of devotion.
Appār	One of the Tamil saints of Śaivism.
Appaya Dīkṣita	One of the Tamil saints of Śaivism.
Apr̥thak siddhi	Inseparable union of the soul and the Supreme Soul. Inseparability of substance and attribute.
Araṇi	A fire-producing plant. Pieces of wood of *araṇi* are used for kindling the sacred fire by friction.
Āraṇyaka	Forest books, religious and philosophical writings to which the Upaniṣads are considered to be attached.

Arcanā	Offering flowers with the recitation of God's name.
Arjuna	One of the Pāṇḍava brothers.
Arka	An image set-up for worship. Incarnation of God by entering into the idols. The sun. Fit to be worshipped. Supreme Consciousness of the knower, means of knowledge, and the knowables (*vahni, arka* and *soma*).
Artha	Meaning. Object denoted by words. Acquisition of wealth.
Asānanda	Name of a devotee who promulgated Rāmānuja's teachings.
Asat	Non-existence.
Āśrama	An hermitage.
Āśraya	Locus, basis.
Aṣṭa Āvaraṇa	Eight protective armours.
Aṣṭāṅga yoga	The eightfold discipline of Yoga: *yama, niyama, āsana, prāṇāyāma, pratyāhāra, dhāraṇā, dhyāna* and *samādhi.*
Aśuddha sattva	Non-spiritual consciousness.
Aśvamedha	Horse sacrifice.
Aśvattha	The Indian fig tree.
Aśvinī	The twin divine physicians.
Ātma darśana	Experience or vision of the soul.
Ātma samarpaṇam	Recognition, acceptance and meditation on the fact that all the souls and the created world in which the souls enjoy are also the precious properties of the Lord.
Ātmattva	Identification with the pseudo-ego.

Avatāra	Descent of God, incarnation of God.
Avidyā	Ignorance, the cosmic principle that is the cause of the worldly illusion. Knowledge that is opposed to true knowledge.
Bādarāyaṇa	Author of *Vedānta-Sūtra*.
Baddha jīva	The soul in bondage.
Bala	Strength.
Basava	Founder of Vīraśaiva Śaivism.
Bhagavān	The Supreme Being endowed with six principal attributes, Viṣṇu.
Bhaja Govindam	One of the poetical works of Śaṅkara.
Bhakta	A devotee of God.
Bhakti	Devotion to God, loving meditation on God.
Bhakti mārga	Path of devotion.
Bhakti rasa	Joy kindled from the experience of divine love.
Bhakti sādhanā	Practice of devotion.
Bhakti-yoga	Observance of unceasing meditation on God as a means to liberation (*mokṣa*).
Bhara samarpaṇam	Recognition and contemplation that only the Lord protects not only the embodied souls but also the world to which the souls are associated with.
Bhārat Mātā	The Mother India, is the Goddess of the Asian subcontinent.
Bhāskara	12th century philosopher.
Bhasma	The Holy Ash associated with Lord Śiva.
Bhāva bhakti	Sentimental devotion based on the sense of

	loving intimacy with Him.
Bhāva liṅga	Manifestation of Śiva's Being (*sat*). Infinite Being.
Bhayānaka	Fearful.
Bhedābheda	Theory of transcendence and immanence of God. A school of Vedānta.
Bhīṣma	Pāṇḍava's and Kaurava's paternal uncle.
Bhogāṅga	One of the three forms of *aṅga* in Śaivism. The state when the soul takes delight only in what is conducive to spiritual growth (*tyāgāṅga, bhogāṅga* and *yogāṅga*).
Bhogāṅgin	One who experiences the delight of the Divine.
Bhūma	One of the meditation techniques.
Bhuma-vidyā	Another name for *brahma-vidyā,* the knowledge of the Infinite.
Bhuman	The Supreme.
Bhūta yajña	Offering food to the animals and birds.
Bībhatsa	Wonder.
Bīja mantra	One lettered *mantra. Bīja mantra* are the seeds to the manifested sounds and matter.
Bījākṣara	Seed-sounds.
Brahmā	The Creator.
Brahma bhakti	Devotion to Brahmā.
Brahma bhūta	State of *Brahman*.
Brahma-Sūtra	Another name for *Vedānta-Sūtra*.
Brahma upāsanā	Meditation on Brahmā.
Brahma-vidyā	Knowledge of the soul, also *ātma-vidyā*.

	Meditation on *Brahman*.
Brahma yajña	Study and teaching of Veda.
Brahmacarya	Celibacy, sense control.
Brahman	The Absolute of philosophy, the ultimate Reality, the personal God according to Viśiṣṭādvaita.
Brāhmaṇa	Theological treatises.
Brahmānaspati	The Lord of prayer. *Brahman*.
Brahmāṇḍa	The bliss of the *Brahman*. A solar system.
Brahmarandhra	The aperture in the crown of the head through which the individual soul is said to leave its body upon death.
Buddhi	Intellect, intelligence. The third of the 25 principles of the Sāṁkhya philosophy, internal organ, one of the *antaḥ karaṇa*.
Caitanya	Absolute Consciousness. The supreme Spirit regarded as the essence of all living beings. *Puruṣa*. Also name of a philosopher.
Cara liṅga	One of the two aspects of *prāṇa liṅga* (*cara liṅga* and *Śiva-liṅga*). The pure luminous *puruṣa*, which is without inward or outward, without any form, also called *ātman*.
Cara sthala	A devotional state when the devotee realises that all his progress is due to *cara liṅga* (a manifestation of Śiva).
Cit	Sentient being, individual self. The Spirit, *Brahman*.
Citta	Consciousness. Mind looked upon as the thinking principle. The intellect (*buddhi*), ego (*ahaṁkāra*) and senses (*indriya*) as one internal

	organ (*antaḥkaraṇa*).
Dahara-vidyā	One of the meditations prescribed in *Chāndogya Upaniṣad*.
Dama	Control of senses.
Daśāṅgula	Ten fingers (space of 10 fingers). Ten directions that the Creator occupies.
Dehin	Empirical self.
Deva	God, Divine.
Devahūti	Sage Kapila's mother.
Devāram	One of the important works on Śaivism.
Devatā	Vedic deity: Celestial being.
Devī	Goddess.
Dhāraṇā	Concentration.
Dharma	A quality of a substance, an attribute, righteousness, religious duty. Merit earned by the performance of duties allotted to each person's *dharma*.
Dhruva	A child devotee who was graced with the vision of the Lord. The planet Jupiter.
Dhruva smṛti	Steadfast meditation.
Dhvani	Undifferentiated sound.
Dhyāna	Contemplation, meditation. A term used in the Upaniṣads to mean *bhakti*.
Dhyāna-yoga	Steadfast meditation.
Divya Prabhandham	The divine sayings. A very important work on devotion written in Tamil by *Vedāntadeśikam*.
Divyonmāda	Divine madness.

Draupadī	Pāṇḍava's wife.
Draviḍa	Southern. Name of the civilisation that prevailed before the arrival of the Āryans.
Duḥkha traya	The three sorts of suffering: *ādhibhautika, ādhidaivika* and *ādhi ātmika*.
Duḥśāsana	One of the brothers of Duryodhana.
Durgā	One of the manifestations of Śakti.
Dvaitādvaita	The Absolute as unity in difference. A system of Vedānta.
Dveṣa	Hatred, aversion. Different forms of aversion are: Anger, ill-will which is a deep-seated inclination, resentment, jealousy and indignation.
Ekānta bhakti	Supreme devotion.
Ekattva	Oneness.
Gajendra	Name of an elephant, whom Viṣṇu saved from the clutches of a crocodile and graced him liberation.
Gaṇa devatā	Group of deities.
Gargara	Violin.
Garutmat	Bird in general. Name of Garuḍa.
Gāyatrī	Considered mother of Veda.
Gāyatrī-mantra	Name of a very important *mantra* in honour of the Sun God.
Girīśa	Name of Śiva. Lord of Mountains.
Godhā	Another name of Āṇḍāl. A musical instrument (lute).
Gopīs	The female cowherd devotees of Śrī Kṛṣṇa.

Gṛhastha	A married man assuming the responsibility of his family life.
Guḍūcī	*Tinospora cordifolia*. One which protects the body.
Guru liṅga	One of the two aspects of *iṣṭa liṅga* (*ācāra liṅga* and *guru liṅga*). Knowledge and power of Śiva assuming the form of a teacher.
Hanumān	Name of the monkey god. Another name of Āñjaneya, a very important character in *Rāmāyaṇa*.
Hari	Another name of Viṣṇu.
Hāsya	Comic.
Hayagrīva	God of knowledge and wisdom.
Hiraṇya Puruṣa	The innermost essence of the visible universe.
Hiraṇyagarbha	The Golden Egg. The Vedic deity entrusted with the function of cosmic creation, Brahmā, name of Viṣṇu.
Hiraṇyakaśipu	Name of a demon king.
Hṛdaya	Heart. The seat of the soul and of the Supreme Soul.
Hṛdayākāśa	The inner space of the heart (where the soul resides).
Icchā	Will. Desire.
Icchā śakti	Will-power.
Idamdra	Another name of Indra.
Ilaya Perumaḷ	Another name of Rāmānuja, the founder of Viśiṣṭādvaita Vedānta.
Indra	A Vedic God.
Indriya	Sense organs.

Īśa	Auspicious. Name of Supreme Lord. Name of Śiva.
Īṣāṇa	The Master. Name of Śiva.
Iṣṭa devatā	Chosen deity.
Iṣṭa liṅga	Manifestation of Śiva's Bliss (*ānanda*). One of the forms of *liṅga* worship.
Īśvara	God, the Supreme Being as the controller of all beings.
Īśvara praṇidhāna	Devotion to *Īśvara*. Abandoning all actions and the fruits of actions to *Īśvara*.
Itihāsa	The two epics — *Rāmāyaṇa* and *Mahābhārata*.
Jāgrat avasthā	Waking state.
Japa	Repetition of *mantra* or God's name.
Japa yajña	Ritualistic repetition of a *mantra* or God's name.
Jayadeva	Author of lyric *Gīta Govindam*.
Jīva	Individual self.
Jīvan-mukta	One purified by true knowledge while still living and therefore freed from the cycle of births.
Jīvan-mukti	The state of devotee's soul after Liberation.
Jīvātmā	The soul residing in a living body.
Jñāna	Knowledge. Usually, the knowledge of the Truth, of the Supreme.
Jñāna bhakti	Devotion based on vivid awareness of the divine majesties.
Jñāna mārga	Path of Knowledge.
Jñāna śakti	Power of knowledge.

Jñāna viśeṣa Devotion as a special kind of knowledge.

Jñāna yajña Devout study of sacred scriptures.

Jyotiṣṭoma A type of Vedic sacrifice.

Kaivalya The state of existence of the Self in its true form as free from bondage, a state of *mokṣa*.

Kālī A manifestation of Śakti.

Kalki An incarnation of Viṣṇu, yet to occur.

Kalyāṇa Auspicious.

Kāma Passion, attachment, desire.

Kapila Author of *Sāṁkhya-Sūtra*. Considered as an incarnation of Mahā Viṣṇu.

Karma Action both mental and physical, rituals, past deeds and their results in the form of merit and sin.

Karma mārga Path of *karma*.

Karma-phala tyāga Renunciation of the fruits or results of actions.

Karma-yoga Observance of religious acts as a means for self-realisation, Yoga of action.

Kārpanyam Feeling of utter helplessness.

Kārttikeya Name of the son of Lord Śiva.

Kāruṇya Compassion.

Kauravas Cousin brothers of Pāṇḍavas. Important characters in *Mahābhārata*.

Kauṣītaki Name of an Upaniṣad.

Kāverī A river in south India.

Keśava Name of Viṣṇu.

Kevala To be alone, general, simple, unalloyed.

Kīrtana	Songs on the glory of God.
Kīrtimata (Vaigai)	One of the rivers of south India.
Kriyā	Activity, the performance of rites.
Krodha	Fury, anger.
Kṣara	Destructible.
Kūrma	The tortoise.
Lakṣmī	Name of Goddess who is the consort of Viṣṇu.
Lakṣmī Tantra	One of the important ritualistic practices of this school.
Liṅga Purāṇa	One of the Purāṇas.
Liṅga sthala	The worshipped form of the formless Śiva.
Liṅgāṅga	The individual souls.
Liṅgāyata	One who wears *liṅga*. The Vīraśaiva devotees.
Lobha	Greed.
Mada	Haughtiness.
Mādhava	Name of Viṣṇu.
Mahābhārata	One of the two great Hindu Epics, the other being the *Rāmāyaṇa*.
Mahabhūta	The primal matter (five in number): *pṛthvī, ap, tejas, vāyu* and *ākāśa*.
Mahādeva	The Great Lord. Name of Śiva.
Mahānadī (Periar)	Name of a river in south India.
Mahātma ghana liṅga	One of the two aspects of *bhāva liṅga* (*prasāda ghana liṅga* and *mahātma ghana liṅga*). That which is completely full in itself, subtle, having neither a beginning nor an end, and is indefinable.

Mahāviśvāsa	Complete faith and conviction.
Mahāyajña	Great sacrifices. The five great sacrifices are: *agnihotra* (domestic sacrifice), *brahma-yajña* (study and teaching of Vedas), *nara-yajña* (service of the guest), *bhūta-yajña* (giving food to the animals and birds) *pitṛ-yajña* (offering of oblations to ancestors).
Maheśvara	Name of Śiva.
Māheśvarī *śakti*	Name of Śakti.
Maitreyī	One of the Vedic sages.
Mala	Impurities.
Manana	Logical reflection.
Manas	Mind.
Mānikka Vācakar	A great Tamil Śaiva saint.
Mantra	Sanskrit language syllables or words signifying spiritual ideas, a Vedic hymn.
Manu	The first man. Father of the race and guide to humanity. Author of *Manu Dharmaśāstra*. Dharmaśāstra is the oldest code of conduct which is followed in Hinduism.
Mārkaṇḍeya	Name of a sage.
Marut	The wind God.
Mātariśvan	The wind God. Name of *Brahman*.
Mātsarya	Hatred.
Matsya	Name of the one of the Purāṇas.
Māyā	Cosmic principle which gives rise to the worldly illusion, the phenomenal character of the universe, the primordial matter (*prakṛti*).

Meykanda Devar	A thirteenth-century philosopher who systematised Śaiva Philosophy.
Mitra	A Vedic God.
Moha	Delusion which prevents the discernment of truth.
Mokṣa	Liberation of the soul from bondage, a complete and comprehensive experience of Brahmā, attainment of *Brahman*.
Mukhya bhakti	Supreme devotion.
Mukta jīva	Librated souls.
Mukti	Immortal freedom or liberation.
Mumukṣu	An aspirant for *mokṣa*, one who is desirous of release from bondage.
Murugan	Son of Lord Śiva.
Nacchiyār Tirumoli	A devotional poetical work of the lady Vaiṣṇava saint Āṇḍāl.
Naciketā	A young philosopher of the *Kaṭha Upaniṣad*.
Nāma	Name.
Namaskr̥ti	Bowing down with reverence.
Nammalvār	One of the important Vaiṣṇava saints of south India.
Nārada	A divine sage, author of *Nārada Bhakti-Sūtra*.
Narasiṁha	Man-lion (an incarnation of Viṣṇu).
Nārāyaṇa	The Supreme Being who is the ground of all sentient and non-sentient entities in the universe and also immanent in them.
Nara-yajña	Service of the guest.
Narmadā	Name of a river in central India.

Nava rasa	The nine emotions.
Navadvīpa	The nine-islands.
Nāyaka	Name for the Supreme Lord.
Nāyanmār	Śaiva saints.
Nididhyāsana	Steadfast meditation.
Nidrā avasthā	Sleep state.
Nimba	Margosa (*Azadirachta indica*).
Nimbārka	Expounder of one of the schools of Vedānta: Bhedābheda.
Nirguṇa	Devoid of all characteristics, undifferentiated, devoid of defiling attributes.
Nirguṇa Brahman	*Brahman* without qualities.
Nirodha	Restricted or restrained.
Niṣkāma karma	Actions that are free from desire for any results.
Nitya mukta	Eternal free souls.
Nitya suri	Eternally existing souls, free from bondage.
Nivṛti	Removal.
Niyama	Observance as an accessory to Yoga comprising cleanliness, contentment, austerities, study of scriptures and devotion to God.
Niyamānanda	Another name for Nimbārka.
Nyāsa-vidyā	The observance of self-surrender as a means to *mokṣa*.
Ojas	Essence of the end-product of the digested food. The fundamental energy behind all activities — physical, mental or spiritual.

Pañca ācāra	Five codes of conduct.
Pāñcarātra	Religious treatises dealing with the modes of worship of God and matters relating to temples.
Pañcākṣara mantra	The five-lettered *mantra* of Śiva: *oṁ namaḥ śivāya*.
Pāṇḍava	The five cousin brothers of Kauravas.
Pāpa	Sin accrued as a result of the performance of evil deeds. Unfavourable disposition of God.
Parā	The highest. The Supreme. The Transcendental.
Parabrahman	The Supreme *Brahman*.
Parama bhakti	Supreme devotion.
Parama pada	The Supreme abode of Viṣṇu.
Parama puruṣa	The Supreme Person.
Paramātmā sākṣātkāra	Direct perception of the form of the Supreme Soul or God.
Paramātman	The Supreme Soul. *Brahman*, God.
Parameśvara	The Supreme God.
Parāśakti	Supreme Śakti.
Parāśiva	Name of Śiva.
Paraśurāma	A minor incarnation of Viṣṇu.
Parātattva	Ultimate principle.
Paratattva	Supreme Entity.
Pārtha	Name of Arjuna.
Pāśa	Bondage.
Paśu	Individual souls.
Pāśupata-Sūtra	One of the most important texts of Śaivism.

Pāśupati	Lord of individual souls. Lord Śiva.
Pati	Lord.
Pattinathor	A Śaiva saint.
Payasvinī (Palar)	Name of a river in south India.
Peria Purāṇa	The big Purāṇa, a sacred Śaiva literature.
Periyālvār	Name of a Śrī Vaiṣṇava saint.
Piṇḍāṇḍa	Part of *Brahman*'s power in man.
Pitṛ	Forefathers (Ancestors).
Pitṛ-yajña	Offerings of oblations to the ancestors.
Prabandha	A composition of Tamil hymns by Āḷvārs.
Prahlāda	The child devotee of *Śrīmad Bhāgavata Purāṇa*.
Prajāpati	A personification of Brahmā.
Prākāra-prākāri	The mode and the substance.
Prakṛti	Primordial matter.
Prāṇa	Vital breath, also applicable to *Brahman*.
Prāṇa liṅga	Manifestation of Śiva's Consciousness (*cit*). Universal divine.
Praṇāma	Salutation.
Praṇava	Original name for *OṀ*.
Prāṇāyāma	Breath control, one of the eight accessories conducive to Yoga.
Prapanna	One who seeks refuge with God. One who adopts *prapatti*.
Prapatti	Total self-surrender to God as the sole refuge.
Prārabdha karma	*Karma* which has already begun to give result.
Prasāda	Favour, grace.
Prasāda ghana liṅga	One of the two aspects of *bhāva liṅga* (*prasāda*

	ghana liṅga and *mahātma ghana liṅga*). That in which one finds the seed of development as consciousness beyond the senses.
Pratyāhāra	The withdrawal of senses from external objects.
Pravṛtti	Activity, initiation into action.
Prema	Affection.
Prīti	Love, devotion.
Priya	Lovely.
Purā bhāvam	Belonging to the past.
Purāṇa	Aged, ancient. Hindu mythological works.
Puruṣa	The supreme Soul. Absolute Awareness. The first of the 25 principles of Sāṁkhya philosophy. Man.
Puruṣārtha	The aim of life of a human being: *dharma, artha, kāma* and *mokṣa*.
Puruṣottama	The Supreme Lord.
Rādhā-Kṛṣṇa	Name of Śrī Kṛṣṇa with His consort Rādhā.
Rāga	Attachment. Passion, that which dwells upon pleasure.
Rāga bhakti	Sentimental devotion.
Rajas	One of the three attributes of *prakṛti* (*sattva, tamas*): the quality which causes suffering, passions, etc.
Rājasika	That which is of the nature of *rajas*.
Rāma-nāma	"Name of Rāma". Name of *Rāma-mantra*.
Rāma-nāma japa	Repetition of Rāma-*nāma*: *rām, rām, rām* . . . Or, *oṁ śrīmrāmrāmrām rāmāya namaḥ*.

Rāmāyaṇa	One of the two important Hindu epics, the other being the *Mahābhārata*.
Raṅganātha	Name of Viṣṇu. Name of the God in Śrīraṅgam, Kāñcīpuram and other important pilgrim centres.
Raudra	Furious.
Ṛṣyamūka	Name of a mountain in central India.
Ṛta	The divine law.
Rudra	A Vedic deity, Śiva as conceived in the post-Vedic period, also synonymous with Viṣṇu according to Rāmānuja .
Rudra Saṁhitā	One of the sections of *Śiva Mahā Purāṇa*.
Rudrākṣa	"Eye of Rudra". The beads used by Śaivaites.
Rūpa	Colour, form.
Saccidānanda	*Sat + cit + ānanda* or Existence, Knowledge and Bliss.
Sadāśiva	Name of Śiva.
Sādhaka	A devotee.
Sādhanā	Method or means adopted to achieve a goal.
Sādhanā bhakti	Practice of devotional means.
Sādhanā saptaka	Sevenfold practice.
Sādhya	What is to be achieved; spiritual goal.
Sādhya upāya	The past pious deeds as means to liberate a soul.
Saguṇa	Endowed with attribute.
Saguṇa bhakti	Devotion attributing qualities to God or the divine object.
Saguṇa Brahman	*Brahman* endowed with attributes.

Sahasra pada	Thousand-footed. An attribute of the Supreme *Puruṣa*.
Sahasrākṣa	Thousand-eyed. An attribute of the Supreme *Puruṣa*.
Śaiva	Worshipper of Śiva.
Śaiva Āgama	The Āgama scriptures of Śaivism.
Śākta	Relating to Śakti. One of the means to attain the Supreme (in Śaivism).
Śakti	The power. The active power of a deity. The Female power in Śaivism.
Sālokya	Entering the abode of God.
Śama	Calmness, tranquillity, mental calmness.
Śambhū	Giver of happiness and prosperity. Name of Śiva.
Samādhāna	Concentration of mind.
Samādhi	Final stage of the *aṣṭāṅga-yoga* discipline. The concentrated attention and mental realisation.
Sāmbhava	Means which awakens the limitless knowledge of the soul.
Saṁgha	The community of monks who followed the Buddha.
Saṁhitā or Saṁhithā	Composition of Vedic hymns. A treatise.
Sāmīpya	Remaining near God.
Sāṁkhya bhakti	Discriminative knowledge of the 24 principles and *Puruṣa*.
Saṁnyāsa	Renunciation.
Saṁsāra	Life-cycles of births and deaths.

Saṁskāra	The subliminal impressions which lie latent in the mind.
Saṁśleṣa	Union with God.
Sanatkumāra	Name of Vedic Sage.
Śāṇḍilya	The author of *Śāṇḍilya Bhakti-Sūtra*. Śāṇḍilya, name of a sage, author of a law book, an Upaniṣad is named after him: *Śāṇḍilya Upaniṣad*.
Śāṇḍilya Bhakti-Sūtra	Śāṇḍilya's aphorisms on Devotion.
Śaṅkara	Propounder of Advaita Vedānta. Name of Śiva.
Sānnidhya	Being in the proximity of God.
Śānta	Peaceful, serene.
Śānta rasa	Emotional expression of peace and calmness of mind.
Śānti	Mental tranquillity.
Saptarṣis	The seven sages.
Sāra	Essence.
Śaraṇa sthala	A devotional state wherein the devotee finds delight and confidence in the service of God.
Śaraṇāgati	Surrendering to God as the sole refuge.
Sarasvatī	Goddess of Learning.
Śarīra-ātmā-bhāva	Concept of God as the owner of the body of the created beings.
Śarīra-śārīra	The inseparable integrity between body and soul.
Sārūpya	Attaining the likeness of God.
Sarveśvara	Lord of all.

Sat	Existence, that which always exists.
Satsaṅga	Assembly of holy persons.
Ṣaṭsthala	A process in Vīraśaivism whereby a devotee progresses in six stages of devotion until he attains oneness with Lord Śiva.
Sattva	One of the three attributes of *prakṛti* (*sattva, rajas* and *tamas*), the quality which represents whatever is fine or light.
Sattva śūnya	Devoid of the three *guṇa*s.
Sāttvika	Pertaining to or characterised by *sattva guna.*
Sāttvika tyāga	Pure renunciation.
Satya	True, truth.
Saundaryalaharī	A devotional composition on the Goddess Devī by Śaṅkara.
Savitā	A Vedic divinity representing one of the manifestations of the Sun God.
Sāvitrī	One of the dynamic forms of the eternal sound. A personification of the Sun God.
Sāyujya	The state of *mokṣa* in which the individual self enjoys equal status with *Brahman.*
Śeṣa-śeṣī	One who exists for the purpose of the Lord, and the Lord. Master-servant.
Śeṣitva	The whole as an attribute.
Sevā	Service.
Śiva	Name of the Supreme Deity of Śaivism. Auspiciousness. Viṣṇu.
Śiva-liṅga	One of the two aspects of *prāṇa-liṅga* (*cara-liṅga* and *Śiva-liṅga*). The symbolic representation of Śiva. The Sanskrit word *liṅgam* means

	symbol, so *Śiva-liṅga* means symbol of Śiva.
Śiva-tattva	The principle of Śiva.
Skanda Purāṇa	One of the Purāṇas.
Smaraṇa	Remembering the glory of the Lord.
Smṛti	Texts based on Revealed Scriptures such as Epics, Purāṇas, Dharmaśāstras, Āgamas, etc.
Smṛti santati	A kind of meditation. An unbroken series of recollection of the object of meditation. A term used in the Upaniṣads to mean *bhakti*.
Soma	Name of a plant. The most important ingredient in Vedic sacrificial offerings. Nectar. Beverage of the Gods. Name of Śiva (Vahni, Arka and Soma).
Spanda	Vibration.
Śraddhā	Faith, synonymous with Lakṣmī, the consort of Viṣṇu.
Śravaṇa	Hearing, comprehending what is taught by the teacher.
Śrī Vaiṣṇava	Worshippers of Viṣṇu and Śrī Lakṣmī.
Śrīkānta	One of the commentators on *Vedānta-Sūtra*.
Śṛṅgāra	Marvel and peace.
Śruti	Revealed Scripture. Vedas including the Upaniṣads.
Sthala	An abode. Reality in Śaivism. Realisation of six truths: *bhakta sthala, maheśvara sthala, prasādi sthala, cara sthala, śaraṇa sthala* and *aikya sthala*.
Stuti	Praise.
Sudarśana	Good looking, beautiful. The discus of Viṣṇu.
Śuddha	Pure.

Śuddha sattva	Pure unalloyed *sattva* quality, transcendental spiritual matter.
Śuddhādvaita	Pure non-dualism of Vallabha.
Sūkṣma śarīra	The subtle body also called *liṅga śarīra*, comprises the mind, the intellect, the ego, the five sense-elements of sound, touch, colour or form, taste and odour, and their sensory functions.
Suniti	Mother of Dhruva.
Suparṇa	A fine-winged bird, a mystical symbol for the Ultimate Reality in Veda.
Sūrya	The Sun God.
Svapna avasthā	Dream state.
Svarūpa	Inherent features.
Svarūpa śakti	Inherent energy.
Tāmraparṇī	Name of a river in south India.
Tanmātra	Subtle elements.
Tapas	Austerity.
Thali	A symbolic representation of *liṅga* made out of the mountain palm leaves.
Tamas	Quality of causing lethargy, darkness; One of the three *guṇas* (*sattva, rajas* and *tamas*).
Thirumurai	Collection of nearly 20,000 verses in 12 sections from 26 Śaiva saints.
Thiruvaimoli	Tamil hymns of Nammālvār.
Tīkṣṇa	Active, penetrating.
Titīkṣā	Forbearance.
Tukārām	A devotee and saint.

Tulasīdās	A devotee. Author of *Rāmacaritamānasa*.
Turīya	The fourth.
Turīya avasthā	The fourth state, the transcendental state.
Tyāgāṅga	One of the three forms of *aṅga* in Śaivism. The state wherein the soul (*jīva*) gives up attachment to worldly objects (*tyāgāṅga*, *bhogāṅga* and *yogāṅga*).
Udgīta	The sacred syllable *OṀ*.
Udgīta-vidyā	A type of meditation.
Ukta	Eulogy, praise. Name of a Vedic sacrifice.
Umā	Lustrous, beautiful. Wife of Śiva.
Umāpati	Śiva. A successor of Meyakandadeva, lived around CE 1300.
Upādhi	Adjunct, a limiting condition .
Upadraṣṭā	The Supreme Lord.
Uparati	Abstaining from sense activities.
Upāsaka	One who worships.
Upāsanā	Meditation. A term used in the Upaniṣads to mean *bhakti*.
Upāsya	The object of worship.
Uṣas	The dawn. A Vedic God.
Vahni	Name of Śiva (Vahni, Arka and Soma).
Vaikuṇṭha	The paradise. Viṣṇu's abode.
Vairāgya	Absence of worldly desires.
Vaiṣṇava	A devotee of Viṣṇu.
Vājaśravasa	A Vedic sage.
Vallabha	Founder of Pure non-dualism of Vedānta

(Śuddhādvaita).

Vālmīki	Author of the great epic *Rāmāyaṇa*.
Vānaprastha	Forest life with celibacy.
Varāha	Boar, the Boar incarnation of Viṣṇu.
Varuṇa	Vedic God of rain.
Vāsanā	Subliminal imprint of an experience but not producing direct results.
Vāsudeva	The Supreme Being as described in the Pāñcarātra system. Viṣṇu.
Vāsudeva-mantra	One of the *mantras* of Viṣṇu: *oṁ namo bhagavate vāsudevāya*.
Vātsalya rasa	Sentiment of affection and tenderness.
Vedanā	Knowledge of *Brahman*. Meditation on *Brahman* according to Rāmānuja.
Vedānta	End of Veda. A system of Hindu philosophy. A term used in the Upaniṣads to mean devotion.
Vedānta Deśika	A disciple of Rāmānuja.
Vibhūti	Property or glory of God.
Vidhātru	The supporter.
Vimoka	Freedom from desires.
Vīra	Heroism.
Vīraśaiva	A branch of Śaivism.
Viśiṣṭādvaita	Non-dualism in the sense of organic unity, a system of Vedānta expounded by Rāmānuja.
Viśleṣa	Separation, disunion, separation from God.
Viṣṇu	The supreme deity of Vaiṣṇavism, the all-pervasive God.

Viśvakarmā	The divine architect.
Viśvedeva	A Vedic God.
Viveka	Discriminatory knowledge.
Vivekacūḍāmaṇi	A philosophical work by Śaṅkara.
Vraja	A village in north India, near Mathurā.
Vrindavan or *Brindavanam*	Name of a place near Mathurā, in north India.
Vyāsa	Compiler of Veda. Author of another great epic, *Mahābhārata*.
Yajña	Vedic ritual of offering libations into the sacrificial fire.
Yājñyavalkya	A Vedic Seer.
Yama	The Vedic God of Death. Five moral disciplines.
Yāmunācārya	Preceptor of Rāmānuja.
Yaśodā	Śrī Kṛṣṇa's foster mother.
Yatna	Effort.
Yoga bhakti	Practice of *prāṇāyāma* and *dhyāna*.
Yogāṅga	One of the three forms of *aṅga* in Śaivism, where the devotee realises the divine peace and presence in everything. Union of *aṅga* and *liṅga* (*tyāgāṅga, bhogāṅga* and *yogāṅga*).
Yogin	A devotee, an ascetic. One who practises Yoga. It also means one who wants to be united to God, a devotee.
Yudhiṣṭhira	The eldest of the Pāṇḍavas.

Bibliography

Adidevananda, Swami (tr.), *Yatindramatadipika of Srinivasadasa*, Chennai: Sri Ramakrishna Math.

Agarwal, Madan Mohan, *Six Systems of Hindu Philosophy*, New Delhi: Chaukhamba Sanskrit Pratishthan.

Āhāra Niyamam, Vedānta Deśika (Tamil *Prabandham*).

Aitaretyopaniṣad with English Transaltion and Notes according to Sri Madhvacharya's Bhashya, K.T. Pandurangi, Sriman Madhva Siddhantonnahni Sabha, Chirtanur (near Tirupati).

Aiyangar, S.K., *History of Vaiṣṇavism in South India*, Oxford University Press.

Aiyer, K. Narayana Swamy (tr.), *Laghu-Yoga-Vāsishta*, The Adyar Library and Research Centre.

———, *Thirty Minor Upaniṣads* (Sanskrit Text with English Translation), New Delhi: Parimal Publications.

Apte, Vaman Shivram, *The Practical Sanskrit-English Dictionary*, Delhi: Motilal Banarsidass.

Ayyangar, Narasimha, *Vedāntasāra of Bhagavad Rāmānuja* (tr.), The Adyar Library and Research Centre.

Bhandarkar, R.G., *Vaiṣṇavism Śaivism and Minor Religious Systems*, Varanasi: Indological Book House.

Bhat, G.P. (tr.), *Skanda Purāṇa*, New Delhi: Motilal Banarsidass.

Bhat, M. (tr.), *Varāhamihira's Bṛhat Saṁhitā*, New Delhi: Motilal Banarsidass.

Bhattatiri, *Nayaraniyam Meppathur Narayana* (tr.), Swami Tapasyananda. Chennai: Sri Ramakrishna Math.

Bhatttacharya, Haridas (ed.), *The Cultural Heritage of India* (6 vols.), Calcutta: The Ramakrishna Mission.

Bhishagrathna K.K. (tr.), *Suśruta Saṁhitā*, Text with translation (3 vols.), Varanasi: Chowkhambha Sanskrit Series Office.

Bhumanand Sarasvati, Swami, *Anthology of Vedic Hymns*, Calcutta: Savitri

Devi Bagaria Trust.

Brahma-Sūtras Śrī-Bhāsya with Text and English rendering of the Sūtras, comments Swami Vireswarananda and Swami Adidevananda Calcutta: Advaita Ashrama.

Caland, W. (tr.), *Vaikhānasasmārtasūtram*, New Delhi: Ramanand Vidya Bhawan.

Chand, Devi, *The Yajurveda*, Sanskrit Text with English translation, New Delhi: Munshiram Manoharlal.

Chari, S.M. Srinivasa, *Advaita and Viśiṣṭādvaita*, New Delhi: Motilal Banarsidass.

———, *Fundamentals of Viśiṣṭādvaita Vedānta* Based on Vedānta Deśika's Thattvamukta Kalāpa, Delhi: Motilal Banarsidass.

———, *Vaiṣṇavism: Its Philosophy*, Theology and Religious Discipline, New Delhi: Motilal Banarsidass.

———, *Philosophy and Theistic Mysticism of the Alwārs*, New Delhi: Motilal Banarsidass.

Chennakesavan, Sarasvati, *Concept of Mind in Hindu Philosophy*, New Delhi: Motilal Banarsidass.

Coburn, T.B., *Devī Māhātmya: The Crystallization of the Goddess Tradition*, New Delhi: Motilal Banarsidass.

Comans, Michael, *The Method of Early Advaita Vedānta*, New Delhi: Motilal Banarsidass.

Cowel, E.B. and A.E. Gough (tr.), *The Sarva-Darśana Saṁgraha of Mādhvācārya*, New Delhi: Motilal Banarsidass.

Cowell, E.B., *The Kauṣītaki-Brāhmaṇa-Upaniṣad*, Varanasi: Chowkhamba Publication.

Dasgupta, Surendranath, *Hindu Mysticism*, New Delhi: Motilal Banarsidass.

———, *A History of Hindu Philosophy* (5 vols.), New Delhi: Motilal Banarsidass.

De Nicolas, Antonio T., *Meditations through the Ṛgveda*, Boulder and London: Shambhala.

Deshpande, N.A. (tr.), *Padma Purāṇa*, New Delhi: Motilal Banarsidass.

Deussen, Paul, V.M. Bedekar, Palsule, G.B. (tr.), *Sixty Upanisads of The Veda* (2 Vols.), New Delhi: Motilal Banarsidass.

Dhananjayan, V.P., *A Dancer on Dance*, Chennai: Bharata Kalanjali.

Dutt, Manmath Nath (tr.), *The Dharma Shastra, Hindu Religious Codes*, New Delhi: Cosmo Publications.

Gambhīrānanda, Swāmī (tr.), *Eight Upaniṣads with the Commentary of Śaṅkarācārya* (2 vols.), Kolkata: Advaita Ashram.

———, *Brahma-Sutra Bhāṣya of Śaṅkarācārya*, Calcutta: Advaita Ashram.

Gandhi, M.K., *Songs From Prison*, Macmillan.

Ganguli, Kisari Mohan (tr.), *The Mahābhārata* (12 vols.), New Delhi: Munshiram Manoharlal.

Gopalacharya, Srinivasa (compiled and edited), *Shabdārtha Kaustubha* (*Sanskrit-Kannada Dictionary*) (6 vols.).

Goswami, C.L., *Śrīmad Bhāgavata Mahāpurāṇa with Sanskrit Text and English Translation*, Gorakhpur: Motilal Jalan.

Griffit, Ralph T.H., (tr.), *The Hymns of The Ṛgveda*, New Delhi: Motilal Banarsidass.

———, *Sāmaveda Saṁhitā*, New Delhi: Motilal Banarsidass.

———, *The Texts of the White Yajurveda or Vājasaneyī Saṁhitā*, New Delhi: Munishiram Manoharlal.

Gupta, Sanjukta, *Lakṣmī Tantra: A Pāñcarātra Text*, New Delhi: Motilal Banarsidass.

Harshananda, Swami, *Śāṇḍilya Bhakti-Sūtra*, Mysore: Prasaranga, University of Mysore.

Hume R.E. (tr.), *The Thirteen Principal Upaniṣads*, Madras: The Oxford University Press.

Iyangara, Srinivasa, *Haṭha-Yoga-Pradīpikā of Svāmīrāma Svāmin* (Text in Devanāgarī and English Translation), Madras: Theosophical Publishing House.

Iyer, S. Venkitasubramania (tr.), *Varāha Purāṇa*, New Delhi: Motilal Banarsidass.

Jagannatha Pandita, *Rasa Gandhāra*, Asiatic Society.

Kale, Moreshwar Ramachandra, *Kumāra Sambhava by Kālidāsa*, New Delhi: Motilal Banarsidass.

Keith, Arthur Berriedale, *The Religion and Philosophy of the Veda and Upaniṣads* (2 vols.), New Delhi: Motilal Banarsidass.

Krishna Warrier, A.G. (tr.), *The Sāmānya Vedānta Upaniṣads*, Madras: The Adyar Library and Research Centre.

Macdonnel A.A. and A.B. Keith, *Vedic Index of Names and Subjects* (2 vols.), New Delhi: Motilal Banarsidass.

Mādhavānanda, Swāmi (tr.), *The Bṛhadāraṇyaka Upaniṣad with the Commentary of Śaṅkarācārya*, Calcutta: Advaita Ashram.

Mahadeva Sastry, Alladi (tr.), *The Bhagavad Gita with the Commentary of Adi Sri Sankaracharya*, Madras: Samata Books.

Manmatha Nath Dutt (tr.), *Viṣṇu Puraṇa*, Prose English Translation, Varanasi: Chowkhamba Publication.

Max, Müller, *Vedānta-Sūtras with Rāmānuja's Commentary*, Delhi: Motilal Banarsidass.

Mukerji, P.N., *Yoga Philosophy of Patañjali Aranya*, Hariharananda University of Calcutta, Rendered into English.

Narasimhachary, M., *Contribution of Yamunācārya to Viśiṣṭādvaita*, Hyderabad: Sri Jayalakshmi Publications.

Nicholson, R.R., *A Literary History of the Arabs*, Cambridge University Press.

Nikhilananda, *Vedānatasāra of Sadānanda Yogīndra* (Sanskrit Text and Translation), Calcutta: Swami Advaita Ashram.

O'Flaherty, Wendy Doniger, *Karma and Rebirth in Classical Indian Traditions*, New Delhi: Motilal Banarsidass.

———, *The Origins of Evil in Hindu Mythology*, New Delhi: Motilal Banarsidass.

Olivelle, Patrick (tr.), *Dharmasūtras (The Law Codes of Āpastamba, Gautama, Baudhāyana, and Vasiṣṭha)*, New Delhi: Motilal Banarsidass.

Pandurangi, K.T., *Bṛhadāraṇyakopaniṣad* with English Transaltion and Notes according to Śrī Mādhvācārya's Bhāṣya, Chirtanus (near Tirupati): Sriman Madhva Siddhantonnahni Sabha.

Panikkar, Raimundo, *The Vedic Experience — Mantramañjara: An Anthology of the Vedas for Modern Man and Contemporary Celebration*, Delhi: Motilal Banarsidass.

Prabhanjanācārya, V. (Kannada tr.), *Harikathāmṛtasāra of Śrī Jangannātha Dāsa*, Bangalore: Aitareya Prakāshana Vyasanakere.

Prabhavananda, Swami, *Narada's Way of Divine Love* (*Narada Bhakti-Sūtras*), Chennai: Sri Ramakrishna Math.

Principal Upaniṣads (2 vols.) Text, English Transaltion and Brief notes according to Sri Ranga Ramanujamuni Anantha Rangacharya (tr.) N.S. Anantha Rangacharya, Bangalore.

Radhakrishnan, S., *Bhagavad Gītā*, New Delhi: Motilal Banarsidass.

———, *Hindu Philosophy* (2 vols.), Madras: Oxford University Press.

Ragavachar, S.S., *Vedārtha-Saṁgraha of Śrī Rāmānujācārya* (tr.), Mysore: Sri Ramakrishna Ashram.

Raghunathan, N. (tr.), *Śrīmad Bhāgavatam* (2 vols.), Madras: Vighneswara Publishing House.

Rajagopalachari, C. (tr. and comm.), *Bhaja Govindam of Sri Sankara*, Bombay: Bharatiya Vidya Bhavan.

———, *Kural: The Great Book of Tiruvalluvar*, Bombay: Bhavan's Book University.

Ramanathan A.A. (tr.), *The Saṁnyāsa Upaniṣads*, Madras: The Adyar Library and Research Centre.

Ramanujachari, C., *Spiritual Heritage of Tyāgaraja*, Chennai: Sri Ramakrishna Matha.

Rangacharya, M. and M.B. Varadaraja Iyengar (tr.), *The Vedānta Sūtra with Śrībhāshya of Rāmānuja* (3 vols.), New Delhi: Munshiram Manoharlal.

Rangacharya, M., *The Philosophy of Conduct: Lectures on the Bhagavadgīta* (3 vols.) New Delhi: Munshiram Manoharlal.

Robert C., *Rāmānuja on the Yoga Lester*, Madras: The Adyar Library and Research Centre.

Rukmini, R.S., *Yogasūtrabhāsyavivaraṇa of Śaṅkara*, Vivaraṇa Text with English translation and critical notes along with text and English translation of *Pātañjala Yogasūtras and Vyāsabnhāṣya* (2 vols.), Delhi: Munshiram Manoharlal.

———, *Yogavārttika of Vijñānabhikṣu*, Text with English Translation and critical notes along with the text and English translation of *Pātañjala Yogasūtras and Vyāsabnhāṣya* (4 vols.), New Delhi: Munshiram Manoharlal.

Saṅgītaratnākara of Śārṅgadeva (2 vols.) (Sanskrit Text and English Translation with comments and notes) R.K. Shingy and Prem Lal Sharma, Delhi: Munshiram Manoharlal.

Sampatkumaran, M.R. (tr.), *The Gītābhāṣya of Rāmānuja*, Bombay: Ananthacharya Indological Research Institute.

Sarasvati, Svami Satya Prakash (tr.), *Atharavaveda Saṁhitā* (3 vols.), Delhi: Veda Pratishthana.

Sarvānanda, Swāmī, *Īśavāsyopaniṣad*, including the original verses, construed text with a literal word by word translation, Madras; Sri Ramakrishna Math.

Sastri, S.S. Suryanārāyana (tr.), *The Saṁkhyakārika of Īśvara Kṛṣṇa*, Chennai: University of Madras.

———, *Vedāntaparibhāsa*, The Adyar Library and Research Centre.

Sastry, Alladi (tr.), *The Taittirīya Upaniṣad with the Commentaries of Śrī Śaṅkarācārya*, Sri Suresvaracharya, Sri Vidyaranya Mahadeva, Madras: Samata Books.

Sharma, B.N.K., *Madhva's Teachings in His Own Words*, Bombay: Bharatiya Vidya Bhavan.

———, *Philosophy of Srī Madhvācarya*, New Delhi: Motilal Banarsidass.

Sharma, P.V., *Caraka Saṁhitā*, Text with translation (3 vols.), Varanasi: Chaukhamba Oritentalia.

Shastri, Hari Prasad (tr.), *The Rāmāyaṇa of Vālmīki* (3 vols.), London: Shanti Sadan.

Shastri, J.L. (tr.), *Liṅga Purāṇa*, Delhi: Motilal Banarsidass.

———, *Śiva Purāṇa*, New Delhi: Motilal Banarsidass.

Singh Bhupala, *Rasārṇava Sudhākara*, Trivendrum Sanskrit Series.

Sinha, Jadunath, *Hindu Philosophy* (3 vols.), New Delhi: Motilal Banarsidass.

———, *The Indian Psychology* (3 vols.), Calcutta: Publishing House.

Srikantha Murti, K.R. *Vāgbhaṭa's Aṣṭāṅga Hṛdayam*, Text with English translations, notes (3 vols.), Varanasi: Krishnadas Academy.

Suzuki, D.T., *Studies in the Laṅkāvatāra Sūtra*, London: Routledge and Kegan Paul Ltd.

Swāhānanda, Swami, *The Chāndogya Upaniṣad*, Containing the original text with word-by-word meaning, notes, Madras: Sri Ramakrishna Matha.

Tagare, G.N (tr.), *Kūrma Purāṇa*, New Delhi: Motilal Banarsidass.

———, *Śrīmad Bhāgavata Purāṇa*, Delhi: Motilal Banarsidass.

———, *Vāyu Purāṇa*, New Delhi: Motilal Banarsidass.

Taimini, I.K., *The Science of Yoga*, Madras: The Theosophical Publishing House.

Tapasyananda, Swami (tr.), *Śrīmad Bhāgavata* (4 vols.), Madras: Sri Ramakrishna Math.

———, *Śvetāśvatara Upaniṣad*, Madras: Sri Ramakrishna Math.

Thakura, Srila Visvanatha Cakravarti, *Rasāmṛta Sindhu*, ISKON.

Tyāgīsānanda, Swāmī, *Nārada Bhakti Sūtra*, Madras: Sri Ramakrishna Math.

Vasu, Rai Bahadur Srisa Chandra, *The Śiva Saṁhitā* (tr.), Delhi: Oriental Books Reprint Corporation.

Vidyalankar, Pandit Satyakam, The Holy Vedas, Clarion Book, New Delhi.

Vijayananda, Swami (tr.), *Nārada Pāncharātram*, Delhi: Parimal Publications.

Vimalānanda, Swāmī, *Mahanārāyaṇa Upaniṣad* Introduction, Translation, Interpreation, Madras: Sri Ramakrishna Math.

Vivekananda, Swami, *Religion of Love*, Vedanta Pr.

Index

sarvejanāh sukhino bhavantu,
sanmaṅgalāni bhavantu.

"Let all beings be happy and peaceful;
Let auspiciousness be in all".